MARRIAGE AMONG THE TRIO

Korokoro (300) returning from a day's fishing on the Paloemeu River

Marriage Among the Trio

A PRINCIPLE OF SOCIAL ORGANISATION

BY

PETER RIVIÈRE

CLARENDON PRESS · OXFORD
1969

*Oxford University Press, Ely House, London W.*1

GLASGOW NEW YORK TORONTO MELBOURNE WELLINGTON
CAPE TOWN SALISBURY IBADAN NAIROBI DAR ES SALAAM LUSAKA ADDIS ABABA
BOMBAY CALCUTTA MADRAS KARACHI LAHORE DACCA
KUALA LUMPUR SINGAPORE HONG KONG TOKYO

PRINTED IN GREAT BRITAIN BY
SPOTTISWOODE, BALLANTYNE AND CO. LTD.
LONDON AND COLCHESTER

TO MY MOTHER'S FATHER

PREFACE

DURING MY MONTHS among the Trio, my world had shrunk to the size of their world. As the aeroplane lifted above the trees, the visual realization of the immensity of the Universe was thrust violently back into my awareness. It was like the reawakening of a long forgotten taste, and as I sat and savoured this unusual experience I came to regret that I had not tried to find out the impression of the few Indians who had travelled by air. I doubt that such a line of inquiry would have elicited any coherent ideas. Could an Indian's eyes and mind have adjusted themselves to comprehend such a vast and undifferentiated view as the jungle affords from the air? I found that Indians who had visited the coast of Surinam were no more competent than I was at explaining to their less travelled compatriots the wonders of civilization. A Trio in his traditional environment may never have a horizon of more than two hundred yards, the diameter of the village clearing. His life is spent in a well, with the sky a bright hole above the forest walls so that even the size of the firmament is restricted by the tree tops. Concepts of distance and direction lose meaning away from this world and the Trio rely on a fund of common experience, unintelligible to the stranger, in giving directions. The Trio word for a village is *pata*, which also means place, and must be contrasted with the forest, *itu*, which is without a place.

Perhaps the most important distinction which the Trio make is that between forest and village. The village is the world of humans, a sanctuary in which animals kept as pets, even those which are normally hunted, will not be eaten if accidentally killed. The forest is the world of spirits and strangers, and uncertainty. But these two worlds are not separate and independent; the jungle forever encroaches on the village, and the Trio by cutting and burning his field is not merely performing an essential agricultural activity, since these acts symbolize for him a far greater battle. The fields are also mediatorial since they stand physically between village and forest, and metaphorically between life and death. This is not to say that the Trio fear the jungle, but their apprehension of the world beyond the village is a collective representation which cannot be ignored. While it is coloured by mythic imagination it is fundamentally not an irrational anxiety but a firmly based and well-founded suspicion which has influenced many facets of Trio life. This point clearly emerges in the course of this work, but here I would like to remedy any injustice to the Trio lest the reader is left with the impression that they are a timid, fearful people cowering in small clearings deep in a dank forest.

I suppose all anthropologists become emotionally involved, to a greater or lesser degree, with their subjects, and I wish briefly to allow my romanticism free rein to express my sentiments about the Trio. My time with these people was spent as their guest, living beneath their roofs, sharing their food and their hunger. The families with whom I lived were kind, generous, and solicitous, my informants long-suffering and patient, and all the Indians tolerant of my stupidity, ineptness, and awkward behaviour. I cannot recall a single case in which an Indian showed any sign of anger or impatience with me; I cannot maintain that I was always equally civil with them. Finally these charming and hospitable people, who looked after me with quite exaggerated care, made strong efforts to make me stay, offering to build me a house, and encouraging me to send for my wife. When my actual moment of departure arrived, I turned from the aircraft door and made the conventional remark of farewell to the Indians assembled, but not a murmur of conventional assent arose. The best news which I have had since leaving Surinam is that the medical care provided by the missionaries appears to be taking effect. It looks as if these Indians will even survive, if not as the Trio they were.

These sentiments find no expression in the following pages, and I would like to make an apology to the Trio if I do not represent them favourably. For reasons which are implicit in the aims of this monograph my apologies extend no further. This work is not readable as a literary narrative because it deals with unembroidered and undiluted facts. Facts are the raw material of all scientific thought, and those produced herein are no different in type and quantity from the evidence regarded as essential in more rigorous disciplines. This point seems to have escaped the attention of too many professional social anthropologists who, disdainful of factual evidence, appear intent on restricting the discipline to a level of impressionistic views and ineffectual conjecture. As recently as 1961 Professor Dumont was provoked to write in an article on 'Marriage in India': 'as a counterweight to top-heavy generalizations, let us demand facts, more facts and always facts' (Dumont, 1961, p. 76). I am fully in sympathy with this plea, and hope that to some extent at least this work fulfils it.

Perhaps before outlining what is attempted in this work I should mention briefly the aims when I started my researches among the Trio, since they do not entirely coincide. The Trio appeared to represent the last Carib-speaking group of a reasonable size whose cultural and demographic state would allow a final chance to answer many of the questions which still exist concerning this linguistic stock. Accordingly the purpose of my researches was not so much the investigation of any specific problems, but a salvage attempt on a people near the brink of cultural extinction, and about whom there is little basic ethnographic information of the type which modern social anthropologists require. On this score I failed; partly because I was a mere twelve months too late in reaching the Trio, and partly because these people were found to possess a culture and social organization which in many aspects are atypical, or at least curiously different from what has been reported among other Carib groups. However, from this angle the research was not a complete failure, since the Trio material does raise some problems and doubts concerning Carib ethnography and points out the need to re-examine some of the 'top-heavy generalizations'. For example, are the Carib-speaking people really matrilineal, as many have glibly asserted? There is certainly no good published evidence on this point, and the present study does not support it.

While work among the Trio was started without any specific problems in mind, a suitable line of inquiry, marriage with the sister's daughter, soon presented itself.[1] The study of this topic occupied much of the fieldwork period, and this monograph contains the results of that research. The way in which the results are presented here is important since it reflects a

---

[1] Curiously enough a subject which Dumont, in the article referred to above, mentions as requiring a more systematic investigation (1961, p. 95).

secondary aim of this work. The monograph is divided into
three parts. The first deals with environmental, historical, and
socio-economic factors, and although this part is entitled
'Background to the Trio', this is not meant to imply that the
subjects of which it treats are relatively unimportant in the
understanding of Trio society. In fact much of it is vitally
important but these are factors which belong to a different level
from the purely sociological facts and the analysis of them
which appear in Part Two, 'Trio Society—The Facts'. In this
part the evidence concerning the main Trio social institutions is
of the type which can be treated quantitatively, and this feature
separates it from Part Three in which the material is of the type
for which there is no means of making objective assessment, and
both the evaluation of the observer and the intellectual pro-
clivity of the analyst have great influence on the conclusion
reached.

In this third part an interpretation is made not simply of the
evidence provided there, but the material from the earlier
parts is drawn into it, so that a whole miscellany of facts is
reduced to a simple coherent scheme.

The divisions of this work represent different levels of approach, and in turn reflect different types of facts, of abstractions, and of analysis. Each different level introduces new facts
but includes and relies on both the facts and the analysis of
them achieved in earlier pages. One of the aims of this work is
to show that one can move from one level to the next, i.e., from
the facts to their function, to the values which maintain them
and the principles which order them. Marriage with the sister's
daughter is a good vehicle for this demonstration because it is
a union which is neither prohibited nor fully approved; it
represents a marital possibility which is partly incestuous and
partly licit. This curious state of affairs is, however, no more
than the empirical solution to a deeper attitudinal conflict
which exists as much at the level of thought as at the level of
action. This, I hope, will become abundantly clear in the
course of this work, but it is also intended to demonstrate that
this marriage form cannot be understood in isolation, since the
motive force is the same principle as that which guides many
other Trio social institutions and practices.

Thus one of the aims of this monograph, alongside with an

elucidation of marriage with the sister's daughter, is to show that there is an interplay between social action and social thought, and that the same principles must underlie both. This is by no means a new idea, but the Trio, because of the small size of their society and its homogeneity, are a good case for the demonstration of this claim.

There is one further point which must be made clear to the reader; much of this monograph is concerned with the examination of Trio social categories, and social categories are treated as facts. If the reader fails to adopt the same point of view much of what is contained in the following pages will not make sense to him. This approach is most obvious in my treatment of the relationship terminology in which the terms are treated as facts on two levels. First, at the level of thought where the whole terminology forms, for a Trio, an ideal model of his society; secondly, at the level of action where the relationship terms can be used as operational tools in everyday social interaction. It is shown that these two levels are not separate but interdependent, and furthermore that the same criteria are at work in the thinking and in the acting.

For those who find the approach and the conclusions unacceptable there remains a great weight of factual data about the Trio. This has its own value, and should allow anyone who is so minded to undertake a re-analysis of the material; something by which I would only be flattered. However, readers will notice that certain aspects of Trio culture have been dealt with more summarily than others. This results from the necessity of keeping within certain bounds of reference and within a certain number of pages. Trio marriage and directly related material is dealt with fully, but the treatment of other institutions, which have more marginal relevance, is limited by the degree to which the understanding of them is essential for the complete explanation of marriage with the sister's daughter and its associated scheme of values.

The conditions under which the fieldwork was conducted between July 1963 and April 1964 were almost ideal. I lived with a Trio family as a member of it, and for much of the time in a house without walls near the centre of the village which allowed a commanding view of all comings and goings, a point well illustrated by Plate XI, a photograph which was taken

xii PREFACE

from the comfort of my hammock which was my vantage point. The readiness of the Indians to accept me in their midst eased my researches to an inestimable degree. All my researches were carried out in the Trio language which is the only language the majority of Indians can speak. I am grateful to the members of the West Indies Mission and to Claude Leavitt of the Unevangelised Fields Mission for help in learning the Trio language, for the occasional services as interpreters, and for the kindness which they and their wives showed me. My thanks are due also to the pilots of the Missionary Aviation Fellowship who several times quickly and safely transported me over distances which it would have otherwise taken weeks to cover. My admiration for their skill and courage in their daily flights in small single-engined aircraft across such terrain is boundless.

I would also like to express my gratitude to Dr. Vera Rubin and the Research Institute for the Study of Man in New York who completely financed my fieldwork by a most generous grant-in-aid and whose generosity extended to making a further grant towards the analysis and preparation of my field notes.

The basis of this monograph is my doctoral thesis presented at Oxford in 1965. Some of the changes which have been made are a result of comments made by my examiners, Dr. Edmund Leach and Mr. Francis Huxley. I am grateful to them for their suggestions but there are certain points which they queried that remain unaltered; I disagreed with their assessment of these points at the time, and continue to do so, so the fault is mine not theirs. My greatest debt of thanks is owing to Dr. Rodney Needham who at every stage has proved an invaluable guide and friend, but I hasten to absolve him also from any mistakes contained herein.

There is obviously no room here for me to thank individually all those who have helped and encouraged me—although my gratitude is no less strongly felt—so I will single out one person to represent them: my wife, who just waited.

P. G. R.

CONTENTS

LIST OF PLATES

Frontispiece

Korokoro (300) returning from a day's fishing on the Paloemeu
River

At End

LIST OF FIGURES

LIST OF MAPS

LIST OF TABLES

2

PART ONE

BACKGROUND TO THE TRIO

THERE ARE two aims in the first part of this monograph: first, to provide an introduction to the Trio and to give the reader some idea of the scene against which the main body of the work is set; secondly, to cover features of Trio culture and the environment in which it exists, which are directly relevant to the problem in hand but, for expository reasons, are best treated separately.

This part is divided into three chapters which deal respectively with the area and environment in which the Trio live, the history and sources of information about these people, and a general review of the way in which they live.

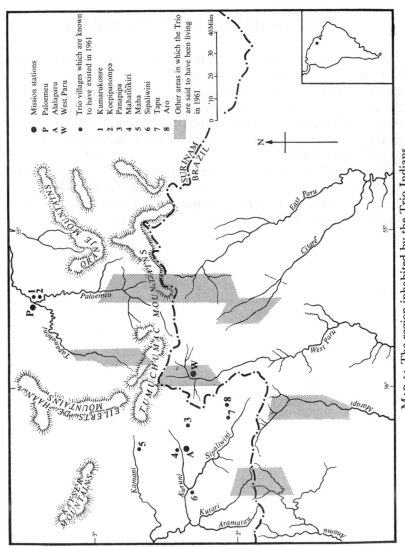

MAP 1: The region inhabited by the Trio Indians.

I

THE SETTING

THE TRIO LIVE in an area approximately bounded by 1 and
3½ degrees North latitude and by 55 and 57 degrees West
longitude. The region is politically divided between Brazil and
Surinam, and the frontier shared by these two countries follows
the watershed which separates the rivers which flow northwards directly to the South Atlantic from those which run
south to join the Amazon. It is an area which, until recent
times, remained remote from the events which occurred at the
mouths of the rivers to which it gave birth, and even today
relatively little of the region is known.

To the east, the watershed is formed by the east–west ranges
of the Tumuchumac Mountains; for the most part these consist
of a series of forest-covered hills which rarely exceed 1,000 ft.
in altitude. These hills are interspersed with massive blocks of
vertical-sided black rock which rise to over 3,000 ft. above the
surrounding forest. In the extreme east of the Trio territory a
spur of the Tumuchumac, the Oranje Mountains, runs northward into Surinam between the basins of the Litani and
Paloemeu Rivers. At about 56 degrees West longitude the main
axis of the Tumuchumac range turns north–south and becomes
the Eilerts de Haan Mountains which separate the Surinam
rivers, the Tapanahoni and the Sipaliwini.

The watershed to the west of this is less well-defined until the
extreme west of the region where it is marked by an eastern
extension of the Sierra Acarai.

The nature of the ground away from these main ranges
varies: the largest rivers have worn wide peneplains which
extend many miles either side of their main course, and their
uniform flatness is only occasionally interrupted by single hills.
Away from the larger rivers the ground is frequently undulating,
and when traversing the country on foot one climbs and descends innumerable steep-sided hills whose presence is barely
discernible from the air.

As topographical features, watercourses are more important

than mountains; the main rivers of Surinam which rise in this region are, from east to west, the Paloemeu, the Tapanahoni, the Sipaliwini, and its tributaries the Kutari and Aramatau. Important right-bank tributaries of the Sipaliwini are the Kuruni and Kamani.

The Amazonian rivers which have their sources in the region are the East Paru, the Citaré, the West Paru, Marapi, and the Anamu, which is an upper tributary of the Trombetas. A feature which the Surinam and Brazilian rivers have in common is that they are blocked along much of their courses by a series of falls and rapids making them of limited practical use as navigable waterways into the interior—a factor which has played an important part in the history and development of the frontier region.

Besides these main rivers the whole area is criss-crossed by a great complex of permanent smaller streams and a multitude of creeks, rivulets, and swamps of which many have only a seasonal life. While the level of the smaller streams will fluctuate quickly and greatly as a result of a single storm, the main rivers rise and fall more sedately. The difference between high and low water levels in a big river is as much as 15–20 ft. Great tracts of the forest are inundated at the wettest time of the year, and during the dry season, the high water mark may be visible above the level of one's head many miles from a large river. During the wet season travel by land is difficult if not impossible, and going by canoe on the main rivers is considered dangerous by the Indians.

There are slight variations in the rainfall régime, depending on the exact location in the area (see rainfall and temperature graphs on p. 6). In general the wet season occurs between April and August, with May and June the wettest months. The main dry season lasts from August to November, with September and October being noticeably the driest months. In November the rains return, but there is a distinct secondary dry season in March before the onset of the main rains.

The rainfall of December and January is normally insufficient to affect the rivers, in which the water reaches its lowest level during March. Precipitation during the dry season falls in occasional storms, but it is rare for more than two weeks to pass without any rainfall. The change from wet to dry season, or dry to wet season, is usually marked by a series of violent storms. The prevailing winds in the area are consistently from the east, except in storms when 180 degree variation in the direction of sharp squalls is experienced.

The dry season is the hottest time of the year, and is also the period when the diurnal range of temperature is greatest. These factors are connected: the early hours of the morning feel very cold, and as soon as the sun rises above the horizon a thick mist develops, particularly over the surface of water, the temperature of which is warmer than the surrounding air. The heat of the sun soon disperses this mist, and the days are hot and clear. After sunset the temperature drops rapidly. In the wet season both the actual temperature and the diurnal range is lower, especially on those days which are overcast and the cloud hangs about the tops of the trees. Deep in the forest there is little difference between the annual and diurnal temperature range, but in a village clearing the diurnal range is in excess of the annual one.

With the exception of two small areas of savannah—one around the headwaters of the Sipaliwini and the other near the sources of the West Paru—the whole region is covered with equatorial rainforest. This type of vegetation is typified by its variety of different species, its abundance, and the magnificence of its development. Although the dense jungle of popular imagination does exist it is not ubiquitous, and over large areas, particularly beneath high trees with massive upper foliage, undergrowth is relatively poorly developed. This more open type of environment is usually restricted to the higher ground; the swampy areas and river banks are distinguished by many species of palm. Not all species are found everywhere and some seem to have a curious distribution; for example the Brazil nut tree flourishes in great numbers to the west of the Alalaparu Creek while to the east there are very few. In the Tapanahoni/Paloemeu area there are said to be none.

Topography also has an important influence in the distribution of animal life: the Indians say that game in the uplands is relatively scarce, and the neighbourhood of large rivers is considered to be the most fruitful hunting ground. It is not possible to assess the animal life of the region but I can merely

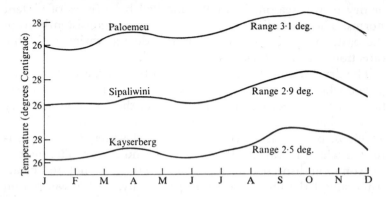

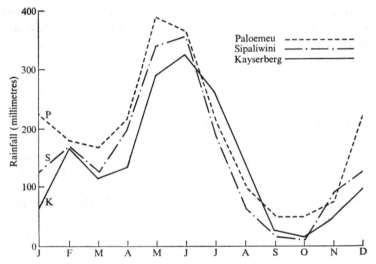

Figure 1 : Seasonal distribution of rainfall and temperature for three sites in the interior of Surinam.

Notes on rainfall and temperature graphs

Meteorological records have been kept at Government airstrips in the interior since they were opened. Since none of these strips had been open more than five years, the graphs which have been prepared are based on averages from the figures collected over four years. Although this is insufficient time to remove the discrepancy of any exceptional season the graphs do provide an objective affirmation of what subjective measurement gave the impression was happening.

say that at one time or another I saw dead or alive all the best known animals of the Guianas.

Geographical and historical reasons can be adduced for the delay, until this century, of the systematic exploration of this watershed region. It has already been mentioned that none of the rivers which flow from this region provides easy access to the interior. This is particularly true of the Brazilian rivers, and of the Courantyne on the Surinam side whose falls prevented ascent by even such an indomitable adventurer as Robert Schomburgk; however, it is only partly true of the Maroni, but the main course of this river does not lead to the territory occupied by the Trio. It is worth noting that the only other main river which flows from the Tumuchumac range to the Guiana Coast is the Oyapock which forms the frontier between Cayenne and Brazil. This river is a relatively easily navigable waterway and the earliest explorations to the source of this river and over the watershed date from the first half of the seventeenth century. However, the physical difficulties of ascending these rivers cannot be taken as the only reason for the delay in exploration or it would be safe to assume that they would still be impassable, which is not the case.

Another difference existed between the Oyapock and the Maroni and Courantyne; from the seventeenth century the French colonized the lower reaches of the Oyapock, but no European settlements were founded near the mouths of the other two rivers until the beginning of the nineteenth century. The reason for this seems to be attributable to the large population of Caribs which we know to have lived on the banks of these rivers, and which were perhaps warlike enough to dissuade the early colonists from settling there.

The role of the Caribs as an obstruction in the way to the interior was taken over in the eighteenth century by the escaped African slaves, the Bush Negroes. These people were sufficiently powerful to prevent European movement into the interior until a peace treaty was signed in 1860. By this date the Bush Negroes had developed a valuable trade with the Indians of the interior, and the difficulties which the Bush Negroes continued to place in the way of would-be travellers until the last decade has generally been regarded as an attempt to preserve their trading monopoly.

Furthermore the great impetus and goal of the early explorers, the search for fantastic riches, had for the great part waned by the nineteenth century. The majority of immigrants arriving in South America during this century came to find wealth in less risky ways.

On the Brazilian side of the frontier, colonization of areas immediately adjacent to the Amazon had begun in the seventeenth century, and although these activities are well documented, little is known about the exploration of the Amazonian tributaries in Pará. There is the record of Francisco de San Mancos who made an ineffectual attempt at exploring the Trombetas in 1725 but as late as 1873 a writer noted that the Trombetas was little known (de Souza, 1873, p. 233). The French explorers of the nineteenth century mention Brazilians whom they met on these rivers, which shows that it is wrong to assume that the area remained unvisited, but merely that accounts are lacking of such journeys, many of which must have been made by illiterate balata-bleeders and diamond hunters, or *mucambeiros*, the Brazilian equivalent to the Bush Negro. The earliest accounts we have of the rivers of Pará come from these French explorers who crossed the eastern end of the Tumuchumac range and travelled down the Yary and East Paru Rivers. It was not until the beginning of the present century that the explorations of the Coudreaus provide the first coherent description of such rivers as the Trombetas and the Cumina. The outstanding feature to be deduced from these accounts is the almost total absence of population on the lower and middle reaches of these rivers.

Up to 1900 only two European travellers had entered the watershed region occupied by the Trio; during this century a number of Dutch and Brazilian expeditions and individuals have traversed the region, and finally in 1959 European settlement started among the Trio. Since our historical knowledge of the Trio is inevitably related to this gradual European infiltration of the area in which they live, the subject more correctly belongs to the next chapter, where it is considered in parallel with the history of the Trio and a review of the ethnographic material.

II

HISTORY OF THE TRIO

THIS CHAPTER begins with a review of the meagre prehistorical knowledge of the area in which the Trio now live,
and then goes on to outline the history of the Trio, of which our
awareness is directly related to the increasing entry into their
territory of people of European and African descent. The chapter ends with a summary of the Trio's demographic state.

I

The most that can be offered under the heading of prehistory
is a series of more or less inspired guesses; there is very little information available which can be considered as established fact.

A Roman Catholic priest, Protasio Frikel, who has probably
had more experience of the area than any other living person,
claims to have identified the following set of culture sequences
(Frikel, 1961, a).

(i) The first inhabitants of the region were pre-ceramic
stone-age hunters and collectors, who survived until the
fifteenth or sixteenth century. He thinks that certain inaccessible Trio sub-groups still retain this type of culture.

(ii) In the sixteenth or seventeenth century these earliest
inhabitants were overrun by immigrants who came from the
west. Frikel has called these people the Proto-Trio of the
Archaic level. These people, although still possessing a stone-
age culture, practised primitive cultivation.

(iii) A further wave of immigrants during the eighteenth and
nineteenth centuries introduced more highly developed forms
of the existing culture traits. These people were the fore-
runners of the present Trio.

(iv) The fourth phase is the one through which the Trio are
currently passing, and the changes are the result of contact with
exotic cultures.

In another work, Frikel (1961, b) has postulated a more
northerly origin for the earliest inhabitants of the Tumuchumac

region. This in itself is not a startling claim, but his evidence is the existence in the area of what appear to be obsolete ceremonial sites and the Indian tradition associated with them. He considers these sites to belong to an extinct people and to be connected with ritual surrounding the winter solstice. This implies a migration of people from outside the tropical forest area, and in this he receives some support from Fock, who considers certain Waiwai culture traits to have sub-Andean associations (1963, pp. 237–8).

The evidence in support of Frikel's conclusions is slight, and no methodical archaeological investigations have been undertaken in the area. Frikel has examined some cave sites on the Brazilian side of the frontier but no detailed report of his findings has so far been published. The little he has written is confusing, since he has made an attempt to correlate his work with that of Evans and Meggers (1960) in Guyana, but seems to have misinterpreted their results (Frikel, 1961, a, p. 14). I have previously demonstrated Frikel's erroneous reading of Evans and Meggers' work (1963, pp. 28–9), and have also questioned the conclusions reached by the American archaeologists (1967).

Frikel claims that older villages were on high ground away from the main watercourses, whereas the modern settlements tend to be on the banks of the larger rivers. There is ample evidence of a similar change in the location of village sites from elsewhere in Guiana, and it is clear that such a movement has taken place in the Paloemeu River region during the last twenty-five years. I do not find so acceptable his claim that old village sites can be dated back 200 years by the Indians being able to trace genealogical relationship through five or six generations to someone who is buried in an old village (Frikel, 1961, a, p. 13). My reasons for doubting this will be found at the beginning of the Index to the Genealogical Table, where I discuss certain problems in the collection of genealogical data.

There is one other prehistorical feature of the area which deserves comment here. Rock grooves[1] have been reported

---

[1] From almost all over the interior of Guiana as well. I use the term Guiana to refer to the 'island' of land formed by the Atlantic Ocean, the Orinoco River, the Casiquiare Canal, the Rio Negro, and the River Amazon (cf. James, 1959, p. 756).

from almost every part of the interior of Surinam. These grooves which can be found at falls and rapids on even the smallest creeks occur in very great numbers. On the Alalaparu Creek I counted over 100 on a stretch of less than a mile. The present Trio have little idea of what they are or how they were made. Some may be the result of natural rather than human agency, but the majority are undoubtedly artificial and are probably the result of grinding stone axes. Disregarding such questions as why and how they were made, these grooves do indicate that a previous aboriginal people were much more widely distributed over the interior of Surinam than has been recorded within historic times, and that this population either lived there for a very long time or its density was far higher than at present, or a combination of these factors.

However, one should not be surprised that indications other than an infrequent stone axe and odd pottery sherds have not been found to support the idea of a large population in prehistoric times; the characteristics of the environment make archaeological investigation very difficult, and the ephemeral nature of the settlements and of the objects in the material culture further militates against the appearance of such evidence. Indeed the prehistory of the Tumuchumac region is likely to remain obscure until it can be seen as a part in the whole picture of the prehistory of Guiana.

II

Trio is the name which is in common usage in Surinam, and almost certainly derives from a Bush Negro corruption of Tïrïyo [1] which the more easterly group of Trio call themselves and are called by their Amerindian neighbours, the Waiyana. The Brazilians use the name Tiriyó. The westerly group of Trio are self-styled Tarəno, and those tribes still further west who are aware of them call them Yawï. [2]

There is evidence to suggest that Trio is a generic term for a number of previously dispersed and autonomous groups. This

[1] A note on the Trio language and its pronunciation will be found in Appendix B.
[2] According to Waiwai mythology, the Yawï-yenna were the children of the Red Macaw and the Buzzard (Fock, 1963, p. 63); this identifies them as the Trio, which Fock was unable to do (ibid., p. 73).

situation no longer exists, but it would be wrong to ignore this possibility, and the history of these groups is included here. Although some of these groups are only nominally and artificially distinct from the Trio, it is easier to separate them and first consider those people who appear in the literature under the name of Trio.

The inhabitants of the Surinam coast were aware as early as the eighteenth century that there lived in the interior a group of Indians called Trio. This information presumably reached them through the agency of the coastal Indians or the Bush Negro since no actual contact between the European colonists and the Trio is recorded in that century. The first recorded meeting between the Trio and a European was in 1843 when Robert Schomburgk found them living near the source of the Anamu River, and on the Kutari (Schomburgk, 1845, p. 85).

The next reference is an extremely brief one in an official document of Cayenne which states merely that 'the Trio are no longer seen' (L. Rivière, 1866, p. 147). The difficulty of this remark is that it obviously implies that the Trio had previously been seen, and except for Schomburgk no such reference appears to exist, and certainly not in relation to Cayenne.

In 1878 the French explorer Jules Crevaux met a few Trio, the survivors of an epidemic, on the upper reaches of the East Paru (Crevaux, 1883, p. 261 sqq.). Coudreau, who never met the Trio, states that they had retired from the Oelemari River region to the Tapanahoni in order to avoid the raids of the Wayarikure (Coudreau, 1893, p. 78). He describes the Trio as being the most numerous of the Guiana tribes (ibid, p. 548) but his estimates always need to be treated with caution.

Thus during the nineteenth century there were only two contacts reported between the Trio and European travellers, and in 1900 as little was known about these people as had been in 1800. In 1904 van Panhuys was able to write, 'Between these Indians and the colonists is no communication' (Panhuys, 1904, p. 8).

In the six years between 1904 and 1910 the situation underwent a sharp change. Three official Dutch expeditions entered the area—the Tapanahoni expedition of 1905, the Tumuchumac expedition of 1907, and the Courantyne expedition of 1910–11. The reports prepared by the members of these expeditions, and particularly those of de Goeje in ethnographic matters, give the first general and clear idea of the region. The reports show that at this time the Trio were living among the headwaters of the East Paru, West Paru, and Paloemeu Rivers, and in the basin of the Sipaliwini—an area stretching between the two points where they had been found in the nineteenth century. The members of these expeditions were told by the Joeka Bush Negroes that when they, the Bush Negroes, first reached the Tapanahoni the Trio were living on its lower reaches. Initially the relations between the Bush Negro and the Trio were good, but they deteriorated, and the Indians retreated into the headwaters of the Paloemeu, and finally their most northerly village was a day's march overland from the source of this river.

Five years after the Dutch Courantyne expedition, the American Farabee crossed the region by the same route as Schomburgk had taken seventy years before and met the Trio in the same area as his predecessor. His work *The Central Caribs* adds only a little to the sum knowledge of the Trio.

The region then remained undisturbed for another decade, and in 1928 a Brazilian expedition under General Rondon visited the area and revealed the presence of some Trio Indians, who had previously been unknown, on the Marapi (Cruls, 1930, and Rondon, 1957). In 1935–8 the Dutch/Brazilian Frontier Commission worked in the region but their report (van Lynden, 1939) is of relatively little ethnographic value. In 1938 two Americans entered the area in search of a compatriot, Redfern, whose aeroplane was thought to have crashed in the area; their search was not rewarded and on their homeward journey one of them was drowned in the Tapanahoni when their canoe capsized on the falls below the Paloemeu mouth.

In 1940–2 a Surinamese of African descent, Lodewijk Schmidt, made three journeys to the area in the course of which he travelled through nearly the whole territory occupied by the Trio.[1] The account which he wrote of these journeys, although not such competent ethnography as the writings of de

[1] I have been told, although I cannot vouch for the story's truth, that the purpose of Schmidt's journey was to ensure that the Japanese had not constructed secret landing grounds in the interior!

Goeje, has proved to be of incalculable value in the preparation of this work. In particular his census of Trio villagers is a remarkable achievement. Schmidt found the Trio living in the same general area as had been recorded by the earlier travellers to the region. The distribution of Trio villages as recorded by Schmidt is shown on Map 2 (p. 36).

Schmidt's journeys among the Trio can be taken to mark the last phase in the exploration of the area, for in 1948 the first visit of Protasio Frikel heralded the initial stage of the present developments in the area. In 1959 Frikel's activities in the area culminated in the Brazilian Air Force making a landing ground on the savannah around the upper reaches of the West Paru, and in the same year a Franciscan Mission was founded near by.

In Surinam, with the exception of an expedition in 1952 which entered the region to investigate a report that the Trio were suffering from a severe influenza epidemic, there was little activity until Operation Grasshopper began. This operation, which involved the opening up of the interior by the cutting of a series of airstrips, did not impinge on the Trio territory until 1960 when work was begun on an airstrip on the Sipaliwini savannah, and another on the left bank of the Tapanahoni opposite the mouth of the Paloemeu. The distribution of Trio villages had undergone one noticeable change since Schmidt's visits: the Indians had moved their villages down the Paloemeu River, and by 1961 there was one Trio village just above this river's junction with the Tapanahoni and another on the Tapanahoni just below the mouth of the Paloemeu.

More important for the Trio than Operation Grasshopper was that in 1959 the Surinam Government granted permission to the American Door-to-Life Gospel Mission to work among them. In the spring of 1960 this mission made its first contact with the Trio in the Sipaliwini basin,[1] and a tiny airstrip was cut alongside the Alalaparu Creek at a point three miles from where it joins the Kuruni River, itself a tributary of the Sipaliwini. After the landing strip had been completed, the site

[1] Some idea of the isolation of the Trio can be gained from this story. At the first Trio village which the missionary Claude Leavitt entered, an old man, since dead, told him that he had seen only three *pananakiri* before. These had been Schmidt and the two Americans looking for Redfern. The Trio call Bush Negroes *mekaro* but classify negroes from the coast as *pananakiri*, as they do all white men except Brazilians who are called *karaiwa*.

was abandoned until August 1961 when the missionary work really began. A little earlier in the same year another station of the same mission had been founded at the Paloemeu airstrip.

In August 1962 the Door-to-Life Gospel Mission collapsed, and the whole organization was taken over by the West Indies Mission under whose auspices both the Alalaparu and Paloemeu stations continue to flourish.

The three mission stations—the two Protestant ones in Surinam and the Roman Catholic one in Brazil—have become centres of Trio population. As early as 1961 the Roman Catholic mission was described as a focus of convergence for all neighbouring Trio sub-groups (Figueiredo, 1961, p. 12). Since this date the distribution of the Trio has undergone some drastic changes, which seem to result from the preference of the Indians for the Protestant mission in Surinam, and there has been a steady drift of population to the stations of this mission during the last four years.

When I began my researches among the Trio in 1963 the following situation existed: all the Trio in the Sipaliwini basin had moved to the Alalaparu mission station, and a few Indians had arrived there from Brazil. The Paloemeu station had attracted all the Trio living in the immediate vicinity, including those from the upper reaches of the Tapanahoni, and a group from the East Paru area had reached the village in 1962. In Brazil Trio villages still existed in the East Paru, West Paru, Marapi, and Anamu regions. When I left the Trio in 1964 this situation had changed; there had been a large-scale migration to the Paloemeu village from the East Paru area, and it is said that there are no Trio still living in this region. A few Indians had moved from the West Paru and Marapi to the Alalaparu village, and it was reported that the Trio of the West Paru were settling round the Roman Catholic mission. Since then the movements have continued, and by the end of the 1964/5 dry season the Marapi villages had been abandoned, and the inhabitants had moved to Alalaparu so that only the Anamu villages remained unaffected by this upheaval. However, by the end of 1965 these villages were being drawn into the net, and some Indians had moved from the Anamu to Alalaparu. During this period other subsidiary movements have also been going on; a group of Indians moved across from Paloemeu to

3

Alalaparu, and went back again the following dry season (1965/6), and some Indians have left Alalaparu to return to the Roman Catholic mission in the West Paru.[1]

It seems likely that there will be minor comings and goings for some time, if not always, but unless there is a further radical change in the influences at work on the Trio the traditional settlement pattern is unlikely to reappear, and the small scattered villages have been permanently replaced by large but more widely separated settlements. Although I was too late to observe the Trio living in their traditional units, I have as far as possible related their social organization to its old setting; indeed many aspects of it are inexplicable in the present social environment. While certain features of the system may already have become obscured, it is equally certain that the stresses involved in this upheaval have thrown into prominence many of their fundamental values.

It is now necessary to turn back and consider the various sub-groups of which the modern Trio are possibly composed.

III

Frikel must be praised for being the first person to make a conscientious and methodical attempt to order and classify the tribes of the whole region. Earlier writers have been satisfied to provide a list of real and imagined people and have given the subject no further thought.

In his original classification Frikel considered the Trio to consist of six 'friendly' sub-groups, and a further six 'wild' ones. These were (Frikel, 1957, pp. 541–62):

Friendly		Wild	
1	Maracho (Pianokoto)	7	Akuriyo
2	Okomoyana (Maipurid-	8	Wayarikure
	jana, Waripi)	9	Wama
3	Prouyana	10	Kukuyana
4	Arimihoto	11	Pianoi
5	Aramagoto	12	Tiriyometesem
6	Aramicho		

[1] This information was provided by the missionary, the Rev. Claude Leavitt, in personal communications dated February 1965, and May 1966.

Three years later he revised this list and suggested the Trio were formed from the following 13 sub-groups (Frikel, 1960, p. 2):

1   The Maracho who are the Pianokoto.
2   The Akuriyo.
3   The Okomoyana.
4   The Prouyana and Ragu.
5   The Arimihoto.
6   The Aramagoto.
7   The Aramicho.
8   The Wayarikure.
9   The Wama.
10 The Tiriyometesem.
11 The Pianoi who are a sub-group of the Aramagoto.
12 The Kukuyana who are a sub-group of the Pianokoto (and also, presumably, of the Maracho).
13 The Kirikirigoto.

The addition to this list is the Kirikirigoto whom Frikel classifies with the Maracho, Okomoyana, Prouyana, Arimihoto, Aramagoto, and Aramiso as being friendly and accessible, while the rest he considers to be wild, or at least inaccessible. In a still more recent article (1964) Frikel proposes some simplifications, but it is easier to review his 1960 list in more detail and consider his further modifications in their appropriate place.

In the following discussion of each of these groups, their name according to the phonetic spelling used for the Trio language elsewhere in this thesis is given after the name used by Frikel. This is followed in brackets by other orthographic equivalents which are to be found in the literature. A comment is also added on the meaning of the name, in which matter I am in general agreement with Frikel, except in the case of Trio itself. Frikel claims that Tïrïyo means 'club' or 'murder people' (Frikel, 1957, p. 559), and although he may be correct in this, I found slight evidence to support his translation. The Trio word for club is *siwarapun* and the stem of the verb to kill is *watïrï* (literally, to make not, to undo); presumably Frikel has derived the meaning of Tïrïyo from the latter. However, a derivation from the stem *tïrï* (to fix, make or do) seems more

probable and fits with Trio ideas about the nature of their own
creation.

1. Maracho—Maraso: 'Eagle [people]'; *maraso* is the Trio
name for a specific white eagle which I have been unable to
identify. It is also the name of a mythical character who by
accidentally answering a tree instead of a rock when he heard a
call caused the Trio to become short-lived like trees.[1]

There does not appear to be any reference to the Maraso in
the literature earlier than the first mention by Frikel in 1957.
In 1963 my Trio informants knew a tribe by this name but said
that they were all dead. Frikel has always bracketed the
Maraso and the Pianakoto and he has recently concluded that
they were essentially the same (Frikel, 1964, p. 100). There
seems to be no reason for doubting this conclusion, nor in fact
for excluding from this simplification the Kukuyana, and
treating all three under the heading of Pianakoto, the advantage in this being that the existence of this last group is better
and more continuously documented from the middle of the
eighteenth century onwards than is any other group in this
area.

Pianokoto—Pianakoto (Pianocoto, Pianoghotto, Pianogoto,
Piannacotou, Piannocotou); 'Harpy eagle people'.

The Pianakoto were first reported in 1755 by Schumann as
living on the upper Courantyne river (de Goeje, 1943, a, p.
340), and in the same area by the English soldier Stedman in
the 1770s (Stedman, 1796, a, p. 405). Robert Schomburgk was
the first European actually to meet the Pianakoto, and in 1843
found them on either side of the Sierra Acarai in the region of
the Anamu-Kutari divide. The Zurumata which he had seen
on the Alto Trombetas he considered to be a sub-group of the
Pianakoto, and the Pianakoto themselves to be a sister tribe of
the Trio (Schomburgk, 1845, p. 64 sqq.). There is in his writing
a clear distinction between the Trio and Pianakoto.

Forty years later the Waiwai told Coudreau that the Pianakoto lived south of the Alto Trombetas and extended eastward
to the country of the Waiyana (Coudreau, 1887, p. 356). On his
last voyage (up the Trombetas) Coudreau was told by his

[1] See p. 262.

guides that the Pianakoto lived on the Anamu, but he failed to see any of these people, although he claimed to have reached the mouth of this tributary (O. Coudreau, 1900, pp. 70–79).

After her husband's death, Olga Coudreau continued to explore the rivers of Pará, and on a journey up the Cumina met a number of Pianakoto dwelling below the junction of the Marapi and West Paru (O. Coudreau, 1901, p. 119).

The reports of the Dutch expeditions which took place in the first decade of this century are notably silent on the subject of the Pianakoto, and de Goeje assumed them to be still living on the Anamu (de Goeje, 1906, p. 4). Farabee also fails to mention the Pianakoto.

General Rondon, in 1928, found this tribe in the same area as Olga Coudreau had seen them (Rondon, 1957, p. 12 and p. 43). The Frontier Commission reported the Pianakoto as living among the upper tributaries of the Anamu (Aguiar, 1943, p. 133). Once again the information from the Brazilian side contrasts curiously with that from Surinam territory. Only a few years after the Brazilian Frontier Commission, Schmidt could find out no more than that the Pianakoto, whom the Trio considered to have been fierce, had once lived in the Sipaliwini basin but that they had now all disappeared. Even in the villages on the Marapi nothing was known of the Pianakoto, and the Bush Negroes said that they had never traded with a people of this name (Schmidt, 1942, pp. 47–48). In 1948 Frikel was told of the Pianakoto living near the source of the Kachpakuru—a middle reach tributary of the Trombetas (Frikel, 1964, p. 98). The Trio of the Sipaliwini basin whom I questioned on this subject in 1963 were mainly ignorant of the name, and even denied the previous existence of such people. Finally, in 1964, Frikel published an article suggesting that the Trio and Pianakoto are basically the same people. Today the name Trio is in use while formerly they were known as Pianakoto, the change in name being the result of inter-tribal mixing in the area (Frikel, 1964, p. 104). This seems a reasonable proposition, the other possibilities being that a tribe of Pianakoto who once lived in the area have died out or moved away. The single certainty is that their existence is not now recognized by the present Trio.

2. Akuriyo—Akuriyo (Acouri, Akolie, Akouris, Akuliju, Akuri). 'Cutting [people]?'

In Surinam the Akuriyo have always been associated with the Trio, and they are frequently considered as optional names for the same people. The use of the name Akuriyo when referring to the Trio was still common at the beginning of this century (see de Goeje, 1906, p. 2). Furthermore there is one eighteenth-century example of a confusion between the Akuriyo and Pianakoto (de Goeje, 1943, a, p. 340).

Today the Trio say that all the Akuriyo are dead, but the name of these people does occur in the mythology and certain current culture elements are considered to have been borrowed from them. In a myth, of which I heard two versions, the second author substituted the Akuriyo for the Okomoyana, who appeared in the first version. When I queried this the author seemed to think they were the same people.

3. Okomoyana—Okomoyana (Comayana, Komajana, Ku-mayena). 'Wasp people.'

Coudreau first reported the Okomoyana as living on the upper reaches of the Aroué River and being related to the Wayarikure (Coudreau, 1893, p. 79). De Goeje wrote that the Okomoyana had formerly (before the coming of the Bush Negroes) lived on the Paloemeu, and had moved to the Kuruni, Sipaliwini and Saramacca River areas (de Goeje, 1906, p. 4). The Okomo-yana were said to have previously fought a bloody war against the Trio in the region of the Paloemeu (Franssen, 1905, p. 131). Bakhuis met an Okomoyana at the Trio village of Apikollo in the Sipaliwini basin, and wrote of him that he spoke and understood the Trio language (Bakhuis, 1908, p. 111). Farabee visited a village of Okomoyana near the junction of the Kutari and Sipaliwini rivers (Farabee, 1924, p. 214).

An Indian mentioned to Schmidt the name of the Okomo-yana but the latter never records meeting any of these people. By the middle of this century Frikel stated that no more than six or eight Okomoyana still existed, and that they lived scattered among other Trio sub-groups (Frikel, 1957, p. 552). According to the information which I collected, the Okomoyana who had once lived in the Sipaliwini basin were, with one exception, all dead. They were killed by colds, whereas Frikel says that they were exterminated by the Kukuyana (Frikel, 1957, p. 552).

It has already been mentioned that there is some confusion between the Akuriyo and Okomoyana.

In his 1957 classification Frikel recognized two Okomoyana sub-groups, the Waripi and the Maipuridjana, but has left both names out of his 1960 list. He would appear to be right in having done this. In Trio a *waripi* is a small wasp, and according to Trio mythology an individual of this name was the first of the Okomoyana and he had his village at the junction of the Sipaliwini and Kuruni Rivers.

The Maipuridjana—Maipurisana are the 'tapir people' (there is doubt about this name being of Trio origin since the Trio word for tapir is *pai*). Trio informants considered this to be an alternative name for the Sikiyana who live on the Trombetas tributaries in the region of the Anamu River. They are said to be very fierce and to have killed many people with clubs and arrows.

This agrees with the warlike nature of the Tshikianas described by Schomburgk (Schomburgk, 1845, p. 84) and of the Chikenas by Farabee (Farabee, 1924, p. 194); the similarity of name, location, and character makes their identification with the Sikiyana appear to be as definite as anything can be in this ethnographic chaos. However, a Sikiyana woman married to a Trio stated that her people had been attacked and slaughtered by the Maipurisana. Regardless of who the Maipurisana are it seems certain that they do not belong among the Trio sub-groups.

4. Prouyana—Pïrǝuyana (Proupe, Pleojana, Prauyana, Praupe). 'Arrow' or 'Arrow-cane people'.

First reference to these people comes from the reports of the Dutch Tapanahoni expedition of 1905, but de Goeje describes them as being like the Waiyana and living in very large houses. Their villages are on the unidentified Pletani River (de Goeje, 1906, p. 4). The name of these people does not appear in Schmidt's list (Schmidt, 1942, p. 18).

Frikel found the Pïrǝuyana in 1950 and again in 1952 living in seven or eight villages on the rivers Kumaruwini, Marapi, and Upper Arakopina in Brazil, and on the Tapanahoni and

Akalapi in Surinam. He was told that the name derived from their practice of always travelling with big bundles of arrows (Frikel, 1957, p. 555).

The information I was able to obtain on these people was rather more sparse. I met no one who claimed to be a real Pïrəuyana, but Eoyari (62)[1] said that his father and Aiyatu's (28) mother had been Pïrəuyana. They had all died as a result of a cold which a Bush Negro called Asuku had given to them. Very long ago the Pïrəuyana had lived at Samawaka, which is an area of white sand located near the headwaters of the West Paru and the Sipaliwini. It is the legendary homeland of all the Trio who later migrated to live in scattered villages. The reasons why the Pïrəuyana were called by that name were that they were always shooting their arrows and because they had long thin legs like arrow canes—a physical feature which was certainly true of Eoyari (62).

No information was forthcoming on the Ragu who are first mentioned by Rondon. Frikel describes them as a sub-group of the Pïrəuyana who had previously been an independent group but had been captured (Frikel, 1957, p. 555).

One informant suggested that the Pïrəuyana were responsible for stopping the Trio from marrying their mothers and their sisters; this in a modified form is identical with the subject of the story in which the Akuriyo and Okomoyana variously figure. This is the single piece of evidence which in any way relates them to the other Trio sub-groups.

5. Arimihoto—Arimikoto (Arimigoto, Arimiyana). 'Spider monkey people.'

According to Frikel this sub-group lived in the Paloemeu, Tapanahoni and Sipaliwini basins and numbered 100–120 souls (Frikel, 1957, p. 545). This coincides with my own information except that they were said to have recently died out.

6. Aramagoto—Aramayana (Aramakoto, Aramogoto, Armagotou, Aramacoutou). 'Sweat bee people.'

I considered these people at some length in a B.Litt. thesis (Rivière, 1963, pp. 171–2), and wrote,

[1] The number which appears after an Indian's name is his reference number in the Index to the Genealogical Table.

Frikel's Aramagoto seem to be directly identifiable with the Armagotou, a tribe which is frequently mentioned during the second
quarter of the XVIIIth century as living on the divide between the
Camopi and Couyary. Sergeant La Haye found them first in 1728,
and saw them again in 1731 in which year his word is substantiated
by Capperon and de Monty. In 1742 a Mon. de Chabrillan was
sent to the Camopi to stop a war that had broken out between the
Armagotu and a tribe called the Caicouchianes. The Census of the
Oyapock in 1749 lists forty-four Armagotu dwelling on the Oyapock.
Prior to this, however, the Armagotu had suffered at the hands of
the Oyampi, who were forcing their way northwards from the
Amazon. The last reference to this tribe is 1769 when Patris'
chronicler, Claude Tony, described the Armagotu as almost
extinct, annihilated by the Oyampi who had been given guns by the
Portuguese. The survivors lived on the Oyapock.

In the following paragraph I suggested that part of this group
fled westwards away from the Oyampi migration—a possibility
to which I can add no more factual evidence but one which I
continue to favour.

Frikel found the Aramayana, numbering about 150, in the
region of the West Paru and Citaré; their name, he states, is
derived from their rather dark complexion (Frikel, 1957, p.
543). A Trio informant in the Sipaliwini area described the
Aramayana to me in the same terms but added that they lived
in hollow trees, and although they knew about cooking preferred to eat their meat raw. Another Indian said that the
Aramayana did not know about fire and that their language
was only slightly like that of the Trio.

Two features from this are worthy of further comment:
Frikel considers that the Trio can be divided into two distinct
physical types, one short, thick-set, and dark skinned, the other
taller, with slender build and light-coloured skin. He believes
the darker type to be the earlier inhabitants of the region, and
the lighter-coloured ones to have arrived more recently (Frikel,
1960). Although some Indians are shorter and more thick-set
than others who are taller and more slender, I cannot admit
there is a correlation between these physical types and the
colour of the skin, nor will I accept that the paler ones, when
angry, will taunt the darker with the colour of their skins, as
Frikel suggests. The skin colour of any individual Trio varies
widely; a few days working in the hot sun and he becomes very

dark, but a week sick in his hammock and he will be as pale as many Europeans.

Secondly, the Aramayana's purported ignorance of fire is of value in trying to identify another group, the Amikouan (Amicuana, Amikwan) of whom I have elsewhere written,

This tribe, which was first seen by Sergeant La Haye in 1728 on the banks of the Kou, caught the popular imagination. The reason for this was La Haye's description of them as being 'long-eared'; this no doubt refers to a habit of piercing and distending the lobe of the ear to take an ornament.

In 1729 Father Lombard wrote a latter saying that the Amikouan were very primitive and even ignorant of fire. I have not seen a copy of this letter but in 1898 Henri Froidevaux published a paper refuting this, and producing as evidence a letter from La Condamine in which the geographer claimed to have discussed the Amikouan with Father Lombard who had admitted that he was wrong about believing this tribe to be unaware of fire.

Although listed as dwelling in the Oyapock basin in both 1730 and 1749, none of the travellers to the interior during this period mentions having met this tribe. In 1769 Patris is told that the Amikouanes live somewhere away to the southwest of the Ouaqui (in the Maroni?) but does not see them. This is the last definite news that is heard of this tribe. Many years later Coudreau suggests that the Amikouanes are the Oyaricoulets (Wayarikure), but gives no reason for making such a proposal.

Some doubt must surround the actual existence of this tribe, though La Haye's testimony on other groups is sound. (Rivière, 1963, pp. 207–8).

The similarity of the Aramayana's and Amikouan's history is remarkable: they were initially reported by the same person, in the same year and in the same area. Both tribes are mentioned as living on the Oyapock by the 1749 census, and the last reference to them is in 1769 when one is described as having moved away to the south-west and the other as having been killed off by the Oyampi. The description of the Amikouan as 'long-eared' is unimportant since all the tribes of the area pierce the lobes of the ear, although admittedly not to the extent that the distension deserves such a nickname. The reputed ignorance of fire can also be explained quite easily without accepting it at face value, but even so there is some reason for assuming the Aramayana and Amikouan to be the same people.

The Pianoi belong under this heading since Frikel has classified them as an inaccessible sub-group of the Aramayana who live near the Citaré. I possess no information about these people and the details recorded by Frikel, which include webbed-feet and the practice of eating the tips of their victims' tongues, seem inadequate grounds on which to believe in their existence.

7. Aramicho—Aramiso (Aramichaux, Aramih.tcho, Aramisho). 'Pigeon [people].'

Once again it is simplest to quote the conclusions of my earlier researches on this sub-group.

On their travels into the interior in 1674, the missionaries Grillet and Béchamel hear of them as a great nation living near the source of the Maroni. They are next heard of on the banks of the River Ouaqui by Mon. de Chabrillan in 1742, and a few are recorded as living on the Oyapock in 1749. In 1766 Simon Mentelle found them well to the west of the Camopi but it is difficult to identify the exact location. Tony, in 1769, is more precise and describes the Aramichaux as having villages on the Ouaqui, Tampoc and Maroni.

They are not again referred to as a tribe although individual Aramichaux Indians are mentioned by Milthiade in 1822 and by Crevaux in 1878; in both cases on the Maroni.

The traditional home of the Aramichaux appears to have been near the Maroni and its upper east bank tributaries. The last record of them in this area as a tribe is very nearly coincidental with the arrival of the Bush Negroes on these rivers. The Aramichaux may well have fled southwards to live on the Amazonian side of the Tumuchumac Mountains, and become part of the Trio complex (Rivière, 1963, pp. 172–3).

In 1955 Frikel found them again near the upper East Paru and on the surrounding savannahs. He estimated there to be about 100 of them living in three villages and their culture to be 'stone age' (Frikel, 1957, p. 545). The information which I collected from the Trio about the Aramiso was that they were all dead, but they had been small people with hairless bodies who were otherwise very like the Trio.

8—Wayarikure; 9—Wama; 10—Tiriyometesem, are the sub-groups which Frikel defines as inaccessible and also un-attached to any of the accessible groups. In 1963 I wrote of these tribes,

Hoff considers the Tiriyometesem and the Wayarikure to be the same and in all probability extinct. Crevaux was the first to hear of the Wayarikure but virtually no specific details about them have ever been recorded. The Wama were contacted by members of the Frontier Expedition in 1937, and again by Ahlbrinck in 1938. These tribes are reputedly Carib-speaking. (Rivière, 1963, pp. 173–4.)[1]

All who have travelled among the Trio have heard fantastic stories about these 'wild' tribes, and in this respect I was no exception since the Wayarikure are a favourite topic of con-versation among the Trio. I hesitate to suggest whether these people exist now, or even did so previously, but since it is certain that they do not at present form part of the Trio it allows me to beg the question. My inclination is to place them with the other extraordinary people who dwell only in the Trio's imagination.

11. Pianoi and 12. Kukuyana have been dealt with under Aramayana and Maraso respectively.

13. Kirikirigoto; I can find no mention of a tribe of this name anywhere in the literature although it appears on some eighteenth-century maps of the region (see Juan de la Cruz Cano y Olmedilla, 1775). *Kirikiri* is the Trio name for a small green parrot, but a widely travelled Indian had not heard of a people by this name.

IV

In conclusion, it is valuable to note that two distinct cate-gories of Trio sub-groups can be recognized. On the one hand there are those which have been reported in the more westerly area, and are distinguished by the interchangeable use of their names not only in the literature but in the present Indian's minds. At some period or another the following equations have occurred: Pianakoto = Trio, Trio = Akuriyo, Akuriyo =

[1] Since going to press it has been reported that a missionary contacted a band of Wama during the summer of 1968 (see *Natural History*, January 1969).

Pianakoto, Akuriyo = Okomoyana, Pïrəuyana = Akuriyo/ Okomoyana. Information about these groups, except for occasional references to a name, is lacking until European travellers entered the region.

In contrast to these are the Aramayana and Aramiso who have a relatively well documented history reaching back to the early eighteenth century and are now considered to constitute the more easterly Trio groups. There is considerable evidence to suggest that these groups migrated from somewhere further to the north and east, probably as a result either of the Tupian migrations or of French intrusion along the Oyapock.

It is also suggested in the literature that the Indians who were found living near the frontier by the early explorers had previously lived further north but had retreated away from the Bush Negroes. It would appear then that the watershed region played its classic role as a retreat area, and although there is no precise knowledge about movements on the Amazonian tributaries, the harsh treatment which the Amerindians received at the hands of the Portuguese and the absence of an aboriginal population on the lower and middle reaches of these rivers indicate that a northward migration of fleeing tribes might be a reasonable supposition.

What happened to the west of the region is still a mystery and is likely to remain so; legends, however, indicate an eastward movement. The Waiwai consider that the Yawĭyenna went to live in the east (Fock, 1963, p. 63), and it is interesting to note that the easterly sub-groups are said by the Trio to have introduced the existing marriage rules. Waiwai and Trio relationship terminologies have a strong structural resemblance.

There is ample if not firm evidence to suggest that the Tumuchumac region has been an area of intertribal mixing, and the vital question is how important are these sub-groups or tribal remnants in the present composition of the Trio and whether there is any advantage to be gained in distinguishing them. It is possible to say with assurance that whatever the distinction may have been previously it is now virtually nonexistent.

The Trio, even if they are composed of previously independent groups who reached the area from different directions at different times, now think of themselves, with the possible exception of the Aramayana on the West Paru, as a single group having a common name, language, and culture. Furthermore while old distinctions have disappeared there are indications that new ones are emerging and are being fostered by the lack of contact between the new large villages. Speaking only of the Surinam Trio, the difference in the influences to which the two villages are exposed is sufficient to cause a diverging development. There already exist slight differences in language (and in the use of relationship terms) between Paloemeu and Alalaparu, and this is even seen in the names by which they call themselves, Tïrïyo at Paloemeu, Tarəno at Alalaparu. Perhaps the most revealing remark on this subject came from a Paloemeu Indian who said, 'The people at Alalaparu are not Tïrïyo'.

The sub-groups are not clans, lineages, totemic, descent, or any other type of formal alliance group. Frikel regularly describes them as sibs, and although he never defines his use of the term, it would appear that he means it to refer to an extended family or a group of interrelated people rather than in the sense of a patri-clan. This is probably a fair assessment of the sub-groups, but one can add to this description a greater or lesser degree of territorial isolation; following my suggestion above that, in this area, separation quickly blossoms into distinction.

If the sub-groups can be defined as groups of closely interrelated people living in one or more villages which are relatively close together but territorially separated from a neighbouring sub-group, their part in the total organization of Trio society becomes clearer. Further discussion of this subject must be delayed until later.

The disappearance of these sub-groups can be explained in two ways. Firstly, the congregation of all the Indians from wide areas into large settlements would obscure the sub-groups which rely for their distinction on isolation. Secondly, there is some indication that the sub-groups were disappearing before the recent population movements. This, I believe but cannot prove, is because of the gradual decrease in the population of the area. Some sub-groups died out completely while others became so numerically weak that they had to merge with other sub-groups in order to survive. It is probable that such integration was sometimes violent, particularly in cases where there was a shortage of women. This, it must be admitted, is basically conjecture, but the past and present demography gives, as we shall see, some idea of their declining numbers.

V

At the beginning of this chapter mention was made of the rock grooves which abound in the interior of Surinam; one way to account for the large number of these is to presuppose a far larger population at sometime in the past. The earlier ethnographic sources are of no help in this matter, and it is not until the first decade of this century that any idea is given of the numerical strength of the Trio.

After the Tumuchumac expedition, Bakhuis estimated there to be about 1,000 Trio (Bakhuis, 1908, p. 110), but at the same date de Goeje assumed fewer, viz., a total of 800, of which 500 lived in Brazil and 300 in Surinam (de Goeje, 1908, p. 1,119). The most valuable information on this subject is provided by Schmidt whose census of the Trio although not perfect is an impressive achievement. He gives a total of 687 Indians of which 226 were in Surinam and 461 in Brazil (Schmidt, 1942, pp. 50–51.) Taking into account that a number of individuals appear more than once in the census (it can be demonstrated that they are not different people with the same name) and that some people inevitably were missed, a figure in the region of 700 seems reasonable.

In 1957 Frikel estimated there to be between 1,000 and 1,200 Trio and this does not include those sub-groups which he describes as 'inaccessible' (Frikel, 1957, p. 514). I consider his figure to be over-optimistic, and certainly my own findings are more in keeping with Schmidt's. In March 1964 there were 157 Trio at the Alalaparu village and a further 219 at Paloemeu, a total of 376 in Surinam. At that time there were, as far as it was possible to ascertain, eight or nine Trio villages in Brazil. Taking 30 as the average number of inhabitants in a Trio village, I estimated there to be between 240 and 270 Indians in Brazil, and a grand total of between 616 and 646 Trio Indians. Since then new information has revealed that the lower rather than the higher figure is likely to be the correct one. Further migrations have increased the Trio population of Surinam to nearly 500 Indians, and only two Trio settlements now exist in Brazil, a small village on the Anamu and a larger one near the Roman Catholic mission on the West Paru savannah. It is unlikely that the combined population of these two settlements greatly exceeds 100 Indians. In round figures, 600 seems to be the fairest estimate of the total number of Trio Indians.

These figures by themselves are inadequate proof of a declining population, although they do seem to indicate it. The Trio themselves admit that they were facing extinction, and were fully aware of the reason. The effect of exotic sickness and disease among Amerindian people is too well documented to require comment here.[1] It will suffice to say that everyone who has visited the Trio has written of deaths caused by foreign ailments. Also the Trio have known for a long time that sickness and death is related to the visits of strangers; it is perhaps in this sense that one must interpret the Pianakoto tradition recorded by Schomburgk that 'the arrival of the first white man betokened the extinction of their race' (Schomburgk, 1845, p. 87). More explicit were the Trio of the East Paru who directly accused the *pananakíri* of bringing disease among them (Crevaux, 1883, p. 273). The same theme continues through all accounts of the Trio, and today their fear of strangers, a particularly well marked feature of the Trio character, has only slightly diminished. The greatest fear is reserved for the Bush Negroes who, because of their greater contact with the Trio, are undoubtedly the most to blame; but this attitude extends also to other Trio who, it is recognized, can equally well be carriers of disease.

As recently as 1952 Frikel noted the death of 25 Indians from colds, and a further 17 in 1958 from the same cause (Frikel, 1960). Even after the arrival of medical aid with the missionaries, the demographic situation remained precariously balanced. In 1963 at Alalaparu there were seven births and eleven deaths of which the most disastrous feature was that of those who died seven were aged 12 and under, and five of them were less than a year old. The situation was a little better at

[1] The destruction of the indigenous population of Oyapock has been described by Sausse who estimated that the number decreased, almost entirely as a result of disease, from 20,000 to 500 between 1700 and 1900 (Sausse, 1951, pp. 67–98).

Paloemeu where there were six births (excluding one stillborn), and five deaths of which two were adults and the other three children of under 4 years. It is obvious that no society can survive this kind of mortality rate, but the continued medical care does seem to have checked the worst effects of the epidemics and the last four years have shown a marked improvement in the situation. In 1964, at Alalaparu, there were twelve births and only one death. In the years 1965, 1966, 1967, there were respectively among all the Surinam Trio 32 births and 10 deaths in a population of 545, 20 births and 7 deaths in a population of 578, and 22 births and 5 deaths in a population of 584. The one black spot in these figures is that children of 12 years and under still account for a half of the deaths (van Mazijk, 1966, 1967, 1968), but otherwise the signs are good.

4

III

SELECTED ASPECTS OF TRIO
CULTURE

THE SELECTION of topics for discussion in this chapter has
been dictated mainly by the requirements for understanding
the subject of this monograph. Some additional and not
directly pertinent information is provided both for sake of
general interest and to fill in gaps in the reader's background
knowledge of these people. Such subjects have not been treated
exhaustively but since they are the ones with which the earlier
ethnographers have dealt, anybody who finds these descriptions too brief can easily turn to other sources for additional
details.

This chapter is based mainly on my own observations, and
only occasionally when I have been suspicious about the
indigenous nature of some trait have I turned to the ethnography for confirmation. The ethnographic present tense is
used through most of the chapter, but it should be remembered
that some cultural features have disappeared and others are
disappearing or changing as a result of the recent developments
in the area and among the Indians.

I

The average height of the male Trio is about 62 ins., but one
or two individuals are as much as 10 ins. above this mean. The
women are mostly a few inches shorter than the men. The
weight of only a few men was recorded, an insufficient number
to suggest a reliable average, but the range is from 100 lbs. to
140 lbs. Both men and women have slender, even graceful
lower halves to their bodies surmounted by waistless, heavy
barrel-like torsos and relatively large shoulders. The apparent
unrelatedness between the upper and lower halves of the
Indians' bodies is one of the most characteristic physical features
of the Trio.

Skin colour varies from light to dark brown, and the little
body and facial hair which does grow is plucked, as are the

eyebrows and eyelashes. The hair of the head is thick and black, and is worn long, down the back by both sexes. From the crown of the head the hair is combed to the front and sides; in front of the eyes the hair is cut level with the centre of the forehead, and allowed to fall either side of the eyes to the cheekbone (on average, but sometimes lower) at which level it is clipped as far back as the ears. This style of haircut is used by the Trio to distinguish themselves from neighbouring Amerindian groups such as the Waiyana who part their hair down the middle, or the Waiwai whose hair is combed forward like the Trio but is then cut in a fringe, above the level of the eyes from ear to ear. This latter style has been adopted by a number of the Trio at Alalaparu who have been influenced by Waiwai Christian missionaries.

The Trio cut off all their hair for one of three possible reasons: an excess of lice, in mourning for a close relative, or, for a girl, at her first menstruation or at the birth of her first child.

The single piece of dress worn by the men is a length of cloth for which the term 'lap' has been generally accepted. The lap is supported by a cotton waistband; one end is tucked through the waistband at the front and several inches allowed to hang down. The rest of the cloth is passed between the legs and fixed in a similar manner at the back. Previously these laps were woven from local cotton but they are now universally made from red trade cloth.

The woman's dress is even more meagre, and merely consists of a small, red cloth apron which, supported from a thin cotton thread, hangs down over the pudenda. A number of women own more elaborate aprons made with coloured glass beads.

Supplements to this basic dress are, for the most part, worn by men and women alike, and any individual may wear all, none, or any combination of the following: armbands, wristlets, calf-bands, and anklets. Today these are often made with glass beads, but previously they were of palm leaves or bark; the calf-bands, which remain unchanged, are woven from cotton and left with long fringes reaching to the ankles in extreme cases. Two items of dress which seem to have fallen into abeyance are the decorated bead armbands worn by adult males, and a device also of beads which the women reputedly wore across the small of the back.

These items, with the exception of the last two, are worn continuously, and could perhaps be considered to belong to the category of dress rather than decoration, although no distinction exists in Trio thought. The strings of beads which both sexes wear round the neck or in bandolier fashion stand somewhere between dress and decoration: some Indians wear beads every day but there is a tendency for the majority to wear more beads on special occasions. Ear ornaments are fitted on most days, and in the manufacture of these glass and aluminium are replacing the traditional snail shell.

Simple feather decorations at the waist or in the armband are fitted on any day, but the more complicated head dresses and crowns are reserved for ceremonial and ritual occasions. The practice of wearing a feather in a hole in the lower lip or septum of the nose seems to have died out. The highly decorated queues which are a feature of the Trio's westerly neighbours are rare, but simple bamboo tubes or fibre bindings are used by men to retain the hair while occupied in strenuous physical labour. The hair is anointed with vegetable oil about once a week, and is then sometimes decorated with white eagle's down.

Tattooing and body-deformation are not practised, but both the body and face are painted, and two types of this can be distinguished. Red paint (*Bixa Orellana*) is used to cover the whole body, or sometimes only the lower half in a single monochrome wash. The pigment is often applied with a mixture of krapa oil (*Carapa guianensis*), and in these cases the strictly practical explanation of body painting as a means for keeping warm or discouraging the attention of mosquitoes has some justifiable validity, especially when its application coincides with a journey. However the Trio see it as a protection against spirits, and, without becoming too involved in a description of Trio beliefs, it is sufficient to note both that the spirits are unable to see objects coloured red and that the smell of red paint is distasteful to them.

On this point it is interesting to note that a large number of Trio spirits are described as being like Bush Negroes, and that the Bush Negroes themselves express great disgust at the Indians' habit of body painting. However, I could never get a Trio informant explicitly to admit the obvious implication.

Black paint (*Genipa Americana*) is never applied indiscriminately all over the body but is either painted in complicated over-all designs, or only on certain parts of the body and in particular over the joints of the lower limbs. The Trio say that the black paint is merely to make themselves more beautiful and attractive to the opposite sex, but the application of the genipa to the joints possibly disputes this, since the spirits are considered to attack a person through these parts. Red and black paint, together with a yellowish one (probably *Bignonia Chica*) are used for executing on the face simple patterns such as straight lines and dots.

II

The disappearance of the traditional settlement pattern which had occurred by the time my investigations began proved the most serious handicap to a full understanding of Trio social organization. To some extent this deficiency has been overcome, partly by my own questioning of informants and partly from the ethnography. Although such a reconstruction can in no way be regarded as a totally adequate substitute for observation of the actual pre-existing situation, I am certain that a high degree of accuracy has been achieved.

The various sources are more or less agreed upon the number and size of Trio villages; at the beginning of this century there were estimated to be 20 to 30 Trio villages (Bakhuis, 1908, p. 110) Schmidt gives the name of 25 Trio villages of which he visited 20 (Schmidt, 1942, pp. 55–62), and Frikel reckons there to be 30 villages or more (Frikel, 1957, p. 514). Relating these figures to the population size considered in the last chapter, it is obvious that these villages are small. Schmidt's census shows that the average number of inhabitants in the Surinam Trio villages is 38 Indians, in Brazil only 24, and an over-all average of 27·8 (Schmidt, 1942, pp. 50–1). Frikel notes, 'Theoretically there is an average of 30 souls per village but the actual figure varies from 15 to 50 although rarely does a village contain more than 50 inhabitants' (Frikel, 1957, p. 514). This size of village is widely reported among the Cariban tropical forest groups of Guiana.

These communities, as well as being small, are scattered; a clear idea of their distribution can be gained from Schmidt's

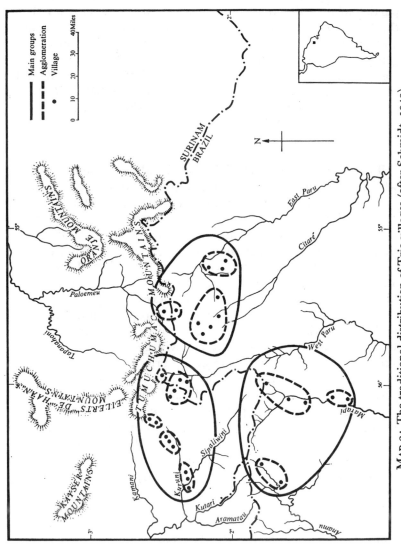

MAP 2: The traditional distribution of Trio villages (after Schmidt, 1942).

accounts of his journeys and his sketch map. On Map 2 the villages visited by Schmidt have been plotted, and when their distances apart in units of day's travel are marked, a distinct pattern emerges. The Trio villages can be divided into three main groups which correspond with the river basins of the Sipaliwini, the Citaré and East Paru, and the Marapi and Anamu. Except in the extreme west, at the Anamu/Kutari divide, a stretch of savannah divides these main groups. The nearest villages belonging to different main groups are separated by not less than 3 to 4 days' march.

Within the main groups clusters of villages, which will be called agglomerations, can be distinguished; the nearest villages of different agglomerations are about two days' march from each other.

Within an agglomeration the villages are normally only a few hours apart, and never more than a day.

For the moment it is only intended to draw attention to the existence of this pattern; its function in Trio economy is discussed later in this chapter, and in Trio social organization in Chapter VI.

The actual location of a village varies greatly; for the most part villages are not built on the banks of large rivers, but this may well be because the Trio live in an area where there are relatively few large rivers. The favourite site seems to be near a smaller but perennial river, but resources other than water are taken into account in selecting a suitable place. One old village which I visited was about a mile from the nearest water in the dry season, but the soil around the village was said to be exceptionally good for cassava.

The Trio, in common with most other tropical forest cultivators, move their villages frequently. A number of different reasons can be shown to account for this but in the case of the Trio it is mainly related to the exhaustion of cultivable land in the immediate vicinity or to the death of an inhabitant. Other factors enter into this, including the infestation of the village by various types of parasites and insects, and the unwillingness of Indians to replace the thatch of an old house and their preference for building a new one. The thatch of a house lasts three to five wet seasons.

It is impossible to gauge how often the Trio used to move

their village sites, and, although de Goeje suggests every five to ten years (de Goeje, 1908, p. 1,102), it is unwise to be too definite about this, and Schmidt records a case of an almost new village being abandoned because a Bush Negro spat in the fire (Schmidt, 1942, p. 32).

It is unusual for the Trio to build a new village more than a short distance away from its predecessor—the reasons for this being that one of the old garden sites will remain productive for another year and that intimate knowledge of the area is a great asset for the hunter.

The number of houses in a village varies, but as many as eight is a large settlement, and four or five is nearer the average size. In Surinam, during 1964, there was an average of approximately five Indians to a house but this figure should be treated with caution since the recent migrations have caused undue pressure on housing while the influence of Christian teaching in persuading nuclear families to live alone has had an incalculable effect. There is no evidence that the Trio have ever lived in the large, communal houses which are a feature of their western neighbours and of many other groups in Guiana.

Four different types of permanent houses are built; two of these are explicitly recognized as having been borrowed from neighbours—a round type from the Waiwai and a rectangular one from the Waiyana. A very recent development is the construction of houses on short stilts—this is probably in imitation of the missionary or airfield staff houses, although such houses were reputedly built by the Galibi of Cayenne at one time, and still are by the Oyampi.

The traditional Trio houses are either a conical shape with the thatch reaching to the ground and with one or two doors, or a shed type which in its simplest form is open at the back and front, but may be closed at one or both ends with a semicircular extension so that in its most complete form it has a lozenge-shaped ground plan. The majority of houses face north or south, a natural adjustment for protection against sun and weather, but the increasing use of walls, made from wood or thatch, is beginning to reduce the preponderance of this alignment. The traditional plan of the village is a number of houses grouped around and facing on to a central open space called the *anna*.

Other less important houses are the temporary shelters which Indians make while travelling or in a village which they are visiting. A few work houses in which the women prepare the cassava may exist, but there are no special houses for men, bachelors, or any other group. A small thatch house, a miniature of the conical type mentioned above, is made for a shaman's séance but this is destroyed after use. Today there is a Christian church at both Alalaparu and Paloemeu and these buildings are very much larger than any other in the village.

All houses are wooden framed and thatched, and they are constructed exclusively by men.

III

The earth floor inside a house will be kept more or less clean but most of the few possessions are stored off the ground on trestles, stuck in the thatch, hung from the roof, or balanced in the rafters.

Every house has its hearth and in the houses without walls the fire is kept going all night and the hammocks of the occupants cluster round within the range of its warmth. Married couples sometimes share a hammock but more often they sleep in separate ones, the woman's slung beneath that of her husband's and in a position from which she can tend the fire without moving from her bed.

Two types of hammock are found among the Trio: a cotton kind (perhaps of Waiyana origin), which is made on a simple loom consisting of two posts in the ground, is woven by women. The preparation of cotton is exclusively confined to women, and their association in Trio idiom is comparable with the term 'distaff' in the English language.

The other kind of hammock, which is woven on a frame by men, is made from silk-grass fibre: the working of this material is as strictly reserved for men as cotton is for women, but it lacks such overt symbolic representation. Both types of hammock are used indiscriminately by men and women.

During the day a man will probably sit on a stool which is sometimes no more than a crudely shaped block of wood, but a number of Indians own carved and decorated ones. These conferred upon their owners some ill defined status; no one borrows or uses such a stool without first trying to ask the owner's permission, but nobody thinks twice about using another person's hammock. Women normally sit on mats made from the inner bark of the Brazil nut tree (the same material is used as a sanitary towel), and do not use stools of their own accord. The only occasion on which I observed a woman sitting on a stool was when I suggested it to her; she did, but with obvious embarrassment.

Most of a man's or woman's possessions are related to their respective roles in the economy. A man owns his hunting equipment, a bow, arrows, a knife, a machete, an axe, a file, a fishing rod with some spare hooks and line, and, in a number of cases, a shot gun. The richer Indian owns a surplus of these items which are stored in a basket or tin canister which is kept in the rafters. As well as these strictly economic tools, a man will also have his various ornaments, feather head dress, beads, and a vanity box containing a comb, little gourds of pigment, a mirror, a pair of scissors, and perhaps some spare lengths of red cloth. These, to a greater or lesser degree, form the total belongings of a Trio male.

A woman's possessions are slightly more extensive since they include all the domestic utensils, although some of these will be shared with other women. The full range of kitchen equipment includes a cassava grater, a cassava squeezer, a sieve, a clay griddle, an assortment of clay or metal pots, and a variety of flat basketwork for use as dishes, plates, or fans for the fire.

There is a startling difference between the basketwork, which is woven by the men and is of a high quality, and the pottery made by the women, of which the technique is poor and the resulting product crude, ill shaped, fragile, and undecorated.

A woman will also own a number of different sized gourds; the larger ones are used as water containers, and a range of smaller ones hang from the roof and contain dried peppers, vegetable oil and other commodities. In a simple palm leaf basket a woman will keep her precious cotton, both the untreated raw material and the balls of spun thread.

Food and drink which is the property of women is kept on shelves or in the rafters out of the reach of animals. None of the animals which are kept as pets has any subsistence value since the Trio strongly decry the eating of any pet even if it is an animal which is regularly shot for food. Most pets are birds such as parrots, toucans, or macaws which have some intrinsic value as trade items and as a source of feathers for making decorations. The Trio also keep chicken but regard them as pets and will not eat their flesh although they will eat the eggs. The missionary at Alalaparu has introduced Muscovy duck and domestic pigs, but it is too early to say what the Indians' attitude to these animals is going to be.

The most important animal in the Trio culture is the hunting dog, and it is valued both for hunting and trading. Men, not women, normally own dogs but there are exceptions to this rule. More often than not a woman will look after her husband's dogs, feeding, watering, and exercising them, but she is not allowed to approach them when she is menstruating. The value of a dog is expressed by the question 'Will it chase pig?'. If a dog hunts well it is well cared for and spends much of its life on a dog table either within the house or in a special kennel just outside; the purpose of this being to prevent it collecting any parasites, such as jiggers, ticks, or fleas, from coming to any harm, or perhaps from injuring anybody. The dogs which will not chase pigs are allowed to wander round the village, ownerless, unfed, fighting with fellow failures for any edible scrap, and kicked by anybody in whose range they come. It is these curs who come rushing and snarling at any stranger who enters the village.

The property of a Trio man and woman is small in amount and simple in its nature; the traditional objects can be created from the resources of the environment and the total technique of their manufacture is known and practised by any adult male/female partnership. Towards such items property concepts are poorly developed, as is shown in the reply of an informant when asked if anyone had ever stolen his bow or arrows: 'Why should anyone take mine? They can make their own.'

In contrast to this is the attitude towards women, in respect of whom the concept of ownership is well developed; women are intrinsically valuable not only as vital economic partners but because they cannot be made or replaced. War is closely related to marriage and trade, and the object of raids on other villages is only conceivable as an attempt to capture women and dogs. Inversely, strangers who come to a village are regarded as a potential threat to the community's female resources. Although the fact did not emerge until some time afterwards, the inhabitants of the first village in the Sipaliwini basin which was contacted by the Protestant missionaries discussed killing them, since they assumed that the missionaries were after their women. It is a truism to say that women are a necessity for the survival and continuance of a community, but the implication of this becomes less trite and more critical when the supply is not assured. A number of Trio institutions can be interpreted as means of preserving the community's female resources. These are examined in Parts Two and Three of this monograph; here it is intended merely to indicate the proprietary attitude of the Trio towards their women.

Between these two extremes lie the attitudes to belongings such as dogs, exotic manufactured goods, and certain cultivated plants. The value placed on these items varies from case to case, and while some informants say that no one would throw away an axe at the death of its owner, others say that even the deceased's dogs may be destroyed. All agreed that it is usual to destroy a dead man's bow or arrows, but his widow is never harmed—'she is a woman'. One must not give the idea of ownership too rigid an application when applying it to women, and indeed the Trio do not recognize in this context the use of either of their words which have this meaning. It is more that women belong to the society, but it is a male society.

IV

The primary economic activities consist of cultivating, hunting including fishing, and collecting, and these occupations provide the raw material upon which the traditional Trio subsistence and material culture is based. It is not absolutely obvious to the observer which of these activities is most important, but to the Trio there is no doubt: 'We can live without meat; without bread we die.'

i. *Cultivation.* The Trio consider the year to begin at the end of the wet season, and this is also the beginning of the agricultural cycle which is marked by the appearance of the Pleiades (*momən*—a container) in the eastern horizon just before dawn. During August or September the new field is cut, for which a sandy, well drained area near the village is selected.

The cut trees are left to lie under the hot sun of the dry season, and then about mid November, when the foliage is brown and withered but before it has fallen, they are burned. The amount of secondary clearing which is required depends on the effectiveness of the burning, but no attempt is made to remove larger trunks or roots, and only the smaller branches are piled in heaps for reburning.

Even before the secondary clearing is completed and with the onset of the December rains the planting of bananas, pineapples, sugar cane, sweet potatoes, eddoes, yams, and maize begins. The earlier operations are performed by men, but both sexes join in the planting. The main crop, bitter cassava, is planted during January, after the December rains but before the arrival of the main wet season which is marked by Orion (Yaraware—a culture hero) beginning to fall from its zenith into the western sky during the early part of the night. The Trio say that the rains fall with Yaraware who owns them.

The task of planting cassava is shared by men and women; men dig mounds of earth with hoes while the women collect cassava stocks from their old fields. These stocks are cut into lengths of about 8 ins. by men or women, and both sexes plant them by pushing a number into the mounds of loose earth.

From this point on the field becomes very much the domain of the woman, and its future care and harvesting of its produce is her job. Bitter cassava has a lengthy growing period; ten months being the minimum time before the root is considered suitable for harvesting. As the women dig the crop they replant, but as the second harvest is collected the field is allowed to fall into disuse, and it soon reverts to secondary forest. Supplementary crops are not normally planted twice in a field. After the second crop of cassava has been lifted a number of visits might be made to pick bananas or cotton which, however, soon become stifled by the undergrowth and weeds. The Indians do not like visiting old gardens for the practical reason that the plants which infest them are thorns and razor grass, and together with fallen trees they make progress difficult and unpleasant. The life of a garden from the time of cutting until it is finally abandoned is about three years.

As well as the food crops other plants are grown in the fields; these include cotton, calabashes, gourds, tobacco, and silk-grass. Cotton and pepper are usually also found growing on the periphery of the village. The bamboo used for arrows is sometimes grown in the neighbourhood of the village.

Agricultural labour does not absorb much of the men's time; at certain periods they may be fully occupied with it but it is a seasonal activity restricted mainly to August–September, and December–January, while the months in between are free from such work. For a man the most unpleasant work is probably that of secondary clearing and digging which take place in the hot sun. The cutting of fields is enjoyed and is considered, quite understandably, exciting work.

Agriculture and the preparation of cassava are the most important female activities and, unlike the men, they have no respite from it.

ii. *Hunting and Fishing.* These activities are only a shade less important than cultivation, but their pursuit is the man's prime role in the subsistence economy. The methods and techniques employed by the Trio show no important variations from those described for other tropical forest hunters of Guiana.

The main weapon of the Trio is the bow and arrow, of which a variety of types can be distinguished and each has its special purpose. A long flat bamboo point is used for the main land game such as wild pig, tapir, or forest deer, a long barbed point with a round cross-section for the larger birds such as bush turkeys, and a small detachable head smeared with curare poison for monkeys. Blow pipes are not used and the idea of them is unknown to the Trio.

A number of Indians own shot guns, and they are a much prized possession. I saw no trace of the spears which the Trio are reported to use by the earlier ethnographers. The clubs they carry are not hunting weapons.

The normal practice is for an Indian to go hunting alone with his dogs, but he may sometimes be accompanied by one or two other men, or a woman, his sister or wife. The task of the dog is to corner the game, and hold it at bay until the hunter can arrive to kill it. About half the ground game killed is credited to the action of dogs. On occasions large parties of men go out on a collective hunt when there is the rare appearance of a herd of white-lipped peccary (*Tayassu pecari*) in the district. Hunting is slightly restricted by the wet season but it is at this time of year that game is most valued because it is at its fattest. One informant could never mention the rainy season without saying in the same breath that it is when the spider monkeys are fat.

It has been noted earlier in this chapter that the lack of suitable agricultural land in the immediate vicinity of a settlement is one of the main reasons for the relatively frequent shifting of village sites. A new village is rarely far from the old one, and the tendency for the community to remain in the same neighbourhood may well reflect the Indians' wish to stay in an area with which they are familiar—an important factor in hunting. It appears, however, that the quantity of game in a given district fluctuates from one year to the next; a fact which provides a clue to the function of the village agglomerations which have been mentioned.

Fishing, in purely quantitative terms, has more seasonal importance than hunting. Fish are caught at any time of year by shooting with a bow and arrow or by use of a line and hook. A harpoon type of arrow is used for fishing which may or may not have feather flights, a detachable head, or three prongs. There may have been bone fish-hooks before the introduction of manufactured metal ones, but it is doubtful if they were adequate for catching the larger fish. Although the Trio appear to know about fish traps I never saw one which had been made by a Trio nor heard of a Trio using one. Women occasionally go fishing with a hook and line, or catch small fish in pots as they jump the falls at the beginning of the dry season.

Fish are most important for subsistence during the dry season, when very large quantities can be caught by the poisoning of pools which have been left by the dropping water level, or even in medium-sized rivers when their flow is greatly diminished. A large-scale fish poisoning is attended by nearly every inhabitant of the village, and in the event of a successful day they will return with a truly prodigious catch. In running water this is always a wasteful process but particularly so with the Trio, who make no effort to dam the stream so that no stupefied fish are swept away. According to the Indians the poisoning of a creek has no detrimental effect on the supply of fish during the following year.

iii. *Collecting*. This third section in the tripartite division of the subsistence economy is no less important for the Trio. It is not always easy to distinguish between hunting or fishing and collecting, or perhaps between cultivating and collecting, but a valid distinction can be made between the collecting of animals or items related to animal life (such as honey or turtle's eggs) which form part of the diet, and objects from plant life which may equally well contribute to the diet or technology.

A slight difference can be noted between the plants collected as food and those as raw materials for manufacture: the former seem to have a more seasonal distribution. Collecting rarely provides the mainstay of the diet, although for a brief period near the beginning of the main rains some palm and other trees bear fruit which the Indians consume in vast quantities, and apparently in preference to the more normal diet. (The abundance of tree fruits at this season presumably explains the fatness of the spider monkey during the rains.)

Raw materials which are used in the manufacture of every item in the Trio's traditional culture are mainly collected as required, and the range of such materials is immense. The greatest proportion are of vegetable origin, and few items come from the animal or mineral worlds. Leather is not used except as a covering for the containers of curare points, while only arrow heads and barbs, and the hooks of cotton spindles, are made from bone. The jaw of a pig is used for carving bows. Clay is collected for making pottery, and stone is used for cassava graters, hearth stones, and was at one time used for axes. Earth eating among the Trio has been reported (de Goeje, 1910, p. 5), but this may have been through lack of salt of which they now have plenty.

Two Trio attitudes are well expressed in their collecting techniques. Time and effort are unimportant in relation to the result; a great deal of both will be expended in cutting down a tree to get a minute quantity of honey, or in the hope that macaw fledglings will survive the fall to become pets. Secondly, they have a not surprising disregard for the resources of their environment, and in particular vegetable ones. The collection of tree fruits is always achieved by cutting the tree down; a practice which is allied to their complete failure to understand my suggestion that the tree could not thus bear fruit next year.

Dietary items are normally collected by either sex as the opportunity arises, but both men and women will make special journeys to collect certain types of food. In the case of raw materials collection is usually restricted to the sex who will process it: a man will go to fetch material for weaving or making a house, but does not go to collect pottery clay, which is done by a woman as she needs it.

In summary, hunting and fishing is mainly a male occupation while farming is a female one, although male help is provided for the heavier tasks. Collecting is performed by both sexes, but in the case of any particular raw material its collection is confined to the sex which is involved in its processing.

V

The description of secondary economic activities is limited to the consideration of the preparation and consumption of food, and does not include such techniques as house building, pottery making, weaving or spinning, although these activities rightly belong under this heading. The reason for this limitation is that food as the basis of subsistence is surrounded by social values and behaviour which provide particularly useful insights into Trio social organization

The Trio eat every bird and animal except carnivores, carrion-eaters, and snakes, the classes of fauna with which Trio beliefs are mainly involved. This division, however, does not extend to fish and amphibians such as the carnivorous *pirai* or the crocodilians which are regularly eaten.

It is not certain which meat the Trio like most, but it is possibly the collared peccary (*Tayassu tajacu*), an assumption based on the oft expressed wish for this kind of meat made by women whose husbands were out hunting. Disregarding the type of animal, the most important consideration is whether or not it is fat—the first question asked of a successful hunter whose return to the village never fails to arouse interest and even excitement.

The kill is normally cut up by a man, but the hair or fur is scraped off by women who dip the skin in boiling water to ease the process. Smaller animals and birds may be entirely treated by a woman. The skin is not removed from the flesh but is cooked and eaten. The meat is usually cooked by the women,
5

and this consists of boiling with peppers. Very little of the animal is considered unsuitable for adding to the pot. Some odd scraps may be cut off and roasted over the fire or in the embers. If there is a surplus of meat or fish it is smoked on a trestle over the fire; meat treated in this way can be stored for several months, but when it comes to be eaten it will also be boiled in water with peppers.

The emphasis on boiling seems only partially related to the preservation of the meat, and seems to be as much connected to the difficulty of eating cassava bread which has not been dipped in liquid. The gravy made by boiling meat is almost public property and anyone may come and ask for some, and indeed it is the epitome of Trio meanness to refuse. This is not true of the meat over which the owner has the right to give or deny, but its distribution, as will be shown later, has considerable meaning in the social organization. During periods when there is no meat or gravy a suitable sauce for softening the cassava bread is made by boiling peppers with water or cassava juice. Meat is not boiled in cassava juice, and in this the Trio differ markedly from some other Carib groups. Salt, a valuable and imported commodity, is not added during cooking but only to the gravy just prior to eating.

In contrast to the excited activity which surrounds the return of a hunter with his kill and the ensuing preparation of it is the dull routine which is connected with the collection and preparation of the cultivated crops. This work is restricted to women, and certain features of the cassava crop, such as its long growing period, absence of a single harvest, and the numerous processes required to turn it into bread, all help to emphasize the monotony of this female occupation.

Although on two exceptional occasions men were seen to carry back cassava from the fields, and more frequently to help in the peeling of the root, no man was ever seen to grate, squeeze, sift, or bake cassava.

In quantitative terms bitter cassava is the only important cultivated plant; the auxiliary crops play only a subsidiary part in the diet, and many of them are consumed in the form of drink. Sweet potatoes, which are used to make a thick gruel, are also roasted in the embers, as are plantains. Bananas and pineapples may be eaten raw or turned into a drink, and sugar cane is mostly chewed. Maize is turned into a coarse flour with a pestle and mortar, and Brazil nuts are grated and the flour baked into bread. The fermented drinks which the Trio used to make from these plants have disappeared since the arrival of the missionaries.

A meal normally consists of meat, or at least gravy, cassava bread, and drink. Meals may be taken at any hour of the day, and often at frequent intervals if meat is available. Food is normally taken in the morning before the day's activity begins, and again towards dusk. It is rare for an Indian to go through the day without additional food. When the men are working in the fields the women take out drink to them, and when out hunting or collecting they usually find something out of which to make a snack—honey, tree fruits, beetle larvae, or small birds or fishes roasted over a quickly kindled fire.

There are two kinds of meal, the family one and the communal one. Those who attend a family meal are normally the residents of a single dwelling, although related people may join in, and anybody who happens to be in the house or even passing may be invited to eat. On occasions a man would go and make a special invitation to someone to come and eat. It is rude to refuse the offer of food although the obligation need not involve more than a mouthful before indicating one has had enough by saying 'naka'. Men and women eat together at family meals except when some unrelated man is present and then the women will eat separately.

At the communal meal which takes place in the *anna*, men and women always eat separately. The food for these meals is provided by several families and the whole affair is presided over by the village leader who calls the people to come and eat, distributes the meat, and to whom '*naka*' is said. The wife of the leader administers the women's food.

The communal meal, as I observed it in the setting of the large newly formed villages, seems to be a development of similar meals which in the traditional-sized settlements would have merely been an extension of the family meal. Indeed at Paloemeu the large influx of immigrants while I was there resulted in a remultiplication of communal meals, which were then eaten in the various sub-divisions of the village, and only on Sunday did the entire community eat together.

The subject of the distribution of food, and in particular who gives what to whom and what the gift means or entails is described in Part Three. The range of such behaviour is wide; the giving of food to a stranger is an accepted obligation and its denial an act of hostility. Commensalism is a mutual acceptance of strangers, and a symbol of both trust and unity. The provision of food or drink of different types to different people may be the reciprocal prestation in a series of obligations, or a single act whereby an individual can invite or encourage one or many to fulfil some well defined role, whether it be for a woman to provide a sexual service, or for a man his assistance in cutting a field. To understand the distribution of food is to understand some of the fundamental aspects of Trio social organization.

VI

The most important and the traditional means of Trio transport is manpower, and the system of communications is by foot along ill defined jungle trails. The Trio did not make extensive use of canoes since even the light-weight barkskin type is difficult to navigate in the narrow creeks which are choked with fallen trees. The use of dug-out canoes and the technique of their manufacture is almost certainly a recent adoption and one borrowed from either the Waiyana or Bush Negroes, but the presence or absence of canoes still depends on the size of the rivers in the area. At Paloemeu the numerous dug-out canoes are in daily use on the wide deep waters of the Tapanahoni and Paloemeu Rivers. At Alalaparu, where the creek contains only a few inches of water in the dry season—the Kuruni is not much deeper—there are only two dug-out canoes; one was built for the missionary by a Mawayana, and another by a Trio who had learnt the art during a stay on the Tapanahoni. These canoes were only used once in the six months of my stay at Alalaparu, and then at the instigation of a Waiwai Indian. Three old barkskins are kept on the Kuruni, but these had been brought from the Sipaliwini, have fallen into disrepair, and are not being replaced.

The usual means of transporting a load is by carrier basket which hangs down the back and is supported by a band round the forehead. Both men and women carry loads in this manner, and considerable weights can be transported for short distances. A woman will carry a basket full of cassava weighing over 50 lbs. back from her field. This figure coincides with the 20–25 kg. which is the load Schmidt considers an Indian capable of carrying on the trail, while he himself claims to carry 80 kg. (Schmidt, 1942, p. 32).

Distance is an important factor in the transport of such weights, and one which must be taken into account when considering the reasons for moving a village site: cassava is a bulky crop and a garden at some distance from the village adds greatly to the women's economic burden. Steward has even suggested that the knowledge of the dug-out canoe coupled with cultivation was sufficient reason to permit the formation of semi-permanent communities of hundreds and perhaps a thousand people (Steward, 1963, e, p. 699).

The Trio travel extensively inside limited areas (most journeys being restricted to the agglomeration and few being outside the territory of the main group). Journeys are made during the dry season and movement is restricted by flood and swamps during the rains. The Indians are unwilling to travel by canoe during high water partly through the danger of navigating the numerous rapids and partly through the slow progress of upstream travel.

There are three reasons why the Trio travel away from their agglomeration (why they travel inside their agglomeration is explained in section VII)   curiosity, search for a wife, and trade. The Trio trade among themselves, with other Amerindian groups, and with the Bush Negroes or *mucambeiros*. The opportunity to trade or work for Europeans (including Brazilians) has recently become a possibility.

Trio trade and contact with other Amerindian groups is now limited, although it was more extensive in the past. At present there is permanent contact in the east with the Waiyana. The Trio and the Waiyana are very different people both in character and appearance; the Waiyana are tall and thick-set, swaggering and demanding. In the East Paru basin the two groups have lived juxtaposed for a long time, and intermarriage had begun by 1878 (Crevaux, 1883, p. 268). Perhaps as a result of a declining population (the Waiyana have suffered even more than the Trio) such marriages now seem to be more frequent than a generation ago; at Paloemeu in March 1964 there were eleven mixed Trio/Waiyana marriages. Six Trio men had Waiyana wives, and five Trio women had Waiyana husbands, but there is only one adult, Marinu (415), who is of mixed parentage. The consensus of opinion among the Trio is that it is bad for a Waiyana man to marry a Trio woman but there is nothing wrong with a Trio taking a Waiyana wife—a conviction in accord with the Trio's general attitude towards their women.

There is no contact between the Sipaliwini basin Trio and the Waiyana, so it is possible to observe at Paloemeu a number of different items and techniques which have obviously been borrowed from the Waiyana. The cultural interchange appears to be on a superficial level and not to have disturbed any important Trio values.

To the west the Trio no longer have any permanent or even regular contact with any Amerindian group. Their neighbours in this direction were the Saluma (who are the Charuma and possibly Taruma[1]) who lived in the Anamu and Trombetas areas. At one time contact and trade with these people seems to have been considerable and de Goeje (1906) describes many Trio objects as being of Saluma origin. Trade with the Saluma ceased sometime in the 1930s as a result of a war between the two tribes. Schmidt, however, is of the opinion that the Saluma withdrew from contact with the Trio because of the 'coughing sickness' which they passed on from the Bush Negroes (Schmidt, 1942, p. 41). The fate of the Saluma is uncertain, and the whole problem of this group, its history, and its linguistic affiliations is too complicated a subject to discuss here, nor, indeed, is it directly relevant (cf. Rivière, 1967). The pertinent fact is that sometime between 1910 and 1940 intercourse, either because of extinction or migration, ceased between the Trio and Saluma.

The older Trio still remember that they use to trade dogs from the Saluma who, in turn, obtained them from the Waiwai. There must also have been some direct contact between the

[1] According to Frikel (1961, a, p. 11), the Charuma are also called the Tunayana; an associate of the Waiwai at Alalaparu was reputed to be a Mawayana but when I asked him to confirm this he said he was a Tunayana. The Mawayana and Taruma languages do not belong to the Carib group; nor presumably does the Tunayana's.

Trio and the Waiwai since there is reputed not so long ago to have been a fight between them and even before the recent developments there was one mixed Trio/Waiwai marriage. A number of Waiwai were introduced among the Trio as Christian missionaries and their cultural influence has been very powerful; it is unlikely that the Protestant missionaries could have achieved the same result in such a short space of time without their help. Unfortunately this intriguing subject has no place in this book.

There are now no indigenous people living to the immediate north and south of the Trio, and it has been suggested in Chapter II that the previous inhabitants of these areas have partly died out and partly constitute the modern Trio.

The diffusion of certain material culture traits among the Waiyana, Trio, and Saluma has been discussed by Frikel (1961,a) with whom I agree on general grounds if not in detail. Finally on this subject it might be noted that no European is recorded as having reached any of these groups prior to the arrival among them of manufactured iron goods. This is partly because of the Amerindian trade routes and partly because of the activities of the Bush Negroes.

The subject of contact and trade with the Bush Negroes is important since in the ambivalent attitude towards these people a certain aspect of Trio ideology finds its most overt expression.

Trio contact with groups of escaped slaves began in the eighteenth century on the Tapanahoni and, as has been mentioned in Chapter II, this resulted in the withdrawal of the Trio to the southern side of the watershed. To begin with, the Bush Negroes may have had partly to depend on the Indians for survival, since those living on the coast were hostile. This dependence developed into a trade which was of equal value to both sides, and the Bush Negroes were trying to safeguard this monopoly until a decade ago. From this trade the Trio received all types of manufactured goods, but in particular axes, knives, machetes, and beads, and the Bush Negroes collected in exchange dogs, cassava squeezers, pets, and basketwork. Dogs were and still are the most valuable trade item; at the beginning of this century a good hunting dog was worth an axe, a sheath knife, an ordinary knife, a pair of scissors, a piece of cloth, and a small bunch of beads (de Goeje, 1906, pp. 28–29). In 1964 I saw a hunting dog sold for two axes, two machetes, a big knife, a metal canister with padlock, a litre bottle of salt, two mirrors, a pair of scissors, and a metal basin.

The Trio accuse the Bush Negroes of being hard and unfair bargainers, but I am not too certain about the scrupulous honesty of the Trio in these affairs; the sign of a good hunting dog is a curly tail, but the Trio ensure this by twisting the tails of young puppies.

Although the Trio have been in touch with the Bush Negroes for almost two hundred years, the total extent of this contact is relatively small since it has been restricted to brief trading visits. The Trio have accepted the material benefits which the Bush Negro has had to offer, but they have not assimilated any of his ideas. Furthermore the possession of more efficient tools has probably had little influence on the basic form of Trio culture other than to make the traditional tasks simpler and quicker. One indirect effect of this trade has already been touched upon: the introduction into the society of property, other than women, which has an intrinsic value, and cannot be replaced by any member of the society out of the resources of the environment.

It is as the provider of valuable manufactured objects, and furthermore the only source of them, which is one view the Trio hold of the Bush Negro.

It was not, one can be certain, the dislike of the Bush Negroes' business methods which caused the Trio to retreat away from them; it was the disease and sickness which they brought with them. This attitude to the Bush Negroes has already been mentioned above (p. 30), and does not need repeating in detail but requires further emphasis.

Schmidt was told that the Trio had abandoned the Kamani River area because the region was too remote and outside the sphere of Bush Negro trade (Schmidt, 1942, p. 34), but a few pages earlier the same ethnographer records an impassioned speech by Pika (39) in which he directly accuses the Bush Negro of coming uninvited, bringing disease and thus killing hundreds of Trio (ibid., p. 20). This fear, horror, and dislike is still plainly present in the Trio attitude to the Bush Negro, and in spite of this Tǝmeta (482) told me that the Trio had moved their villages back down the Paloemeu for the specific purpose of trading with the Bush Negroes.

It is not surprising that this embodiment in a single group of the dual personality of provider and killer has produced conflict in the Trio attitude not only towards it but also to all strangers. In an area of dwindling population the fear of death brought by the traveller is only offset by the necessity of social intercourse if the small isolated community is to survive. The Trio's attitude towards the Bush Negroes reflects plainly the less obvious pattern of hostility and interdependence which exists between Trio villages.

VII

The smallest viable economic unit is the partnership of a man and woman. The combination of an adult of each sex is theoretically capable of existing alone because between them they should know every technique of the traditional culture which the Trio use for exploiting the resources of their environment. Obviously the abilities of individuals vary, but broadly speaking this is true. However, this male/female partnership implies some specialization on the basis of sex.

There are certain jobs which I never saw performed by a man and others never by a woman; for example I never saw a man spinning cotton, fetching water, making a clay pot, or baking bread, nor a woman weaving the more intricate basketry, making or using a bow and arrow, or thatching a house. On the next level are a number of occupations which are recognized as predominantly belonging to one sex but will occasionally be performed by the other; a man might help his wife peel cassava or fetch firewood, or a woman plait herself a simple basket. Finally there are those economic activities such as planting, fishing with a line and hook, or collecting in which both sexes join indiscriminately.

It is obvious that in some of the more strictly sex-linked occupations it may be difficult for the opposite sex to achieve proficiency without the years of childhood practice which they normally involve. However there are tasks such as grating cassava which a man could be equally capable of performing without practice. Even so the Trio are resolute on the division of labour and say that no man could or would attempt to do such a thing, and informants seemed doubtful about it when I suggested a hypothetical situation in which there were no women (not an idea the Trio can readily grasp). For the present purpose it is not important whether the refusal of one sex to participate in certain economic activities of the other is a physical or innate inability or the response to a socially conditioned attitude,[1] but it is fundamental to note such behaviour since the rigid adherence to it emphasizes the economic interdependence of man and woman.

If the male/female partnership is the smallest viable economic unit, what then in the wider sphere is the smallest economic social group? A consideration of this obviously involves a number of factors, but at the moment we are concerned with the economic aspects of the case.

The Trio live in an area of approximately 10,000 square miles of which they are almost the sole inhabitants. With a density of less than one person to 10 square miles there is no strain on the natural resources of the area as a whole. If, as has been suggested, the population of the past was considerably larger than it is at present, then some form of environmental determinism might have influenced the density and distribution of this former population; such a factor can no longer have an influence on the general pattern of settlement.

My first assumption was that the village is the basic economic unit: this I based on the following evidence. The village site is moved at frequent intervals and often as a result of the exhaustion of suitable agricultural land. The new village is built in the same general area which implies that the other natural resources of the region, those obtained by hunting, fishing, and collecting, are not exhausted. Thus the size of a village is in a harmonic balance with the hunting and collecting resources in the neighbourhood, and thus an economically self-supporting unit.

However, there are indications that this assumption is wrong and that the single village is not an entirely independent economic unit; in some years and in some ways it is, at other times and for other things it is not. This state of affairs is re-

---

[1] This value is inculcated at an early age; a small boy who carried some food to the *anna* for his mother was mocked by the other boys with cries of 'woman, woman'.

flected in a number of things. Firstly the size of a village waxes and wanes and, although other than economic factors can help to account for this, there is no doubt that it is partly a response to the exploitation of the area's natural resources. This view is supported by the explicit statement of Indian informants when they said they went to that village to hunt, that one to poison fish, and another to collect Brazil nuts. Secondly, some Indians said they had several villages and a garden at each one.

One has, therefore, the picture of a number of villages together which form the basic independent economic unit. This group is most likely to coincide with the villages which form the fundamental social grouping, and this is the agglomeration as the detailed evidence in Chapter VI shows. It would be useful to be able to associate the agglomeration with tribal subgroups; unfortunately there is not a single shred of evidence to support such a conjecture.

SUMMARY OF PART ONE

This first part of the monograph has been concerned with giving a general background for the Trio Indians. It has been shown that they live in an isolated headwater region, and that their environment is typical of many tropical forest cultivators. Relatively little is known about the prehistory of the area, and what historical knowledge we have indicates that the region has been a retreat area where various tribal remnants have amalgamated to form the present Trio.

Trio contacts with the outside world have mainly been through the medium of the Bush Negroes, who as well as providing useful manufactured goods introduced disease which has not only killed many Trio but also endowed them with a fearful attitude towards all strangers. Recent developments in the area have completely destroyed the traditional settlement pattern of small isolated villages, and the latest contacts, Christian missionaries, will probably change many fundamental Trio attitudes. The medical care now available will almost certainly allow these people to survive.

The material culture and economy show no basic differences from other groups of Guiana. Specialization, with the exception of shamanism, only appears in the sexual division of labour so that the co-operation of the two sexes forms a viable economic partnership. This reliance of men on women is a natural corollary of their proprietary attitude towards them. In the wider social sphere it is the agglomeration of villages which constitutes the basic socio-economic group.

PART TWO

TRIO SOCIETY—THE FACTS

THE FOUR CHAPTERS which make up this second part deal with aspects of Trio society of which the empirical existence is not in doubt and of which much of the material is quantifiable. Chapters IV and V treat of two aspects of the same thing, the criteria of social classification. In Chapter IV the criteria are described, and then used in a formal analysis of the relationship terminology, which in turn leads to the construction of models of the kin term system. In the following chapter it is demonstrated how these same criteria are used by the individual as operational tools in ordering his social world and interacting with other members of society.

Chapters VI and VII deal respectively with residence and marriage. It might be claimed that the chapter on residence should be placed before those concerned with the criteria of social classification. There is some force in such an argument, but I have chosen to leave it in its present position because the evidence presented there is mainly a reconstruction, since I did not observe the traditional pattern of residence; the conclusions, therefore, are less certain. The order of the following chapters does not imply my opinion of the relative importance of their subject matter (this should become abundantly clear), but my confidence in the conclusions. There is no reason why the reader who regards residence as more important or more assimilable than relationship terminologies should not turn first to Chapter VI.

IV

THE CRITERIA OF SOCIAL
CLASSIFICATION

THE EXAMINATION of relationship terminologies is unfashion-
able in so far that little prominence is given to them in modern
monographs. However, I regard the Trio relationship terminology so vital to the understanding of their social institutions
that my starting point for their exposition is a formal analysis
of the relationship terminology. My reason for this is quite
simple: Trio society lacks any type of formal social grouping
and, with the exception of the relationship terminology, any
verbal categories which have absolute rather than relative value,
with which to differentiate members of the society.[1] The basic
social categories among the Trio, both at the level of thought
and action, are kinship categories, and any understanding of
this society must rest on the understanding of them; that is to
say the criteria which a Trio employs in the ordering of his
social world.

A full list of Trio relationship terms, together with their
genealogical specifications, where applicable, will be found in
Appendix A. In this chapter we will only be concerned with
terms 1–17 inclusive, those terms which in fact have genealogical definition, as opposed to purely affinal or descriptive
connotation. These last two classes will be discussed respectively
in Chapter VIII and Chapter IX.

An examination of this terminology reveals the existence of
the following equations:

$$F = FB; \quad B = FBS = MZS; \quad Z = FBD = MZD.$$

---

[1] For example, although, as will be shown in Chapter VI, the household
unit is usually a single nuclear family, the Trio language lacks a word for
family. Attempts to discover such a term inevitably resulted in the informant coining a suitable expression such as *yenuruikaponempəton* which
literally means 'my ones formerly caused to be born', or *yitawərəken* which
literally means 'my particular dawning ones', i.e., those who pass the night
with me.

and the following distinctions:

$$F \neq MB; \quad B \neq FZS, MBS.$$
$$M \neq FZ; \quad Z \neq FZD, MBD.$$

These equations and distinctions together with marriage prescribed with an *emerimpǝ*, which category includes the bilateral cross-cousins, indicate a two-section terminology. However, further examination will reveal certain other equations such as:

$$M = FZD; \quad MB = FZS.$$
$$S = BS = ZS = MBS; \quad D = BD = ZD = MBD,$$

which, while not invalidating the label two-section terminology, do suggest certain complexities that no amount of juggling with the terms and their specifications will clarify. The next and vital step is to consider the principles by which any Trio assigns any other Trio to a particular category, and only after the consideration of these principles will it be safe and worthwhile to tackle the meaning of these terms.

There are three factors which a Trio takes into account in the ordering of his social world; these are genealogical connexion, residence, and age. The first two are clearly differentiated from the last because they receive overt and verbal recognition; they are expressed in the terms *itïpïme* and *imoitï* respectively. The factor of age does not manifest itself at the level of language, and only emerges as a delitescent method of classification when the system is submitted to the closest scrutiny.

Before embarking on a definition of *itïpïme* and *imoitï*, there is one further point which must be made clear. The Trio relationship terminology includes a number of lineal equations but they do not have any definite rule of descent; they are neither patrilineal nor matrilineal. The concept of unilineality is absent from both their social and biological notions, and it is worth making a brief digression to consider their ideas concerning the physical relationship between parents and child.

I

Tǝmeta (482), a normally reliable informant, provided the following account of how the Trio understand conception.

There is a common soul from which reservoir an individual draws his own soul, *amore*. In the beginning, the culture hero, Pərəpərəwa, created this common soul, and on the head of the first man he placed a spiritual male organ on which he then made a magical blowing which caused the soul to travel down through the man to the penis. An erection is caused by the spirit of the child in the penis, and during sexual intercourse both the spirit and flesh of the child flow into the woman, the sex of the child being decided in the penis.

This patrilineal ideology does not receive unanimous support and, while no informants denied it outright, some said that the child's spirit came from both the father and mother, and others that the issue is even more strongly sex-linked, a male child possessing only the spirit of the father and the female child only that of the mother. There is no preponderance of opinion on this subject, about which most Indians are ignorant or uninterested.

However, Təmeta, who favoured patriliny, agreed that the minute soul of the child is nourished by the soul of both parents. Moreover the spiritual connexion between parents and child continues after birth—a belief which receives recognition in Trio couvade practices. This tie is considered strongest between child and mother, since it is seen as a spiritual counterpart to the umbilical cord which, it is said, weakens and disappears after the parents' *amore* has raised and nurtured that of the child.

The behaviour of the parents is not alone in influencing the well-being of the child; Makerepən (434) said that the sickness of her late husband's sister's child was caused by the wickedness of her late husband; a case of the sister's child affected by the actions of the mother's brother.

The ritual behaviour surrounding pregnancy, childbirth, and early childhood suggests that the Trio see the child as the product of both parents, but social fatherhood is as important as actual paternity. One Trio who was seen to practise couvade restrictions was perfectly aware that his wife's child was not his.

The bilateralism which exists in Trio thought concerning physical relationship becomes even more pronounced in the field of social relationships.

6

II

Although the Trio do not recognize descent in its unilineal sense, genealogical connexion between parents and child, and between other close kin, is the foremost criterion in the ordering of social relationships. This connexion is expressed in the term *itĭpĭme*. This word is an adjective formed from the stem *itĭpĭ* and the suffix *-me* which has the connotation 'being'. The word also appears in verb form of which the stem is *itĭpĭhtə*, the suffix *-htə* being a verbalizer. It is doubtful that the basic stem *itĭpĭ* has any meaning by itself, but both the adjectival and verbal forms have the same area of meaning. In its genealogical sense the word applies basically to relationship by descent, although consanguinity may act as the interconnecting link, as will be shown. However, it has a far wider application, and is frequently used in very different contexts although in the same general semantic field. It can mean 'to continue without a break', as, for example, to describe two fields which adjoin each other without any gap or boundary between them. It may be said of someone who is travelling through a place on the way somewhere else without stopping, or at least only briefly.

When applied to people it may be used in a positive or negative form (*itĭpĭmeta*), and a number of factors may decide how any individual is classified. Basically it is as much a social as a biological classification, and certainly the social implications are of far greater importance. An aspect of it which must be made clear is that the term has only a relative not an absolute value. This explains why there is little agreement among informants as to whether certain categories of relatives are *itĭpĭme* or *itĭpĭmeta*. It is unanimously agreed that one's own (man speaking) and brother's children are *itĭpĭme* but there is not the same certainty about a sister's child. One man described a brother's son as being his *yipəri*—literally my branch or tributary—but said that the same word does not apply to his sister's children since they are *itĭpĭmeta*. However this theoretical distinction, although valuable as an indication of descent traced in the male line, collapses in practical application because the relative quality of the term predominates. For example, a brother's child may be considered *itĭpĭme* in comparison with a sister's child, but the latter will take on this value when compared with an unrelated person's child.

The second most important criterion in the ordering of relationships is the fact of co-residence, and this the Trio express in the term *imoitï*. This word describes those who live or have lived in the same village over a period of time. Once again this term has no absolute value, and will vary from individual to individual, depending on how long they have lived together in the same village—or, in other words, how well they know each other. Co-residence can be as closely binding as the ties of genealogical connexion, and in Trio thought they are not truly distinguished. Numerous examples can be given of this, since so closely associated are the two classes that it often proved difficult to persuade an informant to make the distinction, and rarely would an Indian make the distinction of his own accord. For example, Təmeta (482) considered Sipə (490) and Apokïnini (493) to be his brother's son and daughter, and it was only in collecting data for the genealogical table that it emerged that no genealogical connexion exists. On further questioning Təmeta declared, 'Their father is my brother because he is my father's *imoitï*'s son.'[1]

That the Trio often fail to distinguish between the criteria of genealogical connexion and co-residence in the ordering of social relations means that the residential composition of villages has important structural implications. A full examination of the subject will be found in Chapter VI, but here it is intended to continue the formal analysis of the Trio relationship terminology, aware of the factors of *itïpïme* and *imoitï*, and introducing the additional one of relative age. I have elsewhere (Rivière, 1966,a) demonstrated the importance of age in the ordering of social relations—in that article, for expository purposes, the emphasis was placed on the influence of age as a determinant of social classification. This chapter contains much of what appeared in that article but the inclusion of the

---

[1] In December 1967 I had the opportunity to talk with Sr. Protasio Frikel at the Museu Goeldi, Belém. In the course of our conversation we found that we were in agreement about most aspects of Trio social organization, but one exception to this was the meaning of the term *imoitï*. Frikel claims that the Trio are patrilineal and that *imoitï* refers to a man's patrikin; I have maintained my original definition since I have found no evidence to support Frikel's interpretation of this term. However, it is not without interest that my analysis of the terminology, made a long time before our conversation, had suggested the division of the relationship terms into two classes which distinguish a man's patrikin from his matrikin (see p. 66).

influence exerted by the other factors allows a more balanced approach.

The first step in the formal analysis is to make what appears to be a purely arbitrary division of the terms into two sets. This procedure, as will appear in the course of the analysis, is justified, and failure to make it at the outset leads one into great expository difficulties. This division is initially based on the distinction between those terms of the three medial levels which cover genealogical specifications from only one level, and those terms which cover specifications from more than one genealogical level. These two divisions will be referred to respectively as 'patriterms' and 'matriterms'.[1] Their composition is thus:

PATRITERMS	MATRITERMS
tamu	*tamu*
nosi	*nosi*
kuku	*kuku*
ipapa	*tĭ*
wəi	*imama*
ipipi	*pito*
akəmi (*kĭrĭ, wəri*)	*emerimpə*
imuku	*imuku*
emi	*emi*
ipa	*ipa*

As can be seen there are a number of terms which are common to both lines, and these will be dealt with first.

tamu: This term covers all men of the second ascending genealogical level from a male or female ego, and the English denotation 'grandfather' is adequate translation. It will be noted from Appendix A that the genealogical specifications for this term include such individuals as WF and MZH but the existence of such specifications does not contradict the defini-

---

[1] I apologize for these neologisms but all existing terms which might serve have slightly misleading connotations or imply some kind of formal grouping. The best definition for these new terms is a negative one; patriterms are 'those categories which would belong to ego's patriline *if* the society were patrilineal'. Matriterms are 'those categories which would belong to ego's mother's patriline *if* the society were patrilineal'. If Frikel is right about the meaning of the term *imoitĭ*, then the patriterms are ego's *imoitĭ*.

tion of the term just given. The existence of these specifications indicates the presence of inter-genealogical level marriages,[1] but a man does not become a *tamu* as a result of such a union. Let me make this clear: if a man of the second ascending genealogical level (a *tamu*) marries someone whom ego calls *imama* (MZ) then the MZH is called *tamu*. If on the other hand the MZH does not come from the second ascending genealogical level he will not be referred to as *tamu*, but by whichever other term is appropriate, i.e., *ipapa* if he comes from the first ascending genealogical level, or *konoka* if he is a stranger.

nosi: This is a difficult term to understand since it covers the specification FZ as well as FM, MM, etc. In spite of this, the term's definition is 'a woman of the second ascending genealogical level from a male or a female ego'. The pertinent question which now arises is why a woman, who is the sister of a man who unambiguously belongs to the first ascending genealogical level, should be classified together with the women of the second ascending genealogical level. Firstly it must be pointed out that this is how the Trio see it, and however one tackled informants on this problem the answers always came as variants on the theme, 'We call her *nosi* because we call her daughter mother', or 'We call her *nosi* because she is our mother's mother'. Indeed in a number of actual cases the FZ and the MM are the same person, and such terminological usage is well adapted to the practice of marriage with the sister's daughter. Although this may in itself be adequate explanation, there is one further point which needs to be made. Marriage with a *nosi*'s daughter or a

---

[1] I use the expression inter-genealogical level marriages rather than the more common usage inter-generational because in later chapters there is some value in distinguishing between generation and genealogical level. The term generation is used to mean 'the whole body of individuals born about the same period; also, the time covered by the lives of these' (S.O.E.D.). Genealogical level is used where age is not a factor and to mean simply 'offspring of the same parent regarded as a step in a line of descent from an ancestor' (S.O.E.D.). Frequently generation and genealogical level coincide, but not always. Thus ego's FyB may be the same age as ego in which case ego and this man belong to the same generation but different genealogical levels, while ego's F belongs to the same genealogical level as his younger brother but different generations. It will be shown later that inter-genealogical level marriages are infrequently inter-generational ones. I use the term oblique marriages in the same sense as inter-genealogical level marriages.

nosi's son is not only prescribed but is the most popular marriage form (cf. below, Table 27, p. 144). Among the Trio the conventional attitude between mother-in-law and child-in-law is at least respect, which is also the quality of the relationship between the young and the old. Assigning the potential mother-in-law to a higher genealogical level than the one to which she belongs is a simple way of achieving the required respect and is also terminologically economic. The subject of attitudes between different categories of kin and affines is treated in detail in Part Three.

kuku: there is no difference between the meaning of this term and that of *nosi*. Although all the Trio are aware of it and its application, I have no record of its everyday use. At one time I thought it might be used to distinguish between the father's sister and the grandmothers but, if this was ever so, it is certainly not recognized now.

ipa: This is the reciprocal term for *tamu, nosi*, and *kuku*, and thus can be understood to mean 'those of the second descending genealogical level from a male and female ego'. For a woman this category includes her brother's children, which is logically to be expected as they call their father's sister *nosi*.

These terms (*tamu, nosi, kuku*, and *ipa*) indicate that at the second ascending and descending genealogical levels the distinction between patriterms and matriterms disappears. This is a logical result of the intermingling of the genealogical ties which result from bilateral cross-cousin marriage. The grandparents do not distinguish the sex of their grandchildren, but the latter do distinguish between the grandfather and grandmother. The identification of the paternal aunt with the grandmothers and the potential affinal role of the grandparents requires such a distinction to be made.

This leaves the terms *imuku* and *emi* which appear in both sets of terms. They present a considerable problem, but since it is the same one for both, it can be discussed with reference to only one of them.

imuku: this is the generic term for all children but is applied more specifically to male children, i.e., all males of the first descending genealogical level. A man applies this term to his own, his brothers' and his sisters' sons, including the male matrilateral cross-cousin. A woman, however, does not apply this term to her brothers' children (see above) but only to her own, and her sisters' children, including her male matrilateral cross-cousin.

For the moment the cross-genealogical aspect of this term will be ignored, and the failure of a man to distinguish between his own or brothers' children and his sisters' children will be discussed.[1] Because the Trio do not make a terminological distinction between a brother's and a sister's children it does not mean that the relationship is either unknown or unimportant. If an informant is asked how he addresses somebody of the first descending genealogical level, the reply invariably comes in the reverse form, i.e., he calls me father (or mother's brother, as the case may be). In other words, the relationship is known but it is only verbally realized by the member of the junior genealogical level. Ego does not distinguish, in a terminological sense, the relationship of an alter on the first descending genealogical level, but alter does distinguish the relationship of ego. When the Trio are questioned on this matter, they say that they know which are their brother's children and which are their sister's children— a perfectly reasonable claim considering the small size of Trio communities and the low number of social contacts an individual is likely to have in his lifetime. But a social classification based on knowledge can only be built up on experience which comes with age. An adult has the experiential knowledge by which he knows which are his brother's children and which

[1] This is not a common feature of Carib relationship terminologies and for some time I wondered if some term had escaped my notice. I finally convinced myself that it had not when I had the opportunity to check with a number of Trio Indians fluent in the Waiyana language. The Waiyana terminology, also a two-section one, has four terms for members of the first descending genealogical level (S and BS, D and BD, ZS, ZD). While the bilingual informants unhesitatingly made these distinctions in the Waiyana language, they always reverted to just the two terms when speaking Trio.

While this feature of the Trio relationship terminology might reflect, among these people, the relative unimportance of descent compared with co-residence in the ordering of social relationships (see Chapter VI for the high proportion of married brothers and sisters who live in the same village) it would be dangerous to push this idea too far. For example, the Tanala of Madagascar who appear to have a two-section terminology and patrilineal descent have no distinct terms for brothers' and sisters' children (cf. Linton, 1933).

his sister's; a child does not, but instead the information is available for him at a linguistic level by which means he learns to classify correctly the members of his parents' genealogical level. For the purpose of this monograph, I have considered it legitimate to make the distinction from ego's point of view—there seems no other way to reveal a difference which consciously exists in ego's mind but has only passive recognition there. Certainly I would not take this step if there had ever been any difficulty in finding out the exact relationship, but there never was. The two classes of *imuku* which it is intended to use can now be defined.

The *imuku* in ego's patriterms is a male who refers to and addresses ego as *ipapa*. This *imuku* is ego's son, the brother's son, and the sons of male parallel-cousins.

The *imuku* in the opposing descent line is a male who refers to and addresses ego as *tï*. This *imuku* is the sister's son and the sons of female parallel-cousins. Also in this class are specifications from more than one genealogical level, and the term *imuku* in the sense of sister's son also covers the male matrilateral cross-cousin, the mother's brother's son.

All that has been said above equally applies to the term *emi*. For the purpose of this monograph it is intended to distinguish between a class of *emi* who call ego *ipapa* (and are thus daughters, brothers' daughters, and daughters of male parallel-cousins), and a class of *emi* who refer to ego as *tï* (and are the sisters' daughters, the daughters of female parallel-cousins, and the female matrilateral cross-cousin, the mother's brother's daughter).

The way is now open for an examination of the remaining terms; this will be begun by definitions of ego's patriterms. An essential aspect of this set of terms is that the genealogical specifications of each one are limited to one genealogical level, and English denotations do not distort their meaning.

ipapa: the father of a male or female ego and all males of the first ascending genealogical level referred to by the father as *ipipi* or *akɔmi*.

ipipi: an elder brother, the elder male parallel-cousins, and others classified with them, of a male or female ego.

wɔi: an elder sister, the elder female parallel-cousins, and others classified with them, of a male or female ego.

akəmi: a younger brother or sister, the younger male and female parallel-cousins, and others classified with them. This term which fails to make a sexual distinction is the one normally used for referring to a younger sibling or parallel-cousin.

kĭrĭ: This word literally means 'man' as opposed to 'woman', but is also used in referring to a younger brother or younger male parallel-cousin; rarely used except when it is necessary to distinguish the sex of the referent.

wəri: This word literally means 'woman' as opposed to 'man', but it is also used in referring to a younger sister or younger female parallel-cousin; used more frequently than *kĭrĭ.*

imuku: as a patriterm, it refers to those males who address or refer to ego as *ipapa* (see above).

emi: as a patriterm it refers to those females who address or refer to ego as *ipapa* (see above).

Thus the patriterms which refer to men cover ego's fathers, brothers, and those who call him father, and those which refer to women cover the sisters of these men. Genealogy (in both a social and biological sense) is the criterion employed and, because of this well defined horizontal boundaries exist between the categories. Among the matriterms this is no longer so, and in this set all the categories include genealogical specifications from more than one genealogical level. This makes it difficult to isolate and inspect any one category, but because they possess a vertical cohesion from their nature as those from whom ego takes his wife, and to whom he gives a woman in return—a definition which exists both as a conventional marriage rule and as an empirical reality—it is possible to treat the categories as overlapping divisions of a single conceptual unit. The female matriterms will be considered first.

These terms are *imama, emerimpə,* and *emi* (i.e., those who refer to ego as *tĭ*). All three terms cover some aspect of the female cross-cousins, and the discussion is best begun by considering the category of *emerimpə.* This is the term of reference for a potential spouse of either a male or female ego. This category conventionally includes all cross-cousins of the opposite sex, but also covers all unrelated people of the opposite sex until or unless some other relationship is decided upon.

This term is said to lack a direct address form, and I initially accepted this statement, mainly because a similar feature had been reported among the Waiwai (Fock, 1963, p. 190). But such a practice seemed illogical since, unlike the avoidance between affines, freedom of speech, joking (sometimes obscene), and familiarity mark the behaviour between *emerimpə*. Further research showed that such doubt was justified, and experience revealed that convention and practice do not coincide in this matter. This first became obvious when the questioning of various informants about their relationships with all the other members of the community indicated that no one claimed to have an *emerimpə* other than a sibling's spouse. This obviously unviable situation led me to ask informants the more direct question, 'Whom do you consider to be an *emerimpə*?' Answers to this question revealed that a man addresses his *emerimpə* as either *manhko* or *yemi*, and also refers to them in the appropriate terms, i.e., *imama* and *emi*, and a woman addresses her *emerimpə* as either *yetï* or *yimuku*, and refers to them in the appropriate terms, i.e., *tï* and *imuku*. However, it also emerged that ego does not regard every individual in these categories as an *emerimpə*. Thus it can be said that the category of *emerimpə* occurs at an ideal level but not at a practical one, where it is subsumed under two other categories, and the bilateral cross-cousin form which it contains disappears.

Attention has already been drawn to the existence of the equations $FZD = M$, $FZS = MB$, $MBD = ZD$, and $MBS = ZS$, and it is now intended to show very briefly how these terminological equations are well adapted to marriage with the sister's daughter. If ego's father marries his sister's daughter, then ego's mother and father's sister's daughter will be the same person, thus $FZD = M$. In such circumstances the brother of ego's mother will be ego's father's sister's son, thus $FZS = MB$. In this way the patrilateral cross-cousins are transferred to the first ascending genealogical level. If ego's sister marries her (and ego's) mother's brother the offspring of the union will stand in the relationship both of matrilateral cross-cousins and of sister's children to ego, thus $MBD = ZD$, and $MBS = ZS$. The matrilateral cross-cousins appear on the first descending genealogical level, and ego's own genealogical level is occupied only by himself and his siblings. This, however, is an ideal scheme which does not exist, because an individual does not regard all members of the categories concerned as *emerimpǝ*. This is best considered from the male point of view.

The question is quite simply how does a man distinguish between the marriageable and the unmarriageable in the categories of *emi* and *imama*? This question is more simply answered in respect of *emi*, which category includes the specifications mother's brother's daughter and sister's daughter in their widest sense. There is within this category a class with which marriage is prohibited, and this proscription is expressed in two ways, which tend to reinforce each other. Firstly, this is realized at ego's level by the distinction between elder and younger sisters (*wǝi* and *akǝmi*); marriage being conventionally prohibited with the daughter of a younger sister (*akǝmi*). It is also generally agreed that the youngest members of this category are not potential wives 'because they are children'. However, absolute age is important in this, and there are cases in which men not only regard the adult daughter of an *akǝmi* as an *emerimpǝ*, but have actually married one. This topic is amplified in the discussion of Figure 2.

There are no reservations about marriage with the daughter of a *wǝi*, and even those in the closest genealogical relationship may and do marry.

The main difficulty of identification is centred on the category of *imama*, which term covers the mother of a male or female ego, the mother's sisters, and those called sister by the mother, and these include the female patrilateral cross-cousin who is categorically and terminologically indistinguishable from them. This usage derives from the practice of marriage with the sister's daughter, and is a logical adaptation of the relationship terminology to it. The difficulty lies in the fact that the father's sister's daughter is a potential wife, but both in word and thought she is identified with 'mother', which is a prohibited category.

Genealogical relationship offers but a partial solution to this difficulty; both types of mother, marriageable and unmarriageable, are defined as *nosi emi*. This is reasonable since ego's mother may well be his full genealogical father's sister's daughter. However, the marriage of ego with his mother, regardless of any secondary genealogical relationship which may exist, is prohibited, as it is with the mother's sisters. This leaves a class of unrelated women called *akɔmi* by the mother, and which contains ego's potential spouses.

The distinction between these two classes undoubtedly relies, in the first place, on experiential knowledge—it is known within the community which of the women a man calls *manhko* are his potential wives. Such a method of identification should not be the cause of any surprise when one realizes that the average sized village contains only thirty inhabitants and that the nearest neighbouring settlement is at least half a day's march away. The Trio themselves when asked how they know which *nosi emi* they may marry, and which they may not, have no reply other than that they know, and there is no reason to disbelieve them. At this point, it is necessary to reintroduce the qualification of co-residence as expressed in the term *imoiti*. It has been explained above that the Trio often fail to make any distinction between the factor of co-residence and genealogical connexion. To say that a man is your father's *imoiti* means that he will be classed as brother by your father, a father by you, and his children will be your siblings. The reverse of this is that unrelated people are strangers (although there are degrees of unrelatedness and strangeness), and such people are potential spouses, i.e., they are classified by the broad term of *emerimpɔ*. The question which now arises is how the more selective classification as either *imama* or *emi* is made. The answer to this lies in the criterion of relative age, but before an attempt is made to demonstrate this a brief summary is offered.

Ego, within his immediate social milieu, knows by experience his exact relationship with other members of the community, although this knowledge has its roots in his genealogy. Away from his own social sphere, ego's experience is a less reliable guide, and less certain is the genealogical knowledge on which it is based. It is in such a situation, where precedent gives no lead, that age plays its part as a determinant of social classification, although, it must be remembered, it can only be employed within the limits laid down by the relationship terminology.

In turning to the use of age, the first step is to note, although only briefly here because it is dealt with in detail in Chapter VII, that among the Trio the majority of married couples are of the same age, and very few are of widely differing ages.

The point which it is intended to make here is most clearly demonstrated with reference to Figure 2, where, for three male informants—A, B, and C (Muyopɔ (32), Iyakɔpo (52), and Korokoro (300) respectively)—are plotted in graph form the ages of all those women whom they refer to as *imama* or *emi* (those who call the informants *tĭ*).

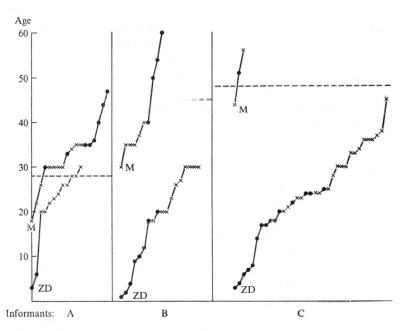

Figure 2: Age as a method of classification for the categories of *manhko* (M) and *emi* (ZD). *Emerimpɔ* marked × ; Informant's age: – – – – – – – – –

Several features of this figure deserve comment.

i. The *emerimpɔ* of informants A and B are grouped round the lower age limit of the *imama* line and the upper age limit of the *emi* line. This is not so apparent in the case of informant C who has only three women whom he considers to be his *imama*.

ii. For informants B and C there is very little overlap in age of the members of the two categories.

iii. In the case of informant A there is a rather greater age overlap between the two categories, but this is useful in demonstrating that genealogical connexion is the foremost criterion. The women aged 26, Tarara (8), and 18, Pakïri (6), are half-sisters having the same mother, who is the informant's FFBD, i.e., father's sister. Thus the two women are FFBDD, or FZD, and are referred to as *imama* and addressed as *manhko*. The woman aged 22, Kïwaraiye (118), is the widow of a man who was the informant's FFBDDS. Now FFBDD = FZD and is thus classified as *imama*. Accordingly her son was brother to the informant and they shared a similar set of relationships. Now this widow was her dead husband's FFBDD (FZD) and was thus *imama* to him, and still is to informant A. This case can be taken a step further since the woman aged 30, Aiyatu (28), who is not his *emerimpə*, was the co-wife of the same man. Informant A does not regard her as a potential wife because she is now married to his wife's father.

iv. The figure shows well certain remarks which have already been made about the category *emi*. In the case of the youngest informant, A, all those women in this category whom he regards as *emerimpə* are the daughters of women whom he considers to be *wəi*. The daughters of his *akəmi* are still very small, so that the prohibition on marriage with the daughters of *akəmi* and the denial of marriage with small girls serve to complement each other where young men are concerned. Against this, informant B, who is older, regards as *emerimpə* four adult women whose mothers he calls *akəmi*. They are Piruru (72), aged 20, Sipakari (274), aged 20, Ikəri (46), aged 23, and Papopə (154), aged 26. This informant does not regard as *emerimpə* any of the young girls, 12 years old and less, who regard him as *tï*. On two further cases he was uncertain whether the girls were his *emerimpə* or not; these two are Atorï (179), aged 20, and Maposi (168), aged 18. The mothers of both the girls he regards as his *akəmi* and the girls consider him to be their *tï*, but Atorï's father the informant calls *pahko*, and Maposi's father *akəmi*.

The situation with informant C is slightly different again, since he makes a clear distinction between the daughters of his *wəi* whom he regards as his *emerimpə* and those of his *akəmi* whom he does not, although some of the latter are older than some of the former. The reason for this lies in the character of the informant who showed himself in a number of ways to be a firm traditionalist, a stickler for convention, and to possess an acute sociological awareness.

In summary, a man's potential wives theoretically belong to the category of *emerimpə*, but in practice they are subsumed under two other categories. The foremost and basic criterion for applying the correct term in any particular case is knowledge of the genealogical relationship, but where this is lacking, age plays an important part in the process of classification. Relative age helps to decide into which category a strange woman will be placed, and will also indicate whether, within that category, she will be classed as marriageable or unmarriageable. Similarly of age to ego is likely to determine her as a marriageable woman, and this is evinced by the similarity in age of most spouses. A similar examinational approach can now be made to the brothers of these women, the male matriterms.

The male categories of the matriterms are *tï*, *pito*, and *imuku* (those who call ego *tï*). From ego's point of view the categories have a conceptual unity as both the husbands of the patriterms' female categories and brothers-in-law of the patriterms' male categories. However, unlike the female categories of the matriterms, all three terms have a direct address form which are *yetï*, *pito*, and *yimuku*. This set of terms will be considered first from the male point of view.

The key to understanding this set of terms lies in accurately determining the status of *pito*. On the face of it there does not appear to be any difficulty about this term since the Trio explicitly state that *pito* is a sister's husband, a wife's brother, an *emerimpə*'s brother, the son of a *nosi*, the son of a *tï*, or the son of both a *nosi* and a *tï*. (Theoretically it would be possible to be related in all these ways to one man.) Broadly speaking these descriptions are true, but as will be demonstrated they are only half truths. For example, the term *pito* is not invariably used to a male cross-cousin; the father's sister's son is frequently identified with *tï*, and the mother's brother's son often equated with *imuku*. A closer inspection of the way in which the term *pito* is applied is necessary.

Two informants, Iyakɔpo (52) and Korokoro (300), were questioned about their relationship to the parents of all the men whom they call *pito*, of which there are thirty-seven between them. The parents of eighteen of these are unknown; of the remaining nineteen the relationships are distributed as shown in Table 1.

TABLE I

Relationships to two informants of the parents of those whom the informants address as 'pito'.

Father	Mother	No. of cases
tï	*wəi*	1
ipipi	*nosi*	2
tamu	*nosi*	6
tamu	*imama*	1
tï	*imama*	1
tï	*nosi*	2
tï	unknown	3
tamu	unknown	2
unknown	*nosi*	1

It can be seen from Table 1 that the number of relationships to be expected for parents of a bilateral cross-cousin (i.e., *tï* and *nosi*), is low, and the slight emphasis on the *tamu/nosi* combination becomes enigmatic when the same process is applied to those whom the same two informants call *tï*. There are thirty-six such cases between them in half of which the parents are unknown. Of the remaining eighteen cases, thirteen are the sons of a *tamu/nosi* combination, four the sons of women called *nosi* and the fathers unknown, and one the son of a father called *tamu* and the mother unknown.

This evidence was enough to suggest that the term *pito* is not genealogically defined. Further support for this assumption was sought, and it emerged when an examination was made of the composition of the relationships within the sphere of the extended family. This revealed that within such a group of genealogically inter-related people there is no one who is addressed as *pito*. In such situations the male cross-cousin does not exist in a bilateral form; the patrilateral cross-cousin invariably is classified as *tĭ* and the matrilateral one as *imuku*. The absence of *pito* within the range of close relatives gains further support from an aspect of intra-tribal trading. It is not possible to have a trading partnership with a close relative since there already exists a series of duties and obligations which render it superfluous. However, it is said that ideally trading partners (*ipawana*) should call each other *pito*.

Can *pito* be defined in an affinal sense? In Table 2 are shown the relationships to four men of the husbands of their living *wəi* and *akəmi* (*wəri*).

TABLE 2

Relationships to four informants of their sister's husbands.

Relationship of ZH	Informants				
	(52)	(32)	(300)	(482)	Total
Pito:	1	4	5	1	11
Tĭ:	1	2	0	1	4
Imuku (ZS):	1	0	5	0	6
Ipipi/akəmi:	5	3	0	0	8
Imuku (BS):	2	1	1	1	5
	10	10	11	3	34

This table shows that nearly one-third of the husbands of the informants' *wəi* and *akəmi* are called *pito*, and that in twenty-one out of thirty-four cases the husbands belong to the group of terms *tĭ*, *pito*, and those who call ego *tĭ*. The rather dispro-portionate number of informants (52)'s and (32)'s *wəi* and *akəmi* who have married *ipipi*, *akəmi*, and those who call the informants *ipapa* is explained in Chapters V and VII.

A similar pattern emerges when this point is examined from the aspect of wife's brother. Iyakəpo (52) recognizes eighteen women as belonging to his potential wife group; nine of these have brothers. Three of these men Iyakəpo calls *yetĭ* (including the half-brother of his actual wife), two *pito*, and four *yimuku* (ZS). This reinforces the conclusion which can be drawn from Table 2—namely that a group of men variously belonging to the categories *tĭ*, *pito*, and *imuku* (ZS) possess a conceptual vertical cohesion as the husbands of the female categories of ego's patriterms or the male categories of ego's matriterms.

7

However, there is still a lack of horizontal boundaries for the category of *pito*.

It is here that the factor of age enters into the analysis. *Pito* is a term reserved for addressing socially distant men, but it must not be assumed from this that all strangers are called *pito*, and that all those addressed as *yetĭ* and *yimuku* are close relatives. Genealogically related individuals will belong to the appropriate category regardless of age, but others will be classified as *tĭ*, *pito*, or *imuku* according to their age relative to ego's. The qualification for *pito* is contemporaneity. These points can be shown with reference to Figure 3 where the ages of those

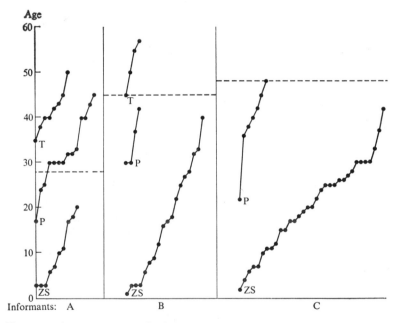

Figure 3: Age as a method of classification for the categories of *tĭ* (T), *pito* (P), and *imuku* (ZS). Informants age: – – – – – – –

individuals whom three different informants call *yetĭ*, *pito*, and *yimuku* are plotted. It can be seen that age has a strong influence on the distribution of these terms, although this becomes much more apparent when this figure (and Figure 2) are compared with Figures 4 and 5. This difference in usage of relative age is discussed further on in this chapter. It will suffice for the moment to give a brief example of how genealogical connexion overrides the relative age criterion. In Figure 3 it can be seen that Iyakəpo (52), informant B, calls three men who are over 30 years old *yimuku*. These three also happen to be those of their category whose ages overlap the age range of those in the category of *pito*. These three are all closely related to the informant; Emopiripə (165), aged 40, is the son of Iyakəpo's father's brother's daughter; Kəsəpə (139), aged 33, is Iyakəpo's mother's half-brother's son; and Kamapə (83), aged 32, is the son of a woman whom Iyakəpo regards as a close sister although no genealogical connexion can be traced and the qualification is that of *imoiti*.

In summary, it can be said that *pito* is a relationship term but not a kinship term. Although the Trio describe *pito* in a cross-cousin specification this merely reflects the term's affinal role. *Pito*, within certain age limits, is applied to the brothers of unknown and unrelated women, who are usually classified as potential wives, although if regarded as sisters their husbands will be called *pito*. The behaviour between unrelated brothers-in-law (when the woman is also unrelated) is very different from that when both parties are related.

Pito is a word which occurs in many Carib dialects, and its meanings, which range from slave (R. Schomburgk, 1848, p. 430), to subject or servant (Crevaux, 1883, pp. 236, 241; Williams, 1932, p. 157), to sister's son or daughter's husband (Farabee, 1924, p. 145; Diniz, 1965, p. 14), all imply subservience of some kind. This connotation does not occur among the Trio where it is a reciprocal term and implies equality of status.

The categories of *ti* and *imuku* can now be more explicitly defined. Although both these categories cover all the specifications listed against them in Appendix A, the presence of any individual in one of the categories relies in the first place on the appropriate genealogical or residential relationship to ego, and *only secondly* on either relative seniority or juniority in age to ego. Ideally there is no age gap between the genealogically related individuals of these two categories, but between the unrelated of similar age the term *pito* is used.

For a woman the categories of *ti* and *imuku*, the latter being those who call her *manhko*, comprise her *emerimpə*, although there

exist the same limitations on age and the closeness of relationship which were described in dealing with a male ego's *emerimpɔ*.
Like a male's *emerimpɔ*, the female's are also divided into two
categories which include both related and unrelated individuals. The same applies in the case of the cross-cousins of the
same sex or the sisters-in-law; a female ego has no equivalent
term to *pito*, and all strange women are classified with related

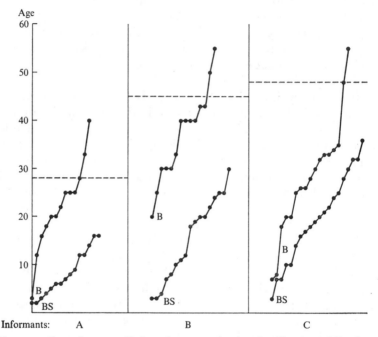

Figure 4: Genealogy, as distinct from age, in the classification of Brothers
(B) and Brother's Sons (BS). Informants age: – – – – – –

women as either patrilateral or matrilateral cross-cousins, i.e.,
in the categories of *imama* and *emi*. This may be because under
a previous post-marital rule of residence there was little social
intercourse between unrelated women.

It is hoped that the reader will be by now satisfied by the
evidence presented that the initial division of the relationship
terms into two sets was justified. Beyond the original criterion
based on the superficial aspect that some terms have cross-
genealogical specifications while others have not, it has been

demonstrated that these two sets of terms are opposed to each other as being both wife-givers and wife-takers to the other. Secondly, the basis on which the original division was made has emerged not simply as a superficial characteristic, but as an observable indication of an important difference in the method of classification employed in the two sets of terms. This point will now be examined further.

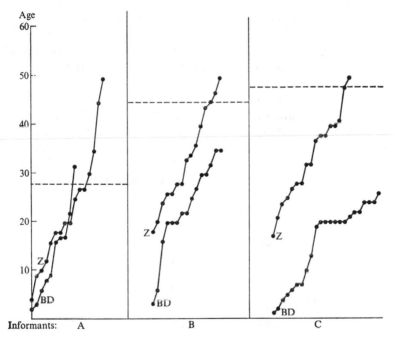

Figure 5: Genealogy, as distinct from age, in the classification of Sisters (Z) and Brother's Daughters (BD). Informant's age: – – – – – – –

The foremost criterion in determining all relationships is genealogical connexion, although residential qualification may be nearly as important. These two factors are overridingly influential within ego's patriterms so that the categories in this set of terms have sharply defined horizontal boundaries between genealogical levels. In the matriterms, although these boundaries are clearly drawn in the cases of genealogically related individuals, it is to these categories that unrelated individuals tend to be assimilated and they are classified by age relative to ego. Among the matriterms the horizontal boundaries between categories are drawn in terms of age; among the patriterms the boundaries are drawn by genealogy which permits a wide overlap of age between adjacent categories without any confusion arising. This can be readily demonstrated.

In Figures 4 and 5 the same procedure has been carried out as in Figures 2 and 3—in Figure 4 are plotted the ages of all those whom the same three informants call *ipipi/akəmi* and those who call the informants *ipapa*, and in Figure 5 those they call *wəi/akəmi* and those who call them *ipapa*. Visual evidence in itself is enough to indicate that the degree of age overlap of adjacent categories is far greater in Figures 4 and 5 than in Figures 2 and 3.

Needham, however, has proposed a simple method of objective assessment to give the degree of age overlap a numerical index (Needham, 1966, p. 14). This index is the number of individuals of different categories whose ages overlap, expressed as a percentage of the total number in both categories. The index for each informant in each figure is as follows:

Informant	Fig. 2	Fig. 3	Average of Figs. 2 & 3
Muyopə (32)	60	16·7 and 50	42·2
Iyakəpo (52)	17·8	27·3 and 0	15
Korokoro (300)	5·3	52·5	28·9
Average	28·0	29·3	28·7

Informant	Fig. 4	Fig. 5	Average of Figs. 4 & 5
Muyopə (32)	57·1	80·8	68·9
Iyakəpo (52)	38·7	70	54·3
Korokoro (300)	91·9	45	68·4
Average	62·6	65·3	63·9

Although there are obvious variations from one informant to another, and from one set of relationships to another, the overall pattern is consistent. In the case of every informant the combined numerical indices of Figures 4 and 5 is greater than that of Figures 2 and 3, and the difference between them is marked—26·7 in the lowest example compared with an average of 35·2. This lowest figure is recorded for Muyope, the youngest informant, while Iyakɔpo and Korokoro who are of similar age have a similar difference between their indices—39·3 and 39·5 respectively. The evidence of the greater use of age as a means of classification among the matriterms than the patriterms is overwhelming, although the Trio themselves seem unconscious of its use. Finally, however, it must be stressed that even among the matriterms age is only used as a principle of classification when genealogical and residential criteria are lacking.

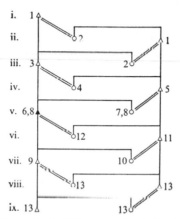

Figure 6. Genealogical diagram of relationship terms.

The Trio relationship terminology can be represented in three different ways: first, as a straightforward system of bilateral cross-cousin marriage which is the way the Trio conceive their own system, i.e., the conscious model. While up to a point this is a perfectly sound and workable model of the society, it is rather too simple a view and conceals nuances which are sociologically important. For expository purposes this model must be rejected because it neither covers all the known facts nor can it be shown to represent any empirical formations. The second way in which the relationship terminology can be represented (see Figure 6) fulfils the latter condition but not the former. It would be wrong to refer to this as the unconscious model because the Trio are not completely unaware of it nor of its implications. I shall refer to it as the 'appetitive' model.[1]

The following definitions of the relationship terms have been used in the construction of the appetitive model:

1 *tamu:* men of second ascending genealogical level.
2 *nosi:* women of second ascending genealogical level.
3 *ipapa:* father and his brothers.
4 *imama:* mother and her sisters including the female patrilateral cross-cousins.
5 *tï:* mother's brother and the male patrilateral cross-cousins.
6 *ipipi:* elder brother.
7 *wəi:* elder sister.
8 *akəmi:* younger brother and younger sister.
9 *imuku:* son and brother's son (those who call ego *ipapa*).
10 *emi:* daughter and brother's daughter (those who call ego *ipapa*).
11 *imuku:* sister's son and male matrilateral cross-cousin (those who call ego *tï*).
12 *emi:* sister's daughter and female matrilateral cross-cousin (those who call ego *tï*).
13 *ipa:* All those, of both sex, on the second descending genealogical level.

This diagram is from the point of view of a male ego; for a female ego it remains basically unchanged except that at level vii the relationship is altered to 13 (*ipa*), because they are the brother's children.

Although this pseudo-genealogical type of diagram has a number of drawbacks, in this particular case it has certain expository advantages. It shows clearly how only brothers and sisters exist at any genealogical level—the cross-cousins being terminologically removed to one of the proximate levels. It can readily be seen how the father's sister becomes identified with the women of the second ascending genealogical level, and accordingly why a woman calls her brother's children by the

---

[1] 'Appetite; one of those instinctive cravings which secure the preservation of the individual and the race' (S.O.E.D.). I have chosen this word since it implies an inclination which may be either conscious or unconscious. Hunger may drive us to eat, but frequently we eat without feeling hunger. As will become apparent this term is very apt in the context of Trio marriage.

same term as that she uses to members of the second descending genealogical level. The equations $M = FZD$, $MB = FZS$, $ZD = MBD$, $ZS = MBS$ are well displayed.

Furthermore, and as has been mentioned above, this appetitive model does represent empirical formations—there are small groups of Trio who can be represented, one-to-one, by such a pattern. In spite of this, the model is inadequate since much of what has been discussed in this chapter cannot be explained in the terms of its structure. For example, it does not allow for the possible marriage with the patrilateral cross-cousin, the existence of such terms as *pito* and *emerimpə*, nor the well defined categories of ego's patriterms compared with the weak horizontal divisions between the categories of the matri-terms. These objections, and others, can be overcome by representing the system in a box type diagram as has been done for a male ego in Figure 7.

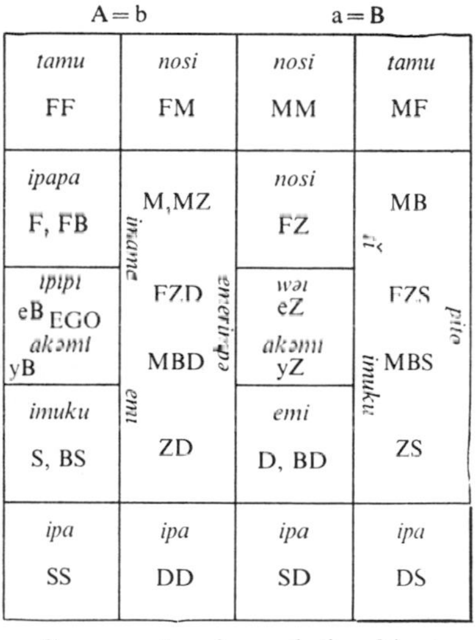

A = b		a = B	
tamu FF	*nosi* FM	*nosi* MM	*tamu* MF
ipapa F, FB	M,MZ	*nosi* FZ	MB
ipipi eB EGO *akɔmɩ* yB	FZD / MBD	*wəi* eZ *akɔmɩ* yZ	FZS / MBS
imuku S, BS	ZD	*emi* D, BD	ZS
ipa SS	*ipa* DD	*ipa* SD	*ipa* DS

Figure 7: Box-type diagram showing relationship terms for a male ego.

In order to accommodate all the features of the terminology, a number of modifications had to be made to the usual shape of such diagrams, the most important alteration being the off-setting of the categories belonging to the opposing sets of terms. This means that at any one level there exist only siblings and parallel-cousins while the cross-cousins overlap the adjacent categories in the vertical sense. Even this diagram, however, is not entirely satisfactory since it has not been possible to devise a two-dimensional diagram which will adequately depict three criteria.

In Figure 7, Columns A and a, which represent the male and female categories of ego's patriterms, have clearly defined vertical and horizontal divisions—the criteria employed being genealogical and residential. Columns B and b, which represent the male and female categories of the matriterms, lack the well defined boundaries between categories. Here, although genealogy is the most important factor, age exerts a great influence in the classification of strangers. Social distance is indicated in the cases of *pito* and *emerimpǝ* by the placing of the terms to one side. Ego takes a spouse from the category contiguous to his own in a horizontal plane.

It can be seen that this model, which will be called the 'existing structure', lies somewhere between the conscious and appetitive models. Although it is a matter of conjecture it seems probable that the existing structure is the result of modification by the appetitive model of the conscious model, in other words the imposition of marriage with the sister's daughter on a system of bilateral cross-cousin marriage. Indeed the differences between Trio convention and practice reflect the differences between these two forms of marriage, and so, in a sense, does the existing structure. Certainly for the present purpose the existing structure must be regarded as the 'correct' model since it is in its capacity alone that all the facts presented in the previous analysis are explicable. In the next chapter it is demonstrated how these facts work within the framework of this structure to allow an individual to operate his social relationships.

V

THE CRITERIA IN ACTION

THE END PRODUCT of the formal analysis of the relationship terminology which was undertaken in the last chapter is the model shown in Figure 7. The purpose of this chapter is to demonstrate the validity of this model, not simply in the ordering of social relationships, but in the understanding of how they are ordered. The aim of this demonstration is to help resolve the confusion which occurs when such a model is regarded as a stereotyped pattern whose rigidity leaves no room for individual preferences. This conception is wrong because such models are not one-for-one representations of empirical facts, but they are models in the terms of which any particular and all relationships are explicable, or again the framework within the limits of which the individual can operate his choice.

This point is easy to show with reference to the Trio because, although their terminology can be represented in a formal model, the actual ordering of relationships is highly individual and appears unstructured. The reason for this is that the Trio relationship terminology includes a number of lineal equations the presence of which allows the terminology to be represented in a formal model, but at the same time its organization from the point of view of any single member of the society tends to be individual and contingent. Only full siblings of the same sex are likely to share an identical set of relationships; a feature characteristic of cognatic systems. Evidence of this is not hard to find, and indeed the nature of the criteria of classification already discussed gives a clue to this, but the tendency is still further increased by the large proportion of marriages between people of different genealogical levels. The offspring of such a union will belong to different categories and to different genealogical levels depending from which side of the family the relationship is viewed. This point is well illustrated by the following example in which I was directly involved.

One evening I was talking to Korokoro (300) and Pisikïkï (312) whom I address as *yetï* and *pihko* respectively. Pisikïkï also calls Korokoro *yetĭ* which is correct since Pisikĭkĭ's mother is Korokoro's father's brother's daughter. We were joined by a 7-year-old boy, Taimu (658), whom Korokoro calls *kami*; I queried this and was told that Taimu's father was the younger brother of Korokoro's father (presumably classificatory since there is no genealogical evidence for this), thus Korokoro who is about forty years older than Taimu calls him *kami* and is reciprocally addressed as *pihko* by Taimu. I then asked if I should call the boy *yetĭ*, and Korokoro laughed and said that I should, but Pisikĭkĭ interrupted to say that this would be wrong and that Taimu should call me *yetĭ* which is the same as he calls Pisikĭkĭ who, in turn, had called Taimu's mother *wɔihko*.

It can be seen from this simple example that with only three people involved there are as many different ways of tracing the relationship between them in spite of the fact that they regard themselves as closely related to each other. On a wider scale this problem is most clearly demonstrated in diagrammatic form; in Figures 8 and 9 the same fifty people are shown from the viewpoint of two different individuals, and these diagrams can be further compared with the same fifty people as they appear on Sheets 4 and 5 of the Genealogical Table. A quick examination will give a rough idea of how the position of an individual varies from one diagram to the next, but the actual variation, in terms of genealogical level, is as follows.

64 per cent of the people appear at the same level in the Genealogical Table and Figure 8.

50 per cent of the people appear at the same level in the Genealogical Table and Figure 9.

44 per cent of the people appear at the same level in Figures 8 and 9.

30 per cent of the people appear at the same level in all three diagrams.

Just one example of the numerous complications which appear in this small sample will be explained more fully. Iyakɔpo (52) calls Arensu (73) *pihko* because he called his parents *pahko* and *manhko*, and he calls Kĭwaipipi (63) *kami* for the same reason. Meanwhile Atu (80) calls Iyakɔpo *pahko* because her father Arensu calls him *kami*, but at the same time she calls Kĭwaipipi, who is her half-sister (same mother, different father), *wɔihko*. Therefore, from Iyakɔpo's point of

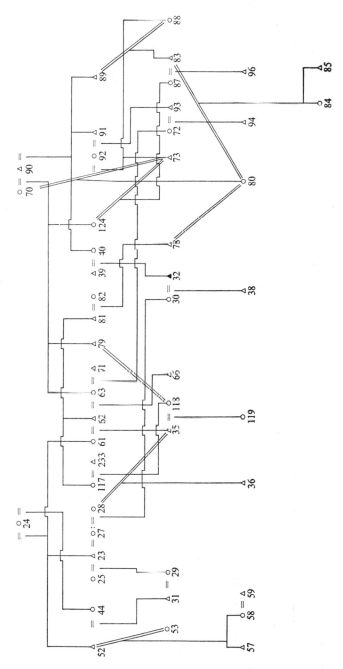

Figure 8: The genealogical position of a sample of 50 Indians according to Muyopɔ (32).

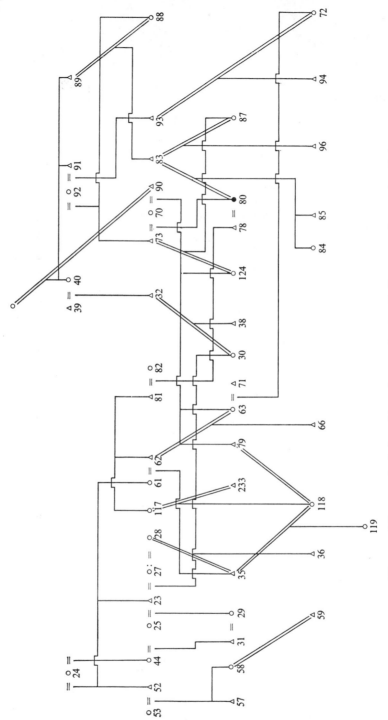

Figure 9: The genealogical position of a sample of 50 Indians according to Atu (80).

view Kïwaipipi belongs to his own genealogical level and Atu to the first descending level. Atu, however, regards Kïwaipipi as belonging to her level and Iyakɔpo to the first ascending level.

Further demonstration of the point that any person organizes his social world along highly individual lines is not required, and it is now the intention to show that although this individuality exists, it is not the result of purely random choice but that most cases are explicable in the terms of the criteria discussed in the previous chapter. For this purpose Iyakɔpo (52) from Alalaparu and Korokoro (300) from Paloemeu are used as controls. In Table 3 are shown the informants' relationships to the offspring of all marriages in which one, or other, or both spouses are classified as *ipipi*, *wɔi*, or *akɔmi* by the informants.

Of the 131 marriages listed in Table 3, 92 of them (70·2 per cent) are between conventionally prescribed categories: these are *wɔi/akɔmi = tï*, *wɔi/akɔmi = pito*, *wɔi/akɔmi = imuku* (ZS), *ipipi = imama*, *ipipi/akɔmi = emi* (ZD). If we consider the two informants' relationships to the children of these unions we can see that for the most part they are ordered in a perfectly orthodox manner, and that 73 of them (79·3 per cent) are related through the sibling connexion. Where exceptions to this practice occur it is safe to assume that some other factors are at work and, in order to find out what these may be, a closer inspection of the 19 cases which fail to follow the conventional pattern is now undertaken.

The single exception in the *wɔi/akɔmi — tï* marriage form concerns Aiyatu (28) and her brothers, Paru (11), who is now dead, and Apipi (399), who lives at Paloemeu. Aiyatu is the wife of Iyakɔpo's full younger brother, Sipi (23), and they all live at Alalaparu. There is no traceable genealogical connexion between Iyakɔpo and Apipi, and the distance has robbed the affinal relationship of its important content. In such a circumstance *pito* is the correct term to apply to a brother's wife's brother.

The informants' relationships to the offspring of the *wɔi/akɔmi = pito* are entirely conventionally ordered, but the children of the marriages *wɔi/akɔmi = imuku* (ZS), which is the female equivalent of *ipipi = imama*, are all classified as *ipa*—which indicates that the relationship is not traced by way of the *wɔi/akɔmi* category but the *imuku* (ZS) one. This procedure is

Table 3

Relationship of two informants to the offspring of marriages involving those called either pihko, wəihko, or kami by the same two informants.

Form of marriage	Number of marriages	Relationship of informant to offspring
wəi/akəmi = tï		
i. Paloemeu:	17	*tï*
ii. Alalaparu:	6	*tï*
	1	*pito*
wəi/akəmi = pito		
i. Paloemeu:	18	*tï*
ii. Alalaparu:	4	*tï*
wəi/akəmi = imuku (ZS)		
i. Paloemeu:	4	*tamu*
ii. Alalaparu:	1	*tamu*
akəmi = imuku (BS)		
i. Paloemeu:	1	*tamu*
wəi = tamu		
i. Paloemeu:	3	*tï*
	3	*imuku*
wəi/akəmi = ipapa		
i. Paloemeu:	2	*ipipi*
ii. Alalaparu:	1	*tï*
ipipi = imama		
i. Paloemeu:	12	*ipapa*
ii. Alalaparu:	4	*ipapa*
	5	*ipipi/akəmi*
ipipi/akəmi = emi (ZD)		
i. Paloemeu:	10	*ipapa*
	6	*tamu*
ii. Alalaparu:	2	*ipapa*
	2	*tamu*
ipipi/akəmi = emi (BD)		
i. Paloemeu:	1	*tamu*
ii. Alalaparu:	2	*tamu*
	1	*ipapa*
ipipi/akəmi = wəi/akəmi		
i. Paloemeu:	4	*tï*
	1	*ipapa*
ii. Alalaparu:	11	*tï*
	9	*ipapa*

completely in agreement with a point raised in the last chapter; for ego to call *imuku* (ZS) the husband of a woman whom he regards as a *wai* or *akəmi* automatically means that he is more closely related to the man than the woman. If ego was not related to the man the term *pito* or *konoka* would have been used. In these cases the informants are tracing the relationship to the offspring of the marriage through the father who is more *itɨpɨme* than the mother; a fact revealed in the choice of relationship terms.

In the *ipipi/akəmi* = *emi* (ZD) form, 60 per cent of the off-spring are regarded by the informants as brothers' children (i.e., *imuku* (BS)), and in the other 40 per cent of the cases they are considered as belonging to the second descending genealogical level (*ipa*), and the relationship has been traced through the woman. It is claimed that ego will trace his relationship to the children of a marriage through the parent to whom he regards himself as most closely related; how far does this 40 per cent support this contention? A complete answer to this question requires a more detailed life history of the informants than was collected—the influence of co-residence combined with mobility of population being the problematic factor—but the point can be demonstrated in some instances.

First will be examined the six cases at Paloemeu in which Korokoro regards the relationship as traced through the woman. In two of these marriages Korokoro is clearly more closely related to the woman than the man:

i. Amasi (476) = ∃kəwiyae (475). Korokoro can trace no relationship to Amasi, but ∃kəwiyae's mother is Korokoro's father's brother's daughter.[1]

ii. Pereresi (656) = Kuramenaru (654). There is no traceable relationship between Korokoro and the man, but the woman is his father's brother's daughter's daughter.

The other four cases are not so clear cut; in the marriage Napeta (336) – Paikə (331) both partners appear equally closely related to Korokoro. The husband is his half-brother,

[1] This is one of those cases referred to in Notes on the Genealogical Table. Although Korokoro insisted that Simore (463) was his father's brother, no evidence for this claim appeared in the collected genealogical data; accordingly the connexion is not shown on the Genealogical Table.

8

and the wife is his mother's brother's daughter and his father's brother's daughter's daughter. Residence may be the important factor here since, as will be shown in Chapter VI, brothers are more likely to live apart than a brother and a sister. No explanation, through lack of details, is available for the marriage Paiye (344) = Kamara (345), although it should be mentioned that Paiye is the elder brother of Amasi whose case has just been described. The example Asoro (435) = Makarepən (434) is interesting; the children of this marriage, which has broken up, are a boy and a girl. The former lives with his father and is regarded by Korokoro as a brother's son, the latter lives with her mother and is regarded by Korokoro as a sister's daughter's daughter—sex and residence appearing to play an influential part. Finally, the last case appears to contradict the claim that relationship is traced through the more closely related person. The man, Nupiyarankə (684), is Korokoro's father's brother's son, but no connexion with the woman, Saere (686), can be found.

The examples afforded by Iyakəpo at Alalaparu are too few to be conclusive, although a distinction exists between the two cases in which relationship is traced through the man, and the two in which it is traced through the woman. Where the offspring are regarded as brothers' children, the two men, Pesaipə (93) and Kinini (79), belong, together with Iyakəpo, to a group of families which are closely inter-related by descent, marriage, and residence. In Pesaipə's case his wife, Piruru (72), is also a member of these families, but Kinini's wife, Kuriya (120), comes from a distance—the Marapi basin. Where the relationship is traced through the women, there are no discernible connexions between the men and Iyakəpo, but the connexion with the women can only be regarded as tenuous. Atorĭ (189), the wife of Muse (182), is related in this manner— Iyakəpo claims that Iyakana (172) was his sister (although no genealogical evidence of this has been forthcoming), and the connexion presumably lies in the fact that Atorĭ's mother is Iyakana's father's brother's daughter. The second example concerns the broken marriage between Taiyape (125), a stranger who has returned to live in Brazil, and Akutapə (60). The family of the latter comes from the Sipaliwini village (see Map 1) which was the original home of Iyakəpo's mother—it

.s possible, therefore, that some undisclosed relationship does exist between Iyakəpo and Akutapə. Alternatively the relationship may have been adjusted in order to take account of the marriage between Iyakəpo's daughter and Akutapə's son.

Although among these examples there appear to be cases which are not directly explicable in the terms of the criteria on which the structure of the relationship terminology is formed, they do not invalidate them. The ordering of social relationships is so individually organized that the ethnographer cannot expect to become acquainted with the nuances which explain every single instance, and indeed the informant himself may have forgotten the reason why he originally chose to adopt one term rather than another. The qualification of *itɨpɨme* can be seen to operate in the majority of cases, and it can be safely assumed that in a number of others where evidence is incomplete the less easily established criterion of co-residence is the influential factor. Age does not seem to play any part in this context: those whom Iyakəpo classifies as brothers' children range from three to eight years, and those he classifies as *ipa* (or *emi*(ZD)'s children) from one to seventeen years. Nor does it seem to make any difference whether the informant classifies the father as *ipipi* or *akəmi*: of Korokoro's cases two are his *ipipi* and four his *akəmi*; of Iyakəpo's cases one is his *ipipi* and three are his *akəmi*.

The relationship to the offspring of the *ipipi* = *imama* type of marriage depends on whether ego regards the woman as a marriageable or non-marriageable *imama*. Where the offspring of such unions are classified with siblings (i.e., as *ipipi, wəi*, or *akəmi*) ego will regard the woman as a non-marriageable *imama*. At Alalaparu, in four out of the five cases this is certainly so and in the fifth case possibly so. On the other hand in three out of the four cases where the offspring of the marriage are classified as *imuku* (BS), ego regards the woman as marriageable. In the fourth case, the woman is not marriageable because she had previously been married to a man whom Iyakəpo refers to as *ipapa* and to the children of that union as *ipipi, wəi*, and *akəmi*.

A similar pattern exists at Paloemeu where Korokoro classifies as *imuku* (BS) all the offspring of such unions, and as marriageable *imama* ten out of the twelve women. In the two outstanding cases there is some doubt; both women had two husbands and the first in each case was *ipapa* to Korokoro and the offspring of those unions *ipipi*, *wəi*, and *akəmi*. The second husbands of both these women are *ipipi* to Korokoro who considers the issue of these second unions to be his *imuku* (BS). The organization of these relationships follows a perfectly logical pattern whose governing principle is degree of relatedness; an *ipipi* who marries a non-marriageable *imama* of ego must be more distantly related to ego than the woman is.

We can now turn to consider the relationship of the informants to the offspring of unorthodox unions, that is to say, those marriages between categories which, if not prohibited, are not prescribed. The reason for such unions is discussed in Chapter VII, and here we are merely concerned with the criteria by which the relationship to the offspring of these marriages is decided. While one can expect to find the same principles at work as in the cases of conventionally ordered unions, the very fact that these unions are not conventionally ordered suggests that one if not both the spouses will come from the periphery of the informants' social world. The reason for this is discussed in the final part of this chapter, but the implication of this for the present discussion is that the relationship to the children of these unions is likely to be readily cognizable or totally inexplicable.

In the single case of *akəmi = imuku* (BS), Korokoro regards the child as his *ipa* and thus traces the relationship through the father, Iyetipə (720), who lives at Paloemeu. The mother, Itamu (724), is dead and, beyond the fact that she was *akəmi* to him, Korokoro could remember nothing about her.

In both the cases at Paloemeu of *wəi/akəmi = ipapa* marriage, the offspring are classified by Korokoro as *akəmi* so that the relationship is traced through the man. The three children of these two unions, all women, are not simply classificatory members of these categories, and their relationship with Korokoro contains many of the features characteristic of a full brother/sister relationship. Since there is no apparent genealogical relationship between these women and Korokoro it seems likely that the dominant factor is co-residence. Today they all live in Agglomeration A at Paloemeu (see Figure 10):

Korokoro lives in 16A; one of the women, Irawĭpən (327), in 20A; and other two, Sintori (437) and Tankuru (438), in 1A. The case of Irawĭpən is slightly complicated by the fact that she and her mother were married to the same man.

The single example of this form of marriage at Alalaparu has already been mentioned; it involves Atorĭ (189), who calls Iyakəpo *yetĭ*, and he in turn regards himself as being closely related to her mother. *Itĭpĭme* is clearly the operating principle in this case.

At Paloemeu in the one case of *ipipi/akəmi = emi* (BD) marriage the relationship to the children is traced through the woman, Patukimpĭ (456). This is in keeping with the value of *itĭpĭme* since she is closely related to a number of people in the residential group of which Korokoro is the centre, and her mother's half-sistei is Korokoro's own son's wife. Patukimpĭ's husband, Səisəi (457), is not related to Korokoro. In two examples at Alalaparu the relationship is also traced through the women who are two sisters, Rĭrĭpə (145) and Taiti (162), both of whom are related to Iyakəpo by marriage. The men involved in these cases are not the present husbands of these women but former ones, now both dead. Rĭrĭpə's former husband was unrelated to Iyakəpo, but Taiti's former husband, Apomita (163), is also related to Iyakəpo by marriage. I have insufficient evidence to resolve these cases. However, it is possible to be more definite in the single case where the relationship is traced through the man; this is Pesami (97), now dead, but the elder brother of Pesaipə (93) with whom it has just been mentioned Iyakəpo regards himself as closely related. The woman, Pipa (99), had come from the Tapanahoni area (she has a sister living at Paloemeu) and is unrelated to Iyakəpo.

The six examples of the marriage form *wəi = tamu*, all of which occur at Paloemeu, are explainable without going into individual details. Korokoro regards all the daughters of these unions as his *emerimpə*, and accordingly classifies them as either *imama* or *emi* (ZD). It has already been shown that relative age is likely to play a part in such classification, and it almost certainly has here. All those whom Korokoro called *manhko* are dead so that their ages are unknown, but all those who refer to him as *tĭ* are alive and younger than him.

Finally, there are the *ipipi/akəmi* = *wəi/akəmi* marriages which represent a sizeable proportion of the whole sample, particularly at Alalaparu. The reason for this large number of prohibited unions is given in Chapter VII. It would be tedious and unnecessary to examine all twenty-five cases in detail and only a few examples will be discussed. The sample selected is those at Alalaparu where the relationship is traced through the man; this is not a purely random decision, but was chosen because it contains some examples which demonstrate particularly well the relative nature of *itĭpĭme*.

There are nine cases at Alalaparu where the offspring of this form of marriage call Iyakəpo *pahko*. There is no doubt surrounding three cases since two of them concern his full brother Sipi (23), and one his half-brother Akuso (114). Two more cases involve other marriages of the same women: Sipi's wife, Warapi (25), now dead, was formerly married to Seni (104), and Iyakəpo is rather vague about his relationship to either of them so his relationship to their children may reflect Warapi's marriage to Sipi. In the other case Akuso's widow, Mikĭpə (20), married Pesaipə (93) to whom, as it has already been noted, Iyakəpo regards himself as closely related.

Two further examples concern Arensu (73) who also belongs to the same genealogically and residentially related complex as Pesaipə (Arensu and Pesaipə are half-brothers), and to whom Iyakəpo also regards himself as closely related. Arensu, who is now dead, was married to Kurapa (13), who is Iyakəpo's WZSD, and who has two full sisters both married to Toropə (107), whom Iyakəpo regards as his *akəmi*. In the case of Toropə's marriages, Iyakəpo traces his relationship to the children through the wives; accordingly Iyakəpo stands in the relationship of *ipapa* to the children of one sister and *tĭ* to the children of the other two sisters. Iyakəpo sees nothing inconsistent in this, since the principle of classification he has employed is that relationship is traced through the parent to which he regards himself as most closely related. A similar situation exists in the marriage between Kanre (202) and Isĭnaoi (201) whom Iyakəpo classifies as *ipipi* and *akəmi* respectively, and whose children refer to Iyakəpo as *ipapa*. Kanre is the son of Iyakəpo's step-father's brother, but no connexion can be found between Iyakəpo and Isĭnaoi. However,

Isĩnaoi has a full sister Kumarau (152) married to Sapə (151), and the offspring of this marriage refer to Iyakəpo as *tĩ*. The reason for this being that Sapə is a stranger at Alalaparu, having arrived there from the East Paru region. These final examples clearly underline the relative way in which an individual employs the criteria of social classification.

Because the Trio relationship terminology contains a number of lineal equations (although they lack any concept of unilineal descent) it is possible to represent the relationship categories in a single, all-inclusive model. This model is not a rigid, unyielding edifice but a flexible control on the individual's ordering of his social world. The important point is that all relationships are, at least to some degree, explicable within the terms of the model, and this is because the principles on which the model is constructed are identical with the criteria which an individual uses in classifying other members of society. These are genealogy, residence, and age. Thus the purpose of this chapter has been to demonstrate that although social relationships among the Trio appear highly individual and contingent, wherever sufficient evidence is available they can be shown to be ordered by this set of criteria. In some cases there may be no option—as in the most direct genealogical relationships—but in more distant cases there may be two, or even more, appropriate relationships to choose from. Finally, there are occasions on which two complete strangers have to decide on a relationship. The last part of this chapter is concerned with such a situation.

A Trio, at intervals through his life, is likely to come into contact with other Trio whom he has not previously met. In such situations, if the liaison is to be maintained, it is necessary for the individuals concerned to agree on a relationship—in other words to decide into which category of the relationship terminology they should place each other. It is difficult, perhaps embarrassing, to communicate with someone whom you do not know how to address, which is tantamount to not knowing their status. Soon after some visitors had arrived at Alalaparu I asked an informant how he addressed one of the new arrivals. He said he did not know. When I pressed the point and asked him what he said when he talked to the stranger the reply was,

'I do not talk to him because I do not know what to say.'[1] On a more personal note I heard the same thing happen several times soon after I arrived at the Paloemeu village. An Indian would come to the hut where I lived with the obvious intention of seeing and talking to me, and on several occasions, often after long pauses, ask the Indian in whose hut I lived what he should call me before he could bring himself to address me.

There are two Trio words for describing the action of deciding upon a relationship—the more frequently heard term is *ikuhtuntə*, the stem of the verb 'to measure', and less often *ikuku*, the stem of the verb 'to try' or 'to test'. Thus a previously unknown person who is measured becomes an *ikuhtu*. This term is not very precise in its meaning and may be used to refer to anyone, be they closely, distantly or not related, with whom the use of a relationship term has been decided. Depending on the circumstances this process of measuring could be informal or formal, brief or prolonged. It is possible that two individuals will be complete strangers to each other, but frequently there is some common basis, such as a past contact between parents or other relatives of the two individuals, on which to start discussion. The criteria used have already been described, but it involves more than merely deciding on a name since the terminology forms a framework for a behavioural content. The nature of the conventionally expected behaviour between different categories of kin is described in Chapter VIII, but it should be noted here that the Trio can make a distinction between those, usually closely related individuals, with whom a term has behavioural content, and more distant or unrelated individuals with whom the term is little more than a name. In the latter case there may not be complete concordance between the relationship term used and the actual content of the relationship as conventionally defined. Take for example the situation in which a strange married couple reach ego's village; if ego calls the man *pito*, his wife should technically be called sister although the behaviour between her and ego is unlikely to resemble that conventionally

---

[1] *Ka* is the stem of the verb 'to say', but it also means 'to address'. For the Trio the question *ati mika iya?* means 'how do you address him?' not 'what do you say to him?', which is the other literal translation. I never found a satisfactory way of asking this latter question.

expected between a brother and a sister, and may well contain some of the opposing relationship, that of *emerimpɔ*. Further-more, should the stranger die, ego's brother might marry the woman and this gives rise to brother/sister marriages.

When, therefore, one leaves the formal level, and enters the field of empirical behaviour one is faced by a dichotomy of the known and unknown, the related and unrelated, or those with whom the terms have content and those with whom they do not. A further point can be made here: within the former group the application of terms is likely to be relatively consistent and coherent because ego inherits them, so to speak, in a block. The further one moves away from ego, the more inconsistent is the use of relationship terms likely to become because ego adds these piecemeal and as the occasion or need arises. I had this fact very clearly brought home to me at Paloemeu where I set out to integrate myself into the relationship system, taking Təmeta (482) as my father and Apari (360) as my mother. It was noticeable that the further away the relationship from my father and mother, the more illogical and discordant the rela-tionships became. Also while it was fairly simple to remember correctly the agreed relationship with people one saw nearly every day, this was not the case with those rarely seen. To some extent my experience must parallel those of the Trio, so that the relationships with those distantly related and rarely seen will tend to be confused, illogical, and even vague.

Before turning to consider the conventional attitudes and actual behaviour between different categories, there are two further steps to be taken. The value of co-residence and marriage in the ordering of relationships has been greatly stressed, and before one can legitimately discuss the content of any relation-ship it is vital to consider who lives with whom and who marries whom. These are the subjects of the next two chapters.

VI

THE PATTERN OF RESIDENCE

In Chapter III a brief outline of the traditional form of the Trio settlement pattern was described and certain economic functions of it suggested. In Chapters IV and V attention was drawn to the importance of co-residence, the factor of *imoiti*, in the ordering of social relationships. This chapter is concerned with the social aspects of the settlement pattern, and what group of relatives constitutes the core of any particular settlement unit. As was made clear in earlier chapters, by the time my investigations among the Trio began, the traditional settlement pattern of dispersed villages had been totally disrupted. However, an attempt has been made in the first part of this chapter to reconstruct the main features of the relationships among village residents by combining the genealogical information collected by myself with the village census made by Schmidt in 1940–2.

Indications from this approach allow an examination of the new large villages along the same lines, and this is done separately for the villages of Paloemeu and Alalaparu. In the second part of the chapter the subject of relationship of house residents is examined.

I

A reconstruction of village residence. In Chapter III the following formation of Trio villages was described: three groups corresponding to three different main river basins, agglomerations of villages within the main groups, and finally the villages which form the agglomerations. With the aid of Schmidt's census (1942, pp. 55–62) it is possible to make a partial reconstruction of the relationships of village inhabitants of one main group—that in the Sipaliwini basin. In this area there are thirteen villages of which eight are inhabited, and these can be divided into five agglomerations.[1]

[1] Some of these villages are undoubtedly abandoned ones but in other cases only temporarily deserted while the inhabitants are at another village of the agglomeration. Schmidt made his journeys at the time of year when the Trio congregate to dance.

Agglomeration 1: Okoimɔ, Tuhori, Inakpo, Paikarakapo.
Agglomeration 2: Turapɔ.
Agglomeration 3: Panapipa, plus one.
Agglomeration 4: Maraka-eeku, plus two.
Agglomeration 5: Akame-eeku, plus two.

In none of these villages has it been possible to identify over 70 per cent of the inhabitants and in some the proportion drops to only 30 per cent. In Table 4 are listed all the Indians which are recorded by Schmidt (1942, pp. 56–59) and which are identifiable in the Genealogical Table. Against each individual are listed his closest relatives (i.e., those listed in the Index to the Genealogical Table) and immediate affines, and these are classified as living in the same village, same agglomeration, same group, or different group. Children have been ignored for the purpose of this investigation, but a brief comment about them is made at the end of the section.

TABLE 4

Distribution of kin and affines in the traditional settlement pattern.

1. *Okoimɔ* (67 per cent recognition)

No.	Village	Agglom.	Grp.	ex-Grp.
(39)	W.WB.WB.	—	—	—
(91)	B.Z.W.S.BW.ZH.SW.SW.	—	—	—
(89)	B.Z.W.BW.ZH.WM.	WB.	—	—
(413)	F.M.W.W.BW.	—	—	—
(603)	W.M.WZ.	—	—	—
(1)	W.	F.	—	—
(630)	—	—	—	—
(40)	H.B.B.BW.BW.	—	—	—
(88)	H.M.HB.HZ.	B.BW.	—	—
(92)	H.D.S.DH.HB.HZ.SW. SW.	S.SW.	—	—
(409)	H.HF.HM.	—	—	—
(571)	H.HF.HM.S.SW.	—	—	—
(560)	Z.H.D.HM.	—	—	—
(459)	Z.ZH.	—	—	—
(3)	H.	HF.	D.DH.	—
(481)	HB.	—	—	—
(604)	M.	—	—	—

2. *Tuhori* (35·5 per cent recognition)

(2)	B.	S.SW.	—	—
(512)	WZ.	—	B.WM.	—
(557)	F.B.W.	—	—	—
(694)	F.B.BW.	—	—	—
(575)	S.S.SW.	—	—	—
(697)	W.	—	—	—
(271)	B.	—	—	—
(150)	ZH.	—	Z.M. ZH.	—
(558)	H.HF.HB.	—	—	—
(722)	H.	—	—	—

3. *Inakpo* (63·6 per cent recognition)

(359)	W.Z.ZH.	B.BW.	—	—
(718)	W.	—	—	—
(73)	W.	M.Z.ZH.	—	—
(405)	W.WM.	—	—	WB.
(71)	W.WM.WB.	—	—	—
(43)	W.WF.WM.	—	B.	—
(45)	W.D.DH.	—	—	—
(482)	W.WB.	WB.	—	—
(79)	M.Z.ZH.	—	—	—
(540)	H.HZ.D.DH.	HB.	—	S.
(719)	H.	—	—	—
(70)	H.S.D.DH.	HM.HZ.	—	—
(356)	M.H.	—	—	B.
(44)	H.F.M.	—	HB.	—
(24)	H.D.DH.	—	B.S.D. SW.DH. BW.BW.	—
(360)	H.B.BW.	B.BW.	—	—
(63)	M.H.B.	—	—	—

4. *Paikalakapo* (56·7 per cent recognition)

(202)	W.WM.WF.WZ.WB.	B.Z.ZH. BW.	—	—
(166)	W.D.DH.	—	B.	—
(187)	W.S.D.D.SW.DH.	—	—	—
(182)	F.M.Z.Z.W.ZH.WF.WM.	—	—	—
(508)	W.	—	—	—
(192)	W.WM.W.DH.	—	—	—

(161)	M.W.WM.WF.	—	—	—
(201)	H.F.M.Z.B.BW.	HB.HZ.	—	—
(167)	H.D.DH.	—	HB.	—
(188)	H.S.D.D.SW.DH.	—	—	—
(191)	H.HF.HM.HZ.HZ.	—	—	—
(509)	H.D.DH.	—	—	—
(244)	H.DH.	—	—	—
(152)	F.M.B.Z.ZH.BW.S.SW.	—	—	—
(162)	H.F.M.HM.	—	—	—
(487)	H.M.	—	—	—

5. *Turapə* (59 per cent recognition)

(529)	WM.	—	B.	—
(68)	—	—	—	—
(382)	W.WM.	—	WZ.	—
(26)	S.	—	—	—
(125)	F.	—	—	—
(11)	W.W.WZ.WZ.	—	—	—
(507)	—	—	—	—
(521)	D.DH.DH.	—	D.DH.	—
(517)	M.H.	—	Z.	—
(111)	H.Z.ZH.	—	—	—
(12)	H.Z.ZH.	—	—	—

6. *Panapipa* (60 per cent recognition)

(62)	W.WB.	—	B.WM. BW.BW.	—
(14)	W.B.WM.	—	—	—
(245)	W.WM.W.WZ.	—	—	—
(52)	W.WZ.Z.ZII.	—	M.	—
(163)	B.	—	—	—
(61)	H.B.BW.	—	M.HB.	—
(18)	H.H.M.	—	—	—
(246)	H.Z.ZH.	—	—	—
(53)	H.Z.ZH.HZ.	—	HM.	—
(283)	D.DH.DH.	—	—	—

7. *Maraka-eeku* (62·5 per cent recognition)

(295)	B.BW.	—	—	—
(104)	—	—	B.BW.	—
(132)	—	—	—	—
(220)	W.	—	—	—

(81)	W.W.	—	B.BW.	—
(577)	—	—	B.BW.	—
(225)	W.W.	—	Z.WM.	—
(227)	W.	—	—	—
(160)	—	—	—	—
(170)	B.W.WM.	—	—	—
(290)	—	—	—	—
(221)	H.	—	—	—
(82)	H.	—	HB.	—
(106)	H.D.DH.	—	HB.	—
(226)	H.	—	HZ.	—
(252)	H.	—	M.HZ.	—
(228)	H.	—	—	—
(237)	—	—	—	—
(219)	H.M.HB.	—	—	—

8. *Akame-eeku* (32·1 per cent recognition)

(203)	WZ.	—	—	—
(155)	B.	—	—	—
(193)	B.	—	—	—
(233)	W.	—	—	—
(117)	H.ZH.	—	—	—

A casual inspection of Table 4 is sufficient to suggest that by far the largest proportion of an individual's closest relatives and affines live in the same village. The precise figures are shown in Table 5 in which is summarized the evidence from Table 4.

TABLE 5

Summary of distribution of kin and affines mentioned in Table 4.

	Village	Agglom.	Group	Ex-Group	Total
Kin	43	5	10	2	60
Affines	43	8	12	1	64
Total	86	13	22	3	124

Table 5 shows that 69·3 per cent of an individual's closest kin and affines live in the same village as himself, the community being equally divided between these two sets of relatives.

It is also clear that all but a very small proportion of relatives live in the same group. Only three relationships are shown as reaching outside the main group, and, in fact, these all lead to the same man, Asanri (451), whom Schmidt records as living in the East Paru basin (Schmidt, 1942, p. 61), while his mother, sister, and sister's husband are shown living in the village of Inakpo. Asanri's stay in the East Paru can have only been of a temporary nature since he married his actual sister's daughter, by whom he has a full grown daughter. Asanri himself is probably not as much as fifty years old, and in 1942 his presence so far from home can well be accounted for by the practice of young Indian men to make extended trips during their youth. Two other examples of this almost certainly occur in Schmidt's census although not listed above, since Schmidt classifies them as children. Asonko (78) is separated from his father, mother, and sister; Anaore (178) is living away from his father, mother, and two sisters.

With the exception of these two young men all children are listed as living in the same village as a parent in every case where identification is possible. The number of adult Indians separated from or united with their parents is shown in Table 6.

TABLE 6

Adults living with or away from parents.

	With Parents	Away from Parents
Men	8	4
Women	12	3

Thus 33·3 per cent of the men live away from their parents, and 20 per cent of the women. Of the four men away from their parents, one is Susuku (10), who is in the next village to that of his father, and he lives in the village of his wife's half-brother. The case of Asanri (451) separated from his mother has already been mentioned. Arensu (73) lives in the village of his much older wife, and in the last case Iyakɔpo (52) lives away from his mother but in the same village as his sister and sister's husband who is also his own wife's half-brother.

Of the three women who live away from their mothers, one, Tasi (252), is with her mother's full brother; one is the sister of

Iyakɔpo which case has been mentioned in the previous paragraph; and the last example lacks any remarkable feature. Thus it appears that in the cases where men or women are separated from parents they are normally found to be living in the same village as some other close relative.

In Table 7 is shown the number of united and separated siblings.

TABLE 7

Number of united and separated siblings.

	United	Separated	Total
Brothers	6	5	11
Sisters	4	1	5
Brother/Sister	7	4	11
	17 (63 per cent)	10 (37 per cent)	27

The single case where sisters are separated involves the same woman as in Table 5, who is living away from her mother but without obvious reason. In the four cases of brother/sister pairs being separated, two have already been commented upon since they concern Asanri (451) and Arensu (73). In the third case, Kanre (202) has left his brother and sister and lives in the village of his wife. The fourth example lacks an explanation.

Of the five separated pairs of brothers, two cases have already been explained; one involves Kanre (202), and one is the husband of the separated sisters who has a brother, married to his own wife's half-sister, living at Turapɔ with their wives' mother.

The other three examples are rather curious, since all three brothers are shown as living at Maraka-eeku where they lack any other identifiable relatives. This is also true of the unexplained example of the brother living away from his sister, and it is a notable feature of all the inhabitants of this village that they lack relationships other than husband/wife ones. There is nothing in Schmidt's writings which can be taken to account for this.

The largest proportion of separated brothers and the smallest of separated sisters offer a hint of matrilocal residence, as does the evidence of Table 6. Before turning to the question of the spouse's parents it should be added that an equal number of united and separated sibling pairs are married or unmarried.

A reconstruction of post-marital residence. While Table 8 shows that there is a tendency for a larger proportion of men to live with their wife's parents than women with their husband's parents, the main emphasis lies on the fact that over three-quarters of the married couples live in the same village as a spouse's parents. When one relates this to Table 6, in which it is shown that a similar proportion of adult children live in their parents' village, one would expect to find examples of married couples living in the same village as both sets of parents. There are, in fact, two examples of this, while there is no single case of a man or woman separated from their own parents and living with the parents-in-law. Thus in all six cases of married couples living away from parents-in-law they are also living away from parents, but the three women living away from their parents-in-law are closely related to the other inhabitants of the village while their husbands are not. Two of the three examples of men living away from their parents-in-law are inexplicable, and in the final case the village is equally divided between the man's kin and affines.

TABLE 8

Men and women living with or away from spouse's parents.

	With	Away	Total
Men	13 (81·2 per cent)	3 (18·8 per cent)	16
Women	6 (66·7 per cent)	3 (33·3 per cent)	9
	19 (76 per cent)	6 (24 per cent)	25

This indicates that brothers-in-law and sisters-in-law can be expected to live together, and this is shown in Table 9.

This table continues to show a tendency, although a slight one, towards matrilocal residence, but it is more usefully diagnostic of another feature which will be considered below. Finally, it can be noted that 61·9 per cent of the Indians live in the same village as their siblings' spouses who are also their own potential wives or husbands.

9

Before attempting a summary of this examination it must be stressed that, in the sample with which I have dealt, it has been possible to identify only 54·5 per cent of all the names recorded by Schmidt. So there are limitations to the conclusiveness of this investigation.

TABLE 9

Men living with and away from brothers-in-law (ZH/WB) and women with and away from sisters-in-law (HZ/BW).

	With	Away	Total
Men	6 (66·7 per cent)	3 (33·3 per cent)	9
Women	5 (55·5 per cent)	4 (44·5 per cent)	9
	11 (61·1 per cent)	7 (39·9 per cent)	18

The feature which recurs throughout is that an individual finds in his own community between two-thirds and three-quarters of his nearest kin and affines, and the proportion is equally divided between the two types. Post-marital residence is neither strongly patrilocal nor matrilocal, although there is a slight tendency towards the latter. This, however, can be explained thus—most marriages occur within the village, but the lack of suitable women will drive a man to search for a wife elsewhere. It is the men who marry outside their own villages who account for the slightly matrilocal flavour which is discernible, since in such circumstances the man remains in his wife's village. I return to this subject in Chapters VII and IX.

Before leaving Schmidt's account it is valuable to attempt one other approach to the study of the composition of a village; this is by considering the relationship of the inhabitants to the village leader. For this purpose two villages have been selected, partly because they contain a high proportion of recognizable members and partly because the leadership changed during the period of Schmidt's journeys, which allows two aspects to be given.

From Table 10 it can be seen that Kurawaka is related to the inhabitants of the village through his siblings or his children; Pika, however, is related to them through his wife, except for two who are a sister and her husband. The same pattern can

TABLE 10

Relationship to successive leaders of Okoimǝ of its inhabitants.

Inhabitants	Kurawaka (91)	Pika (39)
Pika (39)	ZH	—
Kurawaka (91)	—	WB
Sipare (89)	B	WB
Apiyantoni (413)	S	WBS
Nikïratete (603)	SWS	WBSWS
Susuku (1)	ZHZH	ZH
Yarepǝ (630)	—	—
Mauri (40)	Z	W
Pisekane (88)	BW	WBW
Munui (92)	BWM	WBW
Kontina (409)	SW	WBSW
Saripǝn (560)	SWSW	WBSWSW
Sïkuripǝn (459)	SWSW	WBSWSW
Mïkuri (3)	ZHZ	Z
Akǝri (571)	SW	WBSW
Pansina (481)	SW	WBSW
Paiyemipǝ (604)	SWSWD	WBSWSWD

TABLE 11

Relationship to successive leaders of Paikarakapo of its inhabitants.

Inhabitants	Tuna (187)	Kanre (202)
Kanre (202)	DH	—
Tuna (187)	—	WF
Tunareka (166)	DSWF	WZSWF
Muse (182)	S	WB
Yawikǝn (508)	SWFWFS	WBWFWFS
Paseki (192)	SWF	WBWF
Isïnaio (201)	D	W
Imariyae (167)	DSWM	WZSWM
Warepǝ (188)	W	WM
Ikuwaiyï (191)	SW	WBW
Yawinapu (509)	SWFWM	WBWFWM
Pasawatǝ (244)	SWM	WBWM

be seen in Table 11; Tuna (187) is related to the inhabitants of Paikarakapo through the marriages of his children, while for his successor, Kanre (202), the relationships are through his wife.

Finally, in Table 12, are listed the inhabitants of Panapipa, and the relationships which Iyakɔpo (52) considers he has with them. This reveals that Iyakɔpo sees the adult population of this village divided into two genealogical levels—his own, on which he has his brothers and sisters, and a senior one on which there are mothers and their brothers who are also affines. This latter level, from Eoyari's (62) viewpoint, consists of himself and his sisters, and the level below of his sisters' daughters and their brothers who are also his sisters' husbands.

TABLE 12

Relationship of the inhabitants of Panapipa to Iyakɔpo (52).

Eoyari (62)	MB/ZH/WB
Mono (14)	B
Tɔpepuru (245)	B
Apomita (163)	B
Tawiruye (61)	Z
Memɔ (18)	M/BW
Takïnaiu (246)	M/BW/WZ
Siwapun (53)	M/W
Aketɔ (283)	*Nosi*/BWM

Tables 10, 11, and 12 strengthen the earlier conclusions; for a stranger marrying into a village his relationships with the inhabitants will be universally affinal, but for the man who marries within his own village his relationships will be equally divided between kin and affines. These, at least, are the indications suggested by a study of ethnographic sources; it is now necessary to consider how far my own field notes support these conclusions.

An examination of relationships at Paloemeu village. To inspect either the Alalaparu or Paloemeu settlements as single units would obviously prove a valueless task, and accordingly these villages have been divided into segments. This division has been carried out partly rationally and partly arbitrarily.

At Paloemeu the topography of the river bank is such that the settlement is divided into three distinct parts which are separated from each other by shallow water courses. It is assumed that those who had lived together prior to the formation of the large Paloemeu village would tend to cluster together in it, and that examination of these three divisions as distinct entities might provide a useful approach to the problem. One or two general comments must first be made about these village sections.

These divisions hold a population of 41 in the smallest and nearly 100 in the largest so that they are two or three times larger than the size of a traditional village. These divisions are thus considered to approximate to an agglomeration, and no method has been found of identifying smaller units within these three divisions.

Secondly, the population has come from diverse areas—the immediate vicinity, the upper Tapanahoni, the upper Paloemeu, with the East Paru providing the bulk of the inhabitants. It is not possible to say whether or not this area represents a main group, since by 1960 the pattern observed by Schmidt had undergone a number of changes, and not enough is known about them to reconstruct a settlement pattern which existed just prior to the recent upheaval. With these limitations in mind, it is possible to embark upon an examination of the relationships existing within and without these divisions.

Initial investigations showed that an unrealistic view of the situation results if children are included in the study, because they overload the proportion of sibling pairs living together. Accordingly the examination has been restricted to adults who are married or have been married.

Conclusions from the first part of this chapter suggest that a start can be made by considering the unity of sibling pairs, and this is done at three levels; full siblings, or those sharing the same father and mother (as, in fact, has been done in the analysis of Schmidt's census), half-siblings, or those sharing one parent, and parallel-cousins, or the sons and daughters of a father's full brother, or mother's full sister.

Of the four brother/sister pairs which are separated, two live in different divisions at Paloemeu, one has his sister living at Alalaparu, and one a sister living somewhere in Brazil.

TABLE 13

United and separated full siblings at Paloemeu.

	United	Separated	Total
Brothers	3	3	6
Sisters	7	3	10
Brother/ Sister	15	4	19
	25 (71·4 per cent)	10 (28·6 per cent)	35

With the exception of this last case about which I have little information, the other three men are all considered to have transgressed norms of behaviour. Of the two pairs living at Paloemeu, one seems to have little communication with his sister (but I was poorly placed to observe it), but the other man, Koi (390), who had earned the society's disapprobation by putting away his young, nubile wife and taking an older, barren woman, has built himself a house in a relatively isolated position in a different division but is still regularly visited by his mother and sister who bring him gifts of food.

Of the separated brothers, one is married to a Waiyana and lives on the Lawa, and the brothers of the other two are at Alalaparu where they live with their wives' parents.

No common factor marks the separated sisters; one has a sister married to a Waiyana and lives in Brazil, another has a sister at Alalaparu, where she wishes to join her, and the last pair live in different divisions at Paloemeu and there is regular communication between them.

There is a rather higher proportion of separated half-siblings, and it is useful to take the analysis a stage further.

TABLE 14

United and separated half-siblings at Paloemeu.

	United	Separated	Total
Brothers	3	6	9
Sisters	9	3	12
Brother/ Sister	14	11	25
	26 (56·5 per cent)	20 (43·5 per cent)	46

Both parts of Table 15 show that children of the same mother are twice as likely to stay together as are offspring of the same father but different mother.

TABLE 15

i. United half-siblings at Paloemeu showing relationship to parent.

	Same mother	Same father	Total
Brothers	3	0	3
Sisters	5	4	9
Brother/ Sister	10	4	14
	18 (69·3 per cent)	8 (30·7 per cent)	26

ii. Separated half-siblings at Paloemeu showing relationship to parent.

	Same mother	Same father	Total
Brothers	2	4	6
Sisters	1	2	3
Brother/ Sister	2	9	11
	5 (25 per cent)	15 (75 per cent)	20

In Tables 16 and 17 the figures are given in the same way for parallel-cousins which for ease of presentation are shown as brothers and sisters in the tables.

TABLE 16

United and separated parallel-cousins at Paloemeu.

	United	Separated	Total
Brothers	7	4	11
Sisters	18	14	32
Brother/ Sister	20	14	34
	45 (58·4 per cent)	32 (41·6 per cent)	77

The figures in Table 16 show only insignificant differences from those in Table 14, but they both differ significantly from those in Table 13. Furthermore Table 17 continues the indications of Table 15, and matrilateral parallel-cousins are more likely to be found living together than patrilateral parallel-cousins.

TABLE 17

i. United parallel-cousins at Paloemeu showing relationship through parent.

	Mother's Z	Father's B	Total
Brothers	6	1	7
Sisters	10	8	18
Brother/			
Sister	13	7	20
	29 (64·5 per cent)	16 (35·5 per cent)	45

ii. Separated parallel-cousins at Paloemeu showing relationship through parent.

	Mother's Z	Father's B	Total
Brothers	4	0	4
Sisters	2	12	14
Brother/			
Sister	9	5	14
	15 (46·9 per cent)	17 (53·1 per cent)	32

With the information from Tables 13, 14, and 16 a summary of the situation is provided in Table 18.

While nearly two-thirds of the married sister pairs and brother/sister pairs live together, and in the case of full brother/sister pairs this percentage rises to 80 per cent, only half of the brother pairs are united. This fact suggests a matrilocal tendency, and this is supported by the practice of half-siblings of the same mother but different father tending to stay together, while those of the same father but different mother tend to separate. This fact is true, if less emphatically, in the case of parallel-cousins, with matrilateral ones showing a tendency to stay together, although the pattern is not so clearly defined.

TABLE 18

Summary of united and separated full siblings, half-siblings, and parallel-cousins at Paloemeu.

	United	Separated	Total
i. Brothers			
Full	3	3	6
Half	3	6	9
Parallel-cousins	7	4	11
	13 (50 per cent)	13 (50 per cent)	26
ii. Sisters			
Full	7	3	10
Half	9	3	12
Parallel-cousins	18	14	32
	34 (63 per cent)	20 (37 per cent)	54
iii. Brother/Sister			
Full	15	4	19
Half	14	11	25
Parallel-cousins	20	14	34
	49 (62·8 per cent)	29 (37·2 per cent)	78
TOTAL	96 (60·7 per cent)	62 (39·3 per cent)	158

Post-marital residence at Paloemeu. The next stop is an examination of marriage residence. The Trio lack any rule on this subject, and case histories which I recorded show considerable variation in behaviour with frequent movement between the villages of the married couples' respective parents. However, the apparent absence of any rule of post-marital residence, combined with the high proportion of united sibling pairs, leads one to suspect village endogamy, or at least agglomeration endogamy, as the normal practice. The majority of Trio express the opinion that it is best to marry someone from your own village.

Of the forty-nine Trio marriages at Paloemeu, twenty-four couples have a parent from one side or the other still living. Five of these couples both have a parent still alive, and they are distributed in the following manner. Three of them practise matrilocal residence, one lives with both sets of parents, and the fifth couple lives away from both sets. Table 19 shows what form of residence the other nineteen couples practise.

TABLE 19

Men and women living with and away from own surviving parents and spouse's parents (Paloemeu).

	With	Away	Total
i. Men			
Own parents	8	2	10
Wife's parents	8	1	9
	16	3	19
ii. Women			
Own parents	8	1	9
Husband's parents	8	2	10
	16	3	19

Table 19 shows that in the great majority of cases the married couple will live with a surviving parent, whether it be the husband's or wife's. The two cases of a man living away from his parents and one of one living away from his wife's parents involve the same people as the cases of a woman living away from her parents or husband's parents. One of these involves Koi (390) whose case has already been described in this chapter, and in the other examples the surviving parents live in Brazil and I have no adequate information to account for them.

The evidence from the Paloemeu village, although reservations must exist concerning how accurately it mirrors traditional conditions, conforms with the conclusions reached with the aid of ethnographic sources. The village or agglomeration consists of a core of siblings and their spouses together with their own or spouses' parents. The greater proportion of separated brothers can be accounted for by the need of some men to leave their own community and search elsewhere for a wife. This also gives a slight flavour of matrilocal residence since this is the normal practice in such circumstances. Finally, further confirmation can be sought by investigating the Alalaparu population in the same way.

An examination of relationships at Alalaparu village. Any attempt at analysis of Alalaparu similar to that carried out for Paloemeu involves a number of difficulties. First, the settlement cannot be divided by topographical features, and the expansion of the village was limited by the river on the eastern and northern sides, and artificially on the southern side where the Indians have been dissuaded from building houses because this is the fly-in to the airstrip.[1] Secondly, at least one house, and perhaps others, has been built, at the missionary's instigation, elsewhere than the owner wished. The assumption used at Paloemeu that those who now live together lived together previously is not therefore such a useful criterion at Alalaparu, where it has been necessary to be more arbitrary in dividing the village.

The Indians at Alalaparu, who number about 160, all belong to the Sipaliwini group, as territorially recognized from Schmidt's account. When the missionaries first entered the area in 1960, the Trio of the Sipaliwini basin were living in six or seven villages which formed four agglomerations (see Map 1). Within the sphere of the Alalaparu village one of these agglomerations—that consisting of the villages of Təpu and Aro—is clearly distinguishable by its spatial compactness and the limited social intercourse which its inhabitants have with the rest of the villagers. It is this difference in behaviour which first drew my attention to it.

One of the other agglomerations is fairly well defined on the same grounds, but the boundary between the last two is very indistinct, and it is perhaps wrong to consider them as two rather than one agglomeration. The recognition of two divisions rather than one will give the unity figure in the following tables a rather lower value and the separation figure a rather higher one than they should have.

[1] A new airstrip has now been cut, and the approach to it is well clear of the village.

TABLE 20

United and separated full siblings at Alalaparu.

	United	Separated	Total
Brothers	3	4	7
Sisters	4	4	8
Brother/			
Sister	17	5	22
	24 (64·9 per cent)	13 (35·1 per cent)	37

Two of the separated brother pairs, one sister pair and one brother/sister pair have already been mentioned as being divided between Alalaparu and Paloemeu. Three of the brother/sister pairs are divided between the two agglomerations which lack clear distinction, and this is so with one pair of brothers. One pair of sisters is divided because of a marriage with a Waiwai Indian, and one brother/sister pair and two sister pairs as a result of marital conflict surrounding Piwara (156) and Rorï (173). The fourth pair of brothers are practising matrilocal residence, Kəsəpə (139) living in the agglomeration with his wife's siblings, and his younger brother Muyopə (32) with his wife's father.

TABLE 21

United and separated half-siblings at Alalaparu.

	United	Separated	Total
Brothers	3	4	7
Sisters	8	3	11
Brother/			
Sister	12	4	16
	23 (67·6 per cent)	11 (32·4 per cent)	34

The proportion of united half-siblings is appreciably higher than at Paloemeu (see Table 14), and there is also a difference in the proportions of united and separated half-siblings, depending on parentage (compare Tables 15 and 22). At Alalaparu there is little emphasis on children of the same mother but different father staying together as compared with children of the same father but different mother, as is the case at Paloemeu.

TABLE 22

i. United half-siblings at Alalaparu showing relationship to parent.

	Same mother	Same father	Total
Brothers	1	2	3
Sisters	4	4	8
Brother/			
Sister	7	5	12
	12 (52·2 per cent)	11 (47·8 per cent)	23

ii. Separated half-siblings at Alalaparu showing relationship to parent.

	Same mother	Same father	Total
Brothers	2	2	4
Sisters	1	2	3
Brother/			
Sister	2	2	4
	5 (45·5 per cent)	6 (54·5 per cent)	11

In the case of parallel-cousins the trend observed at Paloemeu (see Tables 16 and 17) is more definite at Alalaparu. Table 23 shows that parallel-cousins have an equal chance of being united or separated.

TABLE 23

United and separated parallel-cousins at Alalaparu.

	United	Separated	Total
Brothers	4	2	6
Sisters	10	14	24
Brother/			
Sister	16	14	30
	30 (50 per cent)	30 (50 per cent)	60

Almost three-quarters of the matrilateral parallel-cousins live together, a proportion almost 10 per cent higher than at Paloemeu, although the proportion of types of parallel-cousin pairs is not significantly different. At the same time there is a proportionate increase in the number of separated patrilateral parallel-cousins (compare Tables 17 and 24).

TABLE 24

i. United parallel-cousins at Alalaparu showing relationship through parent.

	Mother's Z	Father's B	Total
Brothers	2	2	4
Sisters	8	2	10
Brother/ Sister	12	4	16
	22 (73·4 per cent)	8 (26·7 per cent)	30

ii. Separated parallel-cousins at Alalaparu showing relationship through parent.

	Mother's Z	Father's B	Total
Brothers	2	0	2
Sisters	2	12	14
Brother/ Sister	7	7	14
	11 (36·7 per cent)	19 (63·3 per cent)	30

When one compares the summary of the figures from Alalaparu with those from Paloemeu (Tables 18 and 25) a number of similarities and differences can be seen. First, the proportion of brother pairs, sister pairs and brother/sister pairs is similar. The proportion of brothers separated and united is identical at the two villages, and the figures for brother/sister pairs bear a close resemblance to each other, the difference being 3·4 per cent. However, the difference in the case of sister pairs is far greater, and only about half the sisters at Alalaparu are united compared with 63 per cent at Paloemeu; this is partly explicable by the arbitrary division of the Alalaparu village.

TABLE 25

Summary of united and separated full siblings, half-siblings, and parallel-cousins at Alalaparu.

	United	Separated	Total
i. Brothers			
Full	3	4	7
Half	3	4	7
Parallel-cousins	4	2	6
	10 (50 per cent)	10 (50 per cent)	20
ii. Sisters			
Full	4	4	8
Half	8	3	11
Parallel-cousins	10	14	24
	22 (51·2 per cent)	21 (48·8 per cent)	43
iii. Brother/Sister			
Full	17	5	22
Half	12	4	16
Parallel-cousins	16	14	30
	45 (66·1 per cent)	23 (33·9 per cent)	68
TOTAL	77 (58·8 per cent)	54 (41·2 per cent)	131

Post-marital residence at Alalaparu. An examination of post-marital residence at Alalaparu shows that there is strong similarity to the situation at Paloemeu. Of the forty-three existing marriages at Alalaparu, twenty-four couples have one or more parents alive but, because of the uncertainty about which division one couple belongs to, the examination is restricted to twenty-three examples.

Out of this number there are five marriages in which both husband and wife have a surviving parent. In three of these cases the married couples and both sets of parents live together. In the other two examples, the brother and sister, Mïtïipï (59) and Wərimuku (216), live with their mother Akutapə (60), whose husband Taiyapə (125) has left her and is said to be living in Brazil. Mïtïipï has recently married Wəripena (58), whose parents live in a different division at Alalaparu; this then is an example of patrilocal residence. Wərimuku is married to Amasina (215) whose father lives at Paloemeu; this is a case of matrilocal residence.

The distribution of the remaining eighteen cases in which only one of the married pair has a surviving parent is shown in Table 26.

TABLE 26

Men and women living with and away from own surviving parents and spouse's parents (Alalaparu).

	With	Away	Total
i. Men			
Own parents	6	3	9
Wife's parents	8	1	9
	14	4	18
ii. Women			
Own parents	8	1	9
Husband's parents	6	3	9
	14	4	18

This evidence confirms the conclusion drawn from the Paloemeu data (Table 19); married couples live with surviving parents regardless of whether they are the husband's or the wife's.

Of the three men who live away from their parents (their wives are the women living away from their husband's parents) one is a young man, Sikamimpə (254), who with his old wife is paying a visit to Alalaparu where neither of them has blood relations. One is Sakakimpə (123) whose father, Taiyapə (125), as mentioned above, has gone to live in Brazil; Sakakimpə lives among a group of his siblings and half-siblings. In the third case a young man, Pepu (22), has married a recently widowed girl and they live among her former husband's children and step-children.

The one woman living away from her parents (her husband is the single man living away from his wife's parents) lives among a group of her husband's siblings and half-siblings. Her parents live at Alalaparu and she has considerable communication with them; it is perhaps wrong to consign her to a different division of the village.

A summary can now be made of the evidence provided in the first part of this chapter. The first point to note is that no important differences can be observed between the figures drawn from three different sources. They all emphasize the following features:

i. Siblings tend to live together. Of the Surinam Trio 72·1 per cent[1] of the full sibling pairs live in the same village division, 62 per cent of the half-sibling pairs, and 61 per cent of the parallel-cousins.

ii. Brother/sister pairs, 80 per cent, remain together more than sisters, 64·7 per cent, and sisters more than brothers, 54·5 per cent.

iii. Half-siblings who share the same mother and matrilateral parallel-cousins remain together more than half-siblings of the same father and patrilateral parallel-cousins, the higher proportion of separated patrilateral parallel-cousins being obviously related to that of separated brothers.

iv. Statistical evidence fails to reveal any set pattern of post-marital residence. Of the 10 marriages in which there are parents from both sides living, 4 practise matrilocal residence, 1 patrilocal residence, 4 live with both sets of parents and the tenth pair live away from both sets. Of the 37 marriages in which the parents of either husband or wife but not of both are alive, 30 couples live with the parents. The practice of living with one's parents, a trait initially apparent in the analysis of Schmidt's material, is a natural corollary of united sibling pairs.

---

[1] The proportion of united siblings is higher when all the Surinam Trio are considered together, because if a man A at Paloemeu has a sister B at Alalaparu this counts as 'separated' in the figures for each place. When the figures are combined this counts as only a single instance. In the case of full siblings there are 4 such occurrences, 1 among the half-siblings, and 14 among the parallel-cousins.

v. The tendency towards matrilocality which is evinced by the higher proportion of separated brothers and parallel-cousins to other types can be interpreted as the need for some men to find their wives outside the immediate community. In such cases matrilocal residence appears to have been the normal practice.

The analysis of Schmidt's material suggests that the village is the important social unit, while the figures for Alalaparu and Paloemeu are assumed to refer to agglomerations. Since the agglomeration is the self-supporting economic unit, and within it Indians regularly move from one settlement to another in order to exploit fully the resources of the area, the idea of the agglomeration as a basic social unit receives further support.

Certainly it is difficult to visualize a village of thirty inhabitants existing as a socially autonomous unit, and since the Indians live in different villages in the agglomeration at different times and co-residence is a criterion of relationship, it seems safe to assume that the agglomeration is both the basic economic and social unit.

Within the agglomeration a man will expect to find the majority of his kin and affines, and his social contacts will be mainly confined to the inhabitants of his agglomeration. The travels of an Indian within an agglomeration allow the constant renewal of these ties, and at the same time satisfy the requirements of subsistence. However, as will be shown in Chapter X, hostility as well as friendship is a feature of the relationship between inhabitants of an agglomeration.

II

The first part of this chapter has dealt with the composition of village and agglomeration populations and the inter-relationship of their inhabitants. This second part is concerned with the inhabitants of single dwellings, and describes the situation at Alalaparu on 1 January 1964 and at Paloemeu on 1 April 1964.

The Trio, as far as we have a record of them, have never lived in large communal houses, although it is possible that they once dwelt in larger houses than they do now. The recent population movements have undoubtedly distorted the traditional pattern as, probably, has the missionary influence.

In the following list the numbers refer to the house and the letter to the agglomeration; A (Fig. 10), B (Fig. 11), and C (Fig. 12) at Paloemeu, and D, E, F, and G (Fig. 13) at Alalaparu. Where, at Alalaparu, the letter is replaced by a question mark it indicates uncertainty as to which agglomeration the inhabitants belong.

Paloemeu　　　　　　　　　　　　　　　　　　　　　　　　No.

1A.　Sapinkɔ (436), his wife, his wife's sister, and her son and daughter. The WZH had recently died.　　　5

2A.　Pikume (365), his wife and daughter.　　　3

3A.　Asanri (451), his wife, married daughter, her husband and two children.　　　6

4A.　Rime (364) and his wife.　　　2

5A.　Pareya (430), his wife and young daughter, also his elder sister whose husband had left her, and her daughter.　　　5

6A.　Naki (420), his wife and baby son.　　　3

7A.　Tɔpepuru (245), and his son by a former wife. These two men are married to sisters one of whom has a son by a former marriage and is also looking after the orphan son of a female parallel-cousin (FBDS). Finally there is a married couple recently arrived from Brazil; the husband is a classificatory brother of the two sisters.　　　8

8A.　Inkiman (417) and his wife. Also Tupiro (679) and his wife, and her younger brother; these three have recently arrived from Brazil.　　　5

9A.　Toropɔti (305), his wife, son, and daughter; also his younger sister with her husband and son.　　　7

10A.　Arena (462)—a widow, with her son and daughter, and her younger half-brother.　　　4

11A.　Waiyana family of Anesi (373) who is married to a Trio woman, and they live in 12A.

12A.　Ankapi (361)—a widow, her married daughter with a Waiyana husband and baby son, a younger daughter, and the son of an older deceased daughter.　　　6

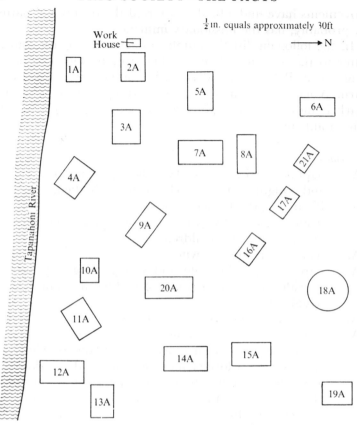

Figure 10: Sketch plan of the middle division of the Paloemeu village (Agglomeration A) in April 1964.

13A. Pisere (381), his wife and daughter. Also a young man and his wife who have recently arrived from Brazil.   5

14A. Napanakɪ̆ (313)—a widow, her son, his Waiyana wife, and their daughter; the Waiyana woman's son by a former marriage; a dead sister's son.   6

15A. Yapi (339), his wife, and her daughter by an earlier marriage; a male parallel-cousin, and a sister with her husband and his dead brother's daughter.   7

16A. Korokoro (300), his wife, and her elder and younger brothers. I lived with this family. 4

17A. Sanəpə (343) and his wife. 2

18A. Keriya (346), his wife and son; his wife's father's brother, his wife, and her younger brother. 6

19A. Koi (390) and his wife. 2

20A. Irawïpən (327), her Waiyana husband, and her two sons by a former marriage; also her half-sister and her husband and young son, and the husband's brother's son; finally a man, Nupiyarankə (684), with his wife and daughter, who have recently arrived from Brazil. 11

21A. This is a work-house, but with the influx of Indians from Brazil a number of immigrants live in it. Koiye (670), his wife, the daughter of a former wife's brother's daughter and her two daughters; Nayïwi (774), a widow, and her three sons. 9

22B. Kiyokiyo (578), his wife, his wife's mother, and a younger half-sister of his wife and a baby son of dubious paternity. Kiyokiyo had once considered himself married to both girls but by April 1964 considered only the one to be his wife. 5

23B. Pokïi (556), his wife, two sons, and his wife's son by a previous marriage; also his wife's married daughter by a previous marriage, and her husband and young son. This family lived for a while in 24B with the husband's family. 8

24B. Saripən (560)—a widow, her married son, his wife, and his son by an earlier marriage; the widow's married daughter, her husband, and her three children—one by the present marriage and the other two by previous marriages; an unrelated girl. 10

25B. Kïsi (616), his Waiyana wife and their two children; his male parallel-cousin and his Waiyana wife. (The two Waiyana women are sisters.) 6

26B. Sini (566), his wife, two children, and a son of his wife by an earlier marriage; also Maruwaikə (577) and his wife, both recently arrived from Brazil. 7

27B. Sirosi (595), his wife and her daughters by a previous marriage, and the husband of one of them. 5

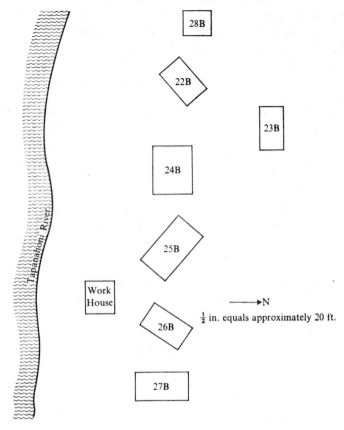

Figure 11: Sketch plan of the downstream division of the Paloemeu village (Agglomeration B) in April 1964.

28B. Yaruwanare (587), his wife and daughter.   3
29B. Unallotted.
30C. Təmeta (482), his wife and two sons.   4
31C. Sareyuna (470), a widow living alone.   1
32C. Sipə (490), and his Waiyana wife.   2
33C. Pĭtĭ (494), his wife and three children; also Asiwapə (716) and his wife who have recently arrived from Brazil.   7
34C. Amasi (476), his wife and son.   3
35C. Poiye (405), his wife, her daughters by a former marriage, and the husband of one of them. Poiye's

half-sister, her son and his Waiyana wife, and the
son of another of her sons. 9

36C. Apari (360), (Tǝmeta's ex-wife), two of her classificatory sisters' sons, and Siki (699), his wife and
three children recently arrived from Brazil. 8

37C. Iyetipǝ (720), his wife and his daughter by a
previous marriage, and his sister and her daughter. 5

38C. Ameniye (725), her Waiyana husband, and her two
children by a former Waiyana husband. 4

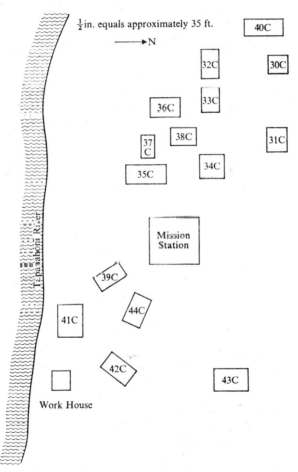

Figure 12: Sketch plan of the upstream division of the Paloemeu village
(Agglomeration C) in April 1964.

39C. Enusasa (400), and her two sons by previous marriages; also Natara (732), his wife, and his son and daughter by an earlier marriage—this family has recently arrived from Brazil. 7

40C. Anoriya (704), her Waiyana husband, and a deceased brother's two daughters. (A number of her husband's Waiyana relatives). 4

41C. Asapoti (376), his wife and his wife's daughter by a previous marriage; also a young man, Simuru (511), the male parallel-cousin of Pesini (528) in a neighbouring house. 4

42C. Supipi (514), his wife and daughter. 3

43C. Surake (744), his dead wife's mother and his three daughters; also Kusene (756), his wife, his son, and two daughters by earlier marriages, the husband of one of the daughters, Kusene's mother, and a small girl in her care. The two families have recently arrived from Brazil. 10

44C. Pesini (528), his Waiyana wife, his daughter and one of his classificatory sisters (FBWZD). (A number of his wife's Waiyana relations.) 4

Alalaparu

1?. Mikïpə (20), her Waiwai husband, her son and daughter by previous husbands, and her father's sister. 5

2D. Akïrïpə (100), his wife, daughter, and adult unmarried sister; joined by Enapere (263) and his wife (whom Akïrïpə considers to be a classificatory sister), when they arrived from Brazil. 6

3D. Kəsəpə (139), with his two wives and six children, and the infant daughter of one daughter. 10

4D. Anaore (178), his wife and two sons. 4

5D. Apirosi (161), his wife, and her daughter by a previous marriage. 3

6D. Emopiripə (165) and his wife. 2

7D. Makïpə (169) and his wife. 2

8D. Sapə (151) and his wife. 2

9D. Itïimare (153), his wife, and her three children by two earlier marriages. 5

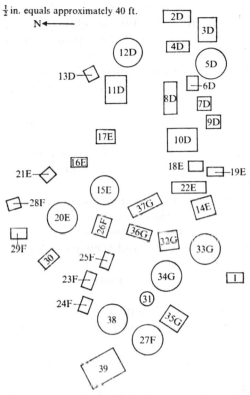

Figure 13: Sketch plan of the village of Alalapaɾu in January 1964.

10D. Asikiri (170), his wife, and their daughter, and his almost full-grown son by an earlier marriage. Sikamimpǝ (254) and his elderly wife are living in this house during a visit from Brazil.   6

11D. Koruyari (195), his wife, and their two young sons. Koruyari and his wife went off on an extended trip and are to be away over a year. The boys have been left in the care of their mother's mother who lives in 13D. This house was then taken over by some migrants from the West Paru; Mooso (273) (who had been Koruyari's mother's husband), and his wife, his wife's half-sister, her husband and son.   5

12D. Muse (182), his wife, and their baby son.   3

13D.   Isĭnaio (201), a widow who lived alone.   1
14E.   Sipi (23), his wife, his daughter by a previous
       wife, her husband, and their young son; a son of
       Sipi's wife by an earlier marriage.   6
15E.   Tawiruye (61) whose husband has recently left her,
       her dead son's son, and a man who lacks any
       relatives.   3
16E.   Matatə (31), his wife, and their common grand-
       mother.   3
17E.   Toropə (107), his wife, their son, his son by a
       former marriage, and her son by a previous
       husband.   5
18E.   Sere (9), his wife, and their daughter.   3
19E.   Mono (14), his wife, and their two sons.   4
20E.   Iyakəpo (52), his wife, and their two sons.   4
21E.   Asapə (43), his wife, and their two daughters.   4
22E.   Susuku (1), his wife, and her adult son and
       daughter by a previous marriage. I lived with this
       family.   4
23F.   Piriuta (77) and his wife.   2
24F.   Pepu (22), his wife, and her daughter by a former
       husband.   3
25F.   Sepĭ (74), his wife, his mother, and his young
       half-brother.   4
26F.   Pesaipə (93), his wife, and their son; also Pesaipə's
       dead brother's son, his half-sister's son, his wife, and
       their son.   7
27F.   Asonko (78), his wife, and her two sons and a
       daughter by a previous marriage.   5
28F.   Sipare (89) and his wife.   2
29F.   Piwara (156) and his wife.   2
30?.   Eoyari (62), his wife, and their son. Eoyari who
       was previously married to Tawiruye then lived in
       15E, but the wife with whom he was living at the
       time of the census belonged to agglomeration F. It
       is not possible to consign them to either agglomera-
       tion.   3
31?.   Kinini (79) and his wife. Kinini belongs to agglo-
       meration F, and his wife to G. They associate with
       their respective groups.   2

32G. Orosisi (126), his wife, and her deceased daughter's two children. Also Misita (134), a widow, with her son and daughter. 7

33G. Maiyinimpə (131), his wife, their son, and her daughter by a previous husband; also Sakakimpə (123), who is Maiyinimpə's wife's mother's son, his wife, and her two children by a previous marriage. 8 The whole of this household went on an extended journey and the house was taken over by Rorĭ (173), his wife, and her two children by a former marriage. Mupi (69), an orphan, also lives with this family and calls the woman 'mother' (probably a patrilateral cross-cousin). 5

34G. Kumiru (117)—a widow, and her daughter's daughter. 2

35G. Siwiri (237)—a widow, her daughter (also a widow), and the latter's two sons and one daughter; the husband of the daughter, and the wife of one of the sons and their baby daughter. 8

36G. Ororinapə (155) and his wife. Sometimes they are joined by his children who otherwise live in 9D with their mother. 2

37G. Waikera (203) and his wife. 2

38 and 39. Waiwai houses.

There is a total of 82 houses at the two villages of which 3 are entirely inhabited by Indians other than Trio. The composition of the residents of the remaining 79 can be classified thus:

i. 35 *houses* (11 Paloemeu; 24 Alalaparu) contain a single nuclear family consisting of a man, his wife, their children, and/or offspring from a previous marriage of either spouse.

ii. 7 *houses* (5 Paloemeu; 2 Alalaparu) contain a single nuclear family as defined in i., plus another unrelated nuclear family. In all but one case (41C) the unrelated family has recently arrived from Brazil and lack alternative accommodation.

iii. 8 *houses* (7 Paloemeu; 1 Alalaparu) contain a parent or other relative of the wife (not child or sibling). The example at

Alalaparu involves Muyopɔ, who has recently arrived from Brazil, dislikes living under his father-in-law's roof, and intends shortly to build his own house.

Of the 7 Paloemeu cases, 2 (12A, 44C) involve marriages with Waiyana, in a further 2 (27B, 35C) the husband is away for long periods on geological survey expeditions, and in one (23B) the couple sometimes live with the husband's mother whose house is next door.

iv. 4 *houses* (3 Paloemeu; 1 Alalaparu) contain a parent or other relative of the husband (not child or sibling). In the single example at Alalaparu (25F), the wife cares for her husband's old mother. Two of the Paloemeu cases (14A, 40C) are associated with mixed Trio/Waiyana marriages, and in the third (7A) a father and son are married to two sisters.

v. 4 *houses* (2 Paloemeu; 2 Alalaparu) contain bilaterally extended families. Two (24B, 35G) are composed of an elderly woman living with a married son and married daughter and their children. The third case consists of a brother/sister pair and their married children. The last case only marginally belongs to this class since it consists of a husband and wife living with their common grandmother (his MM and her FM).

vi. 7 *houses* (all at Paloemeu) are inhabited by a pair of married siblings; in three (1A, 20A, 25B) there are pairs of sisters, although in one (25B) the two men are parallel-cousins as well. In the other four cases (5A, 9A, 15A, 37C) they are brother/sister pairs.

vii. 6 *houses* (3 Paloemeu; 3 Alalaparu) contain widows; two of these live alone (31C, 13D) but close to a married daughter. The other four live with a variety of relatives; one (10A) with her small children and young brother, one (36C) with a deceased classificatory sister's young boys, and two (15E, 34G) with a grandchild.

viii. 8 *houses* (4 Paloemeu; 4 Alalaparu) are difficult to classify except individually since they possess no salient common feature.

While this classification is neither perfect nor comprehensive (the number of variables would result in there being as many classes as examples) it does help to underline some important features. There are relatively few unilateral or bilateral extended families living under one roof, although, as has been demonstrated in the earlier part of this chapter, one can expect to find such relatives living in the same settlement. Complementary to this is the large number of houses containing a single nuclear family, and the proportion of these would be higher if the migrations had not occurred.

Next it is possible to reclassify some of the groups so that eleven houses can be considered to contain married sibling pairs which then form the second largest number in any one category, and together with categories i. and ii. make up two-thirds of the total.

This behaviouristic treatment of Trio village and house residence has been necessitated by the lack of Trio categories. The most important Trio term relating to this subject is *imoiti* which has been described in Chapter IV; an *imoiti* is a closely related person through the qualification of co-residence rather than genealogical relationship, although this distinction quickly becomes submerged. The general mobility of population within the bounds of the agglomeration may result in the *imoiti* status being shared by all the inhabitants of an agglomeration. As has already been mentioned, there is no simple term for a family or a household. Thus it could be said that the lack of formality in the Trio social organization is even discernible at the level of the elementary family or immediate household for which the language lacks precise terms. Accordingly the analysis of Trio residence has involved imposing external and artificial categories which do not exist on the level of Trio thought.

The emphasis on the nuclear family dwelling stresses another aspect of the Trio socio-economic organization. The smallest viable economic unit is the partnership of a man and a woman; this fact has been explained in Chapter III. However, economic activities are sexually divided so that rarely do men and women join in the same task; thus the division of labour means that regular co-operation, as distinct from interdependence, in economic activities is more or less confined to members of the same sex. The large proportion of nuclear family dwellings means, in turn, that most economic co-operation takes place in the sphere of the village and not in the house. Since the inhabitants of a village consist mainly of close relatives, the study of their interactions involves the examination of the attitudes and behaviour, co-operation and obligation, between the different categories of relatives. However, before this can be done there is one more aspect of Trio social organization which must be examined in detail—that is marriage.

VII

TRIO MARRIAGE

MARRIAGE IS the most important social institution among the Trio, since it represents the active part of an otherwise inert structure. Before showing how marriage is the stimulant to social activity, it is necessary to examine in detail Trio marriage practices. This is the subject of this chapter and in it the analysis is carried out at three different levels—first, the conventional rules of marriage; secondly, the extent to which individuals consider that they abide by these conventions; and, thirdly, the actual marriage practices. The final part of the chapter deals with the process of marriage and divorce.

I

The conventional marriage rule has already been mentioned briefly—marriage for a Trio man or woman is prescribed with an *emerimpə*, which term covers the bilateral cross-cousin, but may also include any unrelated individual. The Trio say that there is no direct address term for an *emerimpə*, but this problem has already been examined, and it has been shown that in practice direct address terms are used to *emerimpə*, the patrilateral cross-cousins being equated with members of the first ascending genealogical level, and the matrilateral cross-cousins with members of the first descending genealogical level. This difference between convention and practice becomes even more obvious when the conventional preferences are expressed in genealogical terms rather than categorical ones.

The Trio frequently describe the categories with which marriage is either prescribed or forbidden by reference to the relationship with the parent. This is a more definitive approach than that allowed by the ambiguous *emerimpə* category, and also more revealing. All informants unanimously agree that a man and a woman should marry respectively the daughter and the son of either a *nosi* or a *ti*, with perhaps the slightly greater emphasis being placed on the *nosi*. There is some evidence that, following the marriage to an unrelated person, the parents-in-law will be placed in these categories. For example, Inǝsi (317) has a Waiyana wife and refers to her parents by these terms, but in fact this is an adoption of Waiyana custom and Trio practice will be discussed in Chapters VIII and IX.

In addition to the above categories, some informants express the opinion that it is good for a man to marry the daughter of a *wǝi* or a *tamu*, and for a woman to marry the son of a *tamu*. The informants who say this tend to be those whose marriages follow this pattern, but this is not always so. For example, Eoyari (62) was married to Tawiruye (61) whose mother he called *wǝihko*. When Eoyari was asked if the Trio marry their *wǝi*'s daughters he denied such a practice. When questioned about his marriage to Tawiruye he stressed the conventional aspect of the union since she is also the daughter of a man who was his *tĭ*. It was only after cross-examining him over his relationship with Tawiruye's mother that he admitted that he had married the daughter of a *wǝi* and that such marriages take place among the Trio. Among the informants who assent to the existence of marriage with a sister's daughter, the consensus of opinion is that such a marriage should be only with the daughter of a *wǝi*. However, it has already been noted that age is likely to influence the decision of whether a girl is marriageable or not. There is only one extant case of a marriage with the daughter of an *akǝmi*; this union involves Amasi (476) who is of very similar age to his wife's mother with whom he has no genealogical connexion. He claims that he regards her as his *akǝmi* but in fact has little contact with her.

No informant volunteered the opinion that a woman should marry a *wǝi*'s son, although if a direct question on this topic is asked, such a marriage is said to be suitable if the relationship is distant enough. This type of marriage is the female counterpart to a man marrying someone whom he calls *manhko*, and the reaction to questions about the possibility of such a union is the same. Both these forms of marriage give rise to contradictory claims by the Trio; while it is said that one should marry a *nosi*'s daughter and it is agreed that such a relative is addressed as *manhko*, it is equally claimed that a man does not marry a woman whom he calls *manhko*. In spite of this many informants admit that prior to marriage they called their future wife by this term, and were called *yimuku* by her. The con-

ventional marriage rules only partly accept the existence of
marriage with the sister's daughter and completely fail to take
into account the corresponding difficulties in the classification
of the father's sister's daughter which arise when such a union
occurs. The Trio are unaware of any contradiction here for the
simple reason that two different levels are involved, one of
thought and one of action. Firstly, there is the ideal which
prescribes marriage with an *emerimpǝ* and is expressed in terms
of category. Secondly, individual practice which is in harmony
with the ideal prescription but is expressed in genealogical
terms, and reflects individual choice.

Those relatives with whom marriage is forbidden are clearly
defined; a man should not marry a woman whom he calls
nosi, *wǝihko*, or *akǝmi*, and one who calls him *pahko*. A woman
should not marry a man whom she calls *pahko*, *pihko*, and
akǝmi, and one who calls her *manhko*—allowing for the exceptions
just discussed.

Finally, the majority of informants declared a preference for
marrying someone from one's own village; this means that the
qualification of co-residence, as well as relationship category,
enters into an individual's choice of spouse.

II

This section is concerned with an examination not of what the
Trio say that they ought to do, but what they say they in fact
do. The lack of coincidence between convention and practice
in Trio marriage when seen from an ego centred point of view
(see Chapter IV) makes it imperative to consider this subject
in some detail.

In 1963/4 there were ninety-two all Trio marriages among
those Indians living in Surinam; both partners of all these
unions were asked, 'What do (or did) you call your wife's
(husband's) father and mother?'. In about a third of the cases
the answer was unknown because the informant had not
known the person as a result of their early death. Table 27
shows the results obtained from this inquiry. The conventional
marriage form with the son or daughter of a *nosi* or a *tï* represents a major proportion, except in the case of the husband's
father where the son of a *tamu* has an equal share. However,
nowhere does the conventional relationship far exceed half the

11

total number of cases, and a significant proportion belong to the secondary preferences.[1] If all preferred categories are taken together they represent more than 80 per cent of the total. Thus under one-fifth of the sample consider their own marriage to be outside the conventionally preferred limits. In Tables 28 and 29 the analysis is taken a step further and here are shown the results of re-uniting these relationships in their correct combinations.

TABLE 27

Distribution of relationships of individuals to their child's spouse.

i. Relationship of wife's father to daughter's husband:

tï	tamu	ipapa	ipipi/akɔmi	pito	Total
34	14	8	5	2	63
54 per cent	22·2 per cent	12·7 per cent	7·9 per cent	3·2 per cent	100

ii. Relationship of wife's mother to daughter's husband:

nosi	wɔi/akɔmi	imama	Total
30	21	11	62
48·4 per cent	33·9 per cent	17·7 per cent	100

iii. Relationship of husband's father to son's wife:

tamu	tï	ipapa	ipipi/akɔmi	Total
23	21	6	3	53
43·4 per cent	39·6 per cent	11·3 per cent	5·7 per cent	100

iv. Relationship of husband's mother to son's wife:

nosi	wɔi/akɔmi	imama	emi	Total
32	13	10	1	56
57·1 per cent	23·2 per cent	17·9 per cent	1·8 per cent	100

[1] This assumes that, for a woman, the category *imuku*, i.e. those who call her *manhko*, is a preferred one since 23·2 per cent of the women refer to their husband's mother as *wɔi*. It is interesting to note that the proportion of the prescribed category is highest in this case where the secondary preference is least acceptable. The same thing is reflected in the figures for the relationship of men to their daughter's husband.

From Table 28 it can be seen that the emphasis is on the combination *tĭ/wəi = tamu/nosi*, which are the categories involved when marriage is between the mother's brother and the sister's daughter. The categories involved in a bilateral cross-cousin marriage (*tĭ/nosi = tĭ/nosi*) only occur twice, as do those

TABLE 28

Relationship of men and women to their children's spouses in cases where all four relationships are known.

Relationship of wife's parents to daughter's husband		Relationship of husband's parents to son's wife		No. of Cases
WF	WM	HF	HM	
tĭ	nosi	tĭ	nosi	2
tĭ	nosi	tamu	nosi	1
tĭ	nosi	tĭ	wəi	2
tĭ	wəi	tamu	nosi	8
tĭ	imama	tĭ	nosi	1
ipapa	nosi	tĭ	nosi	1
ipapa	nosi	ipapa	nosi	1
ipapa	wəi	tamu	nosi	1
ipapa	imama	ipapa	imama	1
ipipi	nosi	tĭ	nosi	2
ipipi	imama	tamu	nosi	1
ipipi	wəi	tamu	imama	1
tamu	nosi	tĭ	nosi	1
tamu	nosi	tĭ	wəi	1
tamu	nosi	tamu	wəi	1
tamu	nosi	ipapa	wəi	1
tamu	imama	tamu	imama	1
tamu	imama	tamu	wəi	1
pito	nosi	tĭ	imama	1
			Total	29

expected in the case of patrilateral cross-cousin marriage (*tĭ/nosi = tĭ/wəi*). Of the rest, only one contains none of the conventionally accepted categories and that one is *ipapa/imama = ipapa/imama*. This particular case is the marriage between Sirosi (595) and Asaeye (596); their fathers were *imoitĭ*, and both Sirosi and Asaeye admit that they should not be married.[1] With the exception of this case and the one *ipipi/imama = tamu/ nosi*, the principle applied seems to be that marriage occurs as long as at least one parent of each spouse belongs to a conventionally accepted category.

This approach can be extended to marriages where there is knowledge concerning three out of the four parents.

TABLE 29

Relationship of men and women to their children's spouses in marriages where only three out of the four possible relationships are known (an asterisk indicates the unknown relationship).

Relationship of wife's parents to daughter's husband		Relationship of husband's parents to son's wife		No. of Cases
WF	*WM*	*HF*	*HM*	
tï	*nosi*	*tamu*	*	2
tï	*nosi*	*tï*	*	1
tamu	*nosi*	*tï*	*	1
tamu	*nosi*	*ipipi*	*	1
ipapa	*imama*	*ipapa*	*	1
ipapa	*imama*	*tamu*	*	1
tï	*nosi*	*	*nosi*	1
tï	*wəi*	*	*nosi*	2
tamu	*wəi*	*	*nosi*	1
ipapa	*nosi*	*	*wəi*	1
tï	*	*tamu*	*nosi*	1
tamu	*	*tï*	*wəi*	1
tamu	*	*tï*	*imama*	1
tamu	*	*ipapa*	*imama*	1
*	*wəi*	*tï*	*nosi*	1
*	*wəi*	*ipapa*	*nosi*	1
*	*nosi*	*ipapa*	*wəi*	1
*	*nosi*	*ipipi*	*emi*	1
*	*imama*	*tamu*	*imama*	1
			Total	21

[1] When they were asked why therefore they had married, they answered that there was nobody else. This can be taken to mean nobody suitable in the neighbourhood, which seems to indicate that for some Trio marriage with a conventionally prohibited person is preferable to marriage with strangers.

In Table 29 there is only one further example of a marriage in which none of the parents belongs to the approved relationships for the marriage of their children. Thus, in this sample of 50 out of the 92 existing unions, 94 per cent of the marriages are legitimate, in the sense that they are to some degree within the conventionally prescribed limits. This trend is continued in a further 34 marriages about which less, but some, information is available; in 30 of these cases a correct relationship appears at least once.

Thus it appears that the majority of marriages, when each is considered from the point of view of the participants in it, are between people of approved categories. That this is not so when all the marriages are viewed by any one person has been indicated in Chapter V. This problem was further investigated by an examination of the relationships of four informants to married couples,[1] and a distinction drawn between socially acceptable unions and unorthodox unions as they appear to the informants.[2] The results are shown in Table 30. It can be seen

TABLE 30

Proportions of socially acceptable and unorthodox unions as seen by four informants.

Informants	Iyakɔpo (52)	Muyopɔ (32)	Korokoro (300)	Tɔmeta (482)
Acceptable	18 (45 per cent)	24 (63·2 per cent)	32 (66·7 per cent)	19 (57·7 per cent)
Unorthodox	22 (55 per cent)	14 (36·8 per cent)	16 (33·3 per cent)	14 (42·3 per cent)
	40	38	48	33

[1] The difference in the total number of cases for each informant results both from the limitation of ethnographic data and the ignorance of the informants.

[2] Socially acceptable unions are those in which both spouses belong to categories (as it appears to the informant) between which marriage is approved. Unorthodox unions are those in which one or other or both spouses do not belong to an approved category (as it appears to the informant).

that when all marriages are looked at by a single individual the society seems less conventionally ordered than it appears when each marriage is seen through the eyes of those involved in it. From what has previously been written this is exactly what one might expect to be the case. The more distant, and accordingly more tenuous, any particular relationship becomes, the more illogical is likely to be its ordering. The large number of marriages at Alalaparu which Iyakəpo considers to be between brothers and sisters disappears when examined from the participants' point of view. For example, in the case of the marriage between Sapə (151) and Kumarau (152), Iyakəpo calls the former younger brother and the latter younger sister, so for him this is a brother/sister marriage. Sapə, however, calls his wife's father *yeti* and his wife's mother *nosi*, and Kumarau calls her parents-in-law by the same terms—in other words it is an example of the ideal marriage.

However, if one is going to define marriages in terms of taking place between members of certain categories, a far more difficult problem is posed. A man should marry an *emerimpə* but he classifies these women as either *imama* or *emi*, and the question arises: does marriage with a woman of one of these categories mean marrying into a different genealogical level? There is more than one answer to this question. For the Trio themselves the problem does not really exist because, although there is no ban on marriage between genealogical levels, their own model of the system makes no allowance for it. At the other end of the scale the observer must make an allowance for it if he is to represent the facts in an intelligible form, because some Indians do marry their full genealogical sister's daughters, and in these cases one cannot just explain the marriage by saying that it is a function of the terminology. Such an explanation will account for a large number of cases, and this point is taken up again below, but first are considered some of the problems involved in equating genealogical and terminological data.

This proved a crucial problem in the construction of the Genealogical Table, and the details of the solution devised will be found in the Notes on the Genealogical Table. It is adequate to state briefly that the Genealogical Table is drawn as the slightly modified view of Trio society as seen by two of its members. This results in a rather individual, perhaps distorted view of the society but it has already been shown at the beginning of Chapter V that it is impossible to combine genealogical information from various sources into one diagram. It was also necessary to make certain arbitrary decisions about the genealogical specifications of the relationship categories which covered specifications from more than one level. The criterion applied is that of genealogical qualification in the first place, and then sibling connexion. Thus, because ego's biological mother is called *manhko* and she calls brother and sister those whom her son calls *yeti* and *manhko*, all the members of these two categories are taken as belonging to the first ascending genealogical level. This appears to mean that all conventional marriages take place between people of different terminological/ genealogical levels, but this is not quite so since it depends on where one is standing in the system. The conventional marriages of people of ego's own genealogical level, i.e., his brothers and sisters, appear as oblique, but marriages which do not involve members of his own genealogical level appear horizontal. This example will illustrate the point. Tɔpepuru (245) and his son Ipanapɔ (655) are married to the sisters Napipɔn (653) and Kuramenaru (645), respectively. Tɔpepuru calls his son's wife *yemi* (ZD), as he did his own prior to marrying her. Thus his own marriage is oblique (MB/ZD) but his son's is horizontal (S/ZD). From the son's point of view he calls his father's wife mother, as he used to call his own wife; thus the situation is reversed, and while his father's marriage appears horizontal (F/M), his own is oblique (B/M). Theoretically a horizontal marriage on ego's own level can only take place between brother and sister.

In the Genealogical Table there are represented 399 all-Trio marriages; of these 55·4 per cent are shown as horizontal and 44·6 per cent as oblique. If we restrict this number to existing all-Trio marriages of which there are 92, 46 appear as horizontal, and 46 as oblique, 50 per cent each. These figures do not mean a great deal since, as has already been demonstrated, any particular case changes its form when the observer changes his viewing point. The purpose of introducing these figures is to give additional emphasis to the next step. So far we have been discussing this problem in terms of genealogical levels as they are expressed in the relationship terminology; it is now intended to consider the generational aspect, the age difference between husbands and wives. In Table 31 the ages of the couples in existing all-Trio marriages are listed, and for elucidatory purposes they have been divided into horizontal and oblique types according to the way they appear on the Genealogical Table.

TABLE 31

Ages of couples in existing Trio marriages.

A. *Horizontal Marriages*

Spouses	Ages	Husband older by	Wife older by
346 = 347	26 = 20	6	—
339 = 331	21 = 33	—	12
310 = 306	30 = 24	6	—
343 = 337	17 = 15	2	—
107 = 109	30 = 28	2	—
14 = 8	40 = 26	14	—
9 = 6	20 = 18	2	—
139 = 140	33 = 35	—	2
139 = 145	33 = 30	3	—
215 = 216	17 = 17	—	—
43 = 44	38 = 33	5	—
161 = 162	25 = 30	—	5
178 = 179	24 = 27	—	3
31 = 29	16 = 16	—	—
123 = 120	20 = 30	—	10
32 = 30	28 = 20	8	—
203 = 204	57 = 35	22	—
89 = 88	50 = 45	5	—
100 = 99	25 = 27	—	2
83 = 87	32 = 20	12	—
74 = 75	30 = 18	12	—
153 = 154	22 = 26	—	4
170 = 174	45 = 35	10	—
151 = 152	43 = 40	3	—
169 = 168	28 = 18	10	—
195 = 198	25 = 22	3	—
273 = 274	37 = 20	17	—
269 = 270	30 = 34	—	4

263 = 266	22 = 20	2	—
482 = 485	42 = 24	18	—
399 = 395	33 = 20	13	—
494 = 493	30 = 24	6	—
305 = 354	27 = 30	—	3
720 = 721	32 = 24	8	—
636 = 604	23 = 32	—	9
595 = 596	25 = 30	—	5
602 = 565	24 = 24	—	—
756 = 763	37 = 20	17	—
670 = 673	42 = 38	4	—
660 = 626	40 = 38	2	—
514 = 516	30 = 22	8	—
381 = 368	25 = 20	5	—
365 = 409	32 = 36	—	4
364 = 378	30 = 22	8	—
376 = 345	30 = 34	—	4
577 = 427	36 = 21	15	—

Summary

	Older Husbands	Older Wives	Same Age
Total	30	13	3
Average years Older	8	5	—
Range	2–22	2–12	—

B. *Oblique Marriages*

Spouses	Ages	Husband older by	Wife older by
679 = 680	20 = 18	2	—
684 = 686	18 = 24	—	6
300 = 307	48 = 25	23	—
476 = 475	34 = 18	16	—
254 = 257	19 = 40	—	21
732 = 733	33 = 21	12	—
173 = 110	18 = 28	—	10
1 = 3	43 – 50	—	7
655 = 654	19 = 23	—	4
245 = 653	55 = 21	34	—
165 = 164	40 = 17	23	—
52 = 53	45 = 35	10	—
23 = 28	40 = 30	10	—

TABLE 31—*continued*

62 = 63	50 = 36	14	—
79 = 118	40 = 22	18	—
59 = 58	17 = 20	—	3
126 = 82	40 = 40	—	—
131 = 130	30 = 30	—	—
155 = 46	42 = 23	19	—
156 = 183	30 = 30	—	—
77 = 19	20 = 20	—	—
78 = 80	25 = 32	—	7
22 = 13	18 = 24	—	6
93 = 72	33 = 20	13	—
182 = 189	35 = 20	15	—
716 = 717	20 = 19	1	—
405 = 392	48 = 40	8	—
457 = 456	28 = 22	6	—
451 = 454	48 = 36	12	—
390 = 385	22 = 36	—	14
699 = 696	32 = 28	4	—
566 = 569	27 = 27	—	—
599 = 598	26 = 18	8	—
587 = 590	45 = 28	17	—
556 = 559	28 = 40	—	12
641 = 638	26 = 20	6	—
752 = 755	20 = 18	2	—
578 = 581	24 = 22	2	—
417 = 415	30 = 23	7	—
435 = 633	25 = 17	8	—
430 = 414	25 = 20	5	—
645 = 644	20 = 20	—	—
351 = 354	33 = 20	13	—
420 = 423	30 = 20	10	—
436 = 437	22 = 25	—	3
688 = 689	28 = 24	4	—

Summary

	Older Husbands	Older Wives	Same Age
Total	29	11	6
Average years Older	11	8	—
Range	2–34	2–21	—

It should be remembered that an error of 10 per cent is assumed in the estimation of ages, and thus the slight difference in average age between the two types of marriage can be considered to be unimportant. Furthermore in the Oblique list there are two examples of much older men and one of a much older woman which almost entirely account for the higher average in the Oblique form. In the examples where the husband is much older, and this applies also to the single example in the Horizontal list in which the gap is over 20 years, the husband, by Trio standards, is a very old man. Each is about 50, and has lost a former wife or wives who have been replaced by a much younger woman. None of these men has had a child by these younger women. The case in which the wife is many years older than her husband is described later in this chapter.

If the figures from both parts of Table 31 are combined, the average age difference between husband and wife is 8 years, and 68 (73.9 per cent) of the husbands are the same age or older than their wife. Over half (56 per cent) of the marriages fall within the average difference of 8 years, and in 94.6 per cent of the cases the difference in age is 20 years and less. If we assume that a Trio generation is approximately 20 years, then only just over 5 per cent of the marriages occur between people of different generations, as compared to 94 per cent of the married couples from the sample in Tables 28 and 29 who regard their marriage as in some way conventionally ordered and thus between different terminological/genealogical levels.

The first two sections of this chapter can now be briefly summarized. The Trio do not follow the theoretical ideal which they describe, although most marriages do take place within a wider set of conventions. In the process, certain adjustments which are not entirely recognized have been made to the relationship terminology, which has meant that the potential spouse has been transferred to a category on the first ascending or descending genealogical level. Accordingly any single conventional marriage is between individuals of different terminological genealogical levels although when age is taken into account the spouses will almost certainly be found to belong to the same generation. The next step is to examine the genealogical relationships between spouses to see how far Trio marriages occur between genealogical levels but within the same generation.

III

Very few of the existing Trio marriages are between people of traceable genealogical connexion, and all ten examples are listed in Table 32. This is a rather low figure which can be accounted for in a number of ways. Firstly, there are un-doubtedly a number of relationships missing from the Genea-logical Table. I must accept responsibility for some of these lacunae, but not all. There are numerous cases where an in-formant stressed the closeness of a relationship, and said, for example, that a man was indeed his own father's very own brother. Further questioning would then reveal that the two men shared neither a common father nor a common mother. Accordingly, in the absence of substantive evidence it is as-sumed that no genealogical connexion exists in spite of any emphatic claims on an informant's part. The tendency for *imoitï* to become indistinguishable from kin has already been explained.

Further it seems improbable, considering the size of the villages and the preference for village endogamy, that such a small number of married couples' parents are related.

After the examples of genealogically connected spouses is a sample of marriages in which a rather more tenuous relationship between spouses can be traced.

TABLE 32

i. The cases of genealogically connected spouses (relationship in brackets are those considered to exist by the couple concerned). Last figures are age. (T = tamu; N = nosi; P = pito.)

1. Inkiman (417) = Marinu (415); Inkiman's mother was the full sister of Marinu's father. FZS = MBD (MBD/? = ?/?). 30 = 23.
2. Asanri (451) = Eukiye (454); Eukiye's mother was Asanri's full sister. MB = ZD (TS/NS = MBD/ZD). 48 = 36.
3. Pesaipə (93) = Piruru (72); Pesaipə's father's half-sister is Piruru's mother. MBS = FZD (MBS/NS = BD/ND). The relationship FFDD = MFSS is also traceable. 33 = 20.

4. Kamapə (83) = Mori (87); Kamapə's mother's full brother is Mori's father and his father's half-sister her mother. MBS/FZS = MBD/FZD (MBS/*N*S = MBD/*N*D). 32 = 20.

5. Korokoro (300) = Ukərе (307); Korokoro's father's brother's daughter (i.e. female parallel-cousin or sister) is Ukərе's mother. MFBS = FBDD (*T*S/*N*S = MBD/ZD). 48 = 25.

6. Muyopə (32) = Mïkəripə (30); Muyopə's father's half-sister's son is Mïkəripə's father. FMMSS = FMDSD (*T*S/*N*S = MBD/?). This is an interesting case since the relationship is traced by Muyopə through his mother whom Mïkəripə's father called sister. 28 = 20.

7. Matatə (31) = Numepə (29); Matatə's mother is a half-sister of Numepə's father. FMDS = MMSD (*N*S = MBD). 16 = 16.

8. Naraeyiyi (310) = Minori (306); Naraeyiyi's mother's male parallel-cousin (i.e. brother) is Minori's father. FFBDS = MFBSD (*T*S/? = MBD/?). Minori did not know her husband's mother but knows that her father had called her husband's father, mother's brother. 30 = 24.

9. Pesoro (602) = Iriuna (565); Pesoro's mother's half-sister's daughter (a female parallel-cousin or sister of Pesoro) is Iriuna's mother. MMMDS = MMDDD (*N*S/? = MBD/ZD). 24 = 24.

10. Pïtï (494) = Apokïnini (493); Pïtï's half-sister is Apokïnini's mother. Same father, different mother. MB = ZD (TS/NS = MBD/ZD). 30 – 24.

ii. Examples of other relationships between spouses.

1. Asonko (78) = Atu (80); Asonko's father's brother's wife is Atu's elder half-sister. (MBS/*N*S = BD/*N*D).

2. Orosisi (126) = Sine (82); traced off the Genealogical Table this relationship is WFSD = FFDH which formally reduces to WBD = FZH.

3. Pepu (22) = Kurapa (13); FMZDHZ = BWMZSS. This set of terms can be reduced formally thus:

FMZ to FM.	BW to M.
FMZD to FZ.	BWM to MM.
FMZDH to MB.	BWMZ to MM.
FMZDHZ to M.	BWMZS to MB.
M to FZD.	BWMZSS to MBS.

4. Natara (732) = Anïtiye (733); this is a complicated case—the traceable relationship is BWZHFBDHZ = BWFBSWZHB.

This can be reduced formally thus:

BW to W.	BWFBS to BWB.
BWZ to W.	BWBW to Ego.
BWZH to Ego.	BWBWZ to Ego.
BWZHFB to F.	BWBWZH to Ego's H.
BWZHFBD to Z.	BWBWZHB to Ego's H.
and thus to ZHZ.	

A ZH is likely to be either MB or ZS and thus the wife M or ZD, and vice-versa for a female ego. The relationship is considered to be ?/$NS = MBD/ZD$.

5. Kirïmesa (752) = Ponsikini (755); The connexion would appear to be that Kirïmesa's half-sister is Ponsikini's mother, but to be precise it is FWMS = MDHD. (?/? = PD/?).

6. Sipare (89) = Pisekane (88); This case results from an unorthodox marriage. The tie is MHB = BWD. Sipare married the daughter of his brother's wife by a former marriage. (MBS/$NS = MBD/MD$).

7. Itïimare (153) = Papopә (154); This is MBSWB = ZHFZD. It is not possible to make a rational analysis of this example. If one takes ZHF to be MB then it is a B and Z marriage; if ZHF is taken as *tamu*, as in fact Itïimare considers the relationship, then ZHFZD is M. MBSWB inevitably equals B, but then Papopә calls her HM, *Manhko*. (MBS/MS = TD/?).

8. Sikamimpә (254) = Mirәrә (257); this is another tenuous link. ZHBWZHFBD = FBSWZHBWB which can be formally reduced to ZHZ = BWB. Since ZH is likely to be either MB or ZS, then ZHZ will be M or ZD. Since BW is likely to be M or ZD, then BWB will be MB or ZS. (BS/ZS = ?/?).

9. Arumumpә (351) = Natәtә (534); This one is BDHZHZMD = MDBWBWFB. This one reduces on both sides to F = D.

10. Asapoti (376) = Kamara (345); This case is complicated by the presence of a woman who has had a child by both a man and his son. The connexion is MDHWFDS = MFDHWMD when traced through the mother which reduces to ZS = M. When traced through the woman's father the connexion is FZHWFDS = MFDHWBD which reduces to FZS = MBD.

The cases in the first part of Table 32 are important for several reasons. They demonstrate that genealogically related as well as classificatory members of the prescribed categories marry. On the other hand none of these marriages is between genealogically related persons of prohibited categories, nor even, as the Trio claim, between closely related mother's sister/sister's son. Of the ten cases there are five between mother's brother and sister's daughter, three with the matrilateral cross-cousin, and one each with the patrilateral cross-cousin and bilateral cross-cousin. Thus half of the cases are between people of different genealogical levels, but only one of these is between individuals of different generations. The average age difference for the five sister's daughter marriages is 9·8 years, and for the cross-cousin marriages it is 7·6 years. Both these figures are very close to the over-all average.

The second part of Table 32 is also interesting since in these cases the relationships between spouses are mainly an adjunct of some previous marriage, and they contain a strong element of exchange or repetition. Most of the terms when formally reduced to their simplest factor show a coincidence with conventional marriage rules. Furthermore, and this applies to the whole of Table 32, there is a general agreement between the actual or reduced genealogical relationship between spouses and that claimed by them. This suggests that in other cases where it has not been possible to trace a relationship, the claimed one may have some factual basis.

It is now possible to make some general statements about Trio marriage, and the oblique aspect in particular. Nearly all marriages take place between people of the same generation, and this includes that proportion of marriages which occurs between people of different genealogical levels. Such types of alliance can only be attested in the form of marriage with the sister's daughter, but the relationship terminology in its empirical usage, by reflecting this marriage form, bestows the characteristics of obliqueness on all conventional unions. It could, therefore, be said that the terminology distorts the actual facts since in such cases the apparent oblique character of the unions is simply a function of the terminology. The problem centres on the patrilateral cross-cousin, not because she is accessible to both father and son, but because she may be the latter's mother and in so being belongs, by usual definition, to the first ascending genealogical level whither she draws after her, in a terminological sense, all those others that stand in the relationship of *nosi emi* to her son. In fact it is her marriage which is oblique and not that of her son when he marries someone whom he calls *manhko*.

To summarize all this, ideally there are no oblique marriages, in terms of generation there are few, terminologically all conventional alliances are oblique, and in practice it is only marriage with the sister's daughter which takes place between genealogical levels. All this reflects an interplay between the conscious and the appetitive models, and is consistent with the terms of the existing structure.

IV

In this section certain secondary forms of marriage practised by the Trio are examined to see how far they fit in with the scheme already outlined.

i. Polygamy: a weakly developed institution which is disappearing under missionary influence. The following cases were recorded:

1   Kəsəpə (139) has two wives and formerly had a third. The two wives are unrelated and there are indications that he wishes to be rid of the elder one by whom he has had five children.

2   Kiyokiyo (578) was married to the half-sisters Tawi (581) and Napiyo (582), but early in 1963 stated that Napiyo was no longer his wife. Napiyo continued to live in the same house as her mother, half-sister and ex-husband, and in January 1964 gave birth. It is mainly assumed that Kiyokiyo is the father, which he does not deny. Others, however, say that Simuru (511) is responsible.

3   Supipi (514) had previously been married to the sisters Rena (516) and Tapiro (519) but the latter is no longer his wife.

4   Ororinapə (155) had been married to the sisters Papopə (154) and Ikəri (46). He had apparently taken them when they were still young and brought them up. Papopə, the elder, who had borne him two children, recently left him. She went off with Piwara (156) for a short time (it was said that she ensnared him with love magic), but he left her and she is now married to Itïimare (153). Ikəri continues as Ororinapə's sole wife.

5 Toropə (107), when I first met him, was married to the two sisters, Sore (109) and Mairupə (110). They had formerly been married to Toropə's brother, Rapu (108), while another sister, Tukupə (113), had been Toropə's wife. Both Rapu and Tukupə had died, and Toropə inherited his brother's widows. (This is the only example of widow-inheritance which I recorded, but a widow's potential husband will almost certainly be a brother of her deceased husband; this is a function of the wider marriage rules and not a leviratic practice.) Toropə's polygamous marriage broke up under missionary influence.

6 Təmeta (482) had been married to both Apari (360) and Kara (485), but has put away Apari under the influence of Christian teaching.

7 Sipi (23) had been married simultaneously to Aiyatu (28) and Makarakara (75), but when I met him he had only Aiyatu as his wife. Aiyatu had previously been the co-wife with Kïwaraiye (118) of Kurumuku (35).

8 Iyakəpo (52), whose main wife is Siwapun (53), had a curious relationship with Isaruwiyae (55). Initially I assumed that this was a brother/sister relationship, and in fact he called another woman of the same parents elder sister. It was difficult to get a straight answer from him on this subject until one day Isaruwiyae moved to another house, and Iyakəpo told me that he had sent his second wife away because God did not like it.

9 Eoyari (62) had two wives, Tawiruye (61) and Kïwaipipi (63). When this double marriage broke up Eoyari at first stayed with Tawiruye, but then changed his mind and built a new house for himself and Kïwaipipi.

Finally there are two examples of very short-lived polygamous unions, and the taking of a second wife seems to be one of the main reasons for the disintegration of an earlier marriage. Atu (80) left Kamapə (83) when he married her half-sister, Mori (87); Tasi (252) left Təpepuru (245) when he married Napipən (653).

Although polygamous marriages do occur there are insufficient examples in these few cases to suggest that it could in any way be described as a popular practice. Polygamy is one

12

of the few social practices to have caught the earlier ethnographers' attention. Schmidt observed nine cases of polygamy among the Trio, six men with two wives, two with three and one with four (Schmidt, 1942, p. 50). Frikel, who says that cross-cousin marriage is the ideal Trio form, although MB/ZD marriage is relatively common, considers that polygamy, except in the case of village leaders, is a recent innovation borrowed from the Charuma or Waiyana (Frikel, 1960). Out of the nine examples listed above five of the men had their own village. Frikel also mentions a case of polyandry—a practice of which I have no record, although an unmarried young man does seem to have some right of access to his elder brother's wife, who will be his *emerimpɔ*.

ii. Woman married to father and son: this type of union has already been mentioned as being theoretically possible, and there are two examples of its actual occurrence. This is not a polyandric union since the men were married successively, not simultaneously.

1   Iporika (231) was married to Ponoriu (15), and at his death Iwana (235), his son by an earlier marriage, took Ponoriu as his wife. Isaruwiyae (55), who is the daughter of Iporika and Ponoriu, called Iwana brother, as she also calls Mono (14), who is the son of Iwana and Ponoriu.
2   Akowani (550) was married to Yawinapu (509), and at his death Yawikən (508), his son by an earlier marriage, took his step-mother as wife.

This form of marriage has the same structural significance as that of two sisters married to a father and son. The case of Təpepuru (245) and Ipanapə (655) has already been described; other examples include

1   Saimane (68) and his son Supipi (514) who are married to half-sisters.
2   Asonko (78) and his father's brother Eoyari (62) who are married to half-sisters.

The third possible arrangement is for a father to marry a dead son's wife, but I have failed to discover an example of this.

iii. Man married to mother and daughter: this practice is widely reported among Carib-speaking people, and recent examples have been reported from the Waiwai (Fock, 1963, p. 202), and Patamona (Henfrey, 1964, pp. 122–3). There are no extant cases of it among the Trio but there is a record of two such unions.

1 Arensu (73) was married to Tïnaiye (70) and her daughter Marere (124). This may have been a polygamous union. Tïnaiye, the only survivor of this marriage, is an old woman and difficult to understand. The general consensus of opinion is that it was a bad thing, but Arensu's sister, Pisekane (88), said it was good because there were very few marriageable men when it occurred.

2 Sanutu (326) was married to Narui (330), and when she died he took her daughter Irawïpən (327). He was not married to them both at the same time. An informant told me that when Sanutu did this, people gossiped and said it was bad of Sanutu to behave thus.

Such marriages are anomalous, being conventionally wrong, socially disapproved of, and structurally unsound. They seem to be based on sentiment and an attempt to maintain pre-existing conditions, a feature characteristic of Trio behaviour.

iv. Child marriage: this institution is a practice whereby a man takes into his care a young (normally under ten years old) sister's daughter whom he brings up and may, when she reaches adolescence, make his wife. The man is said to be the girl's *arimikane*, her nurturer, and this term must be distinguished from husband (*inyo*), which implies a sexual relationship. Most girls who were brought up under this system mentioned both the relationships, and in those cases where they did not one can perhaps assume only one aspect. The system is falling into disuse, but the following examples were collected.

1 Kara (485) said that her mother's brother had been a 'little' husband to her.

2 Səisəi (457) said that he had been both the husband and *arimikane* of Sinrapə (615).

3 Nouku (590) said that Inkiman (417) had been both her husband and *arimikane*.

4 Ororinapə (155) had brought up the sisters Papopə (154) and Ikəri (46) and had then taken them as his wives.

5 Mooso (273) took his sister's daughter Pakïwapə (275) to the West Paru, but when they returned to the Sipaliwini area the girl went back to living with her mother.

There is a single case of an older woman Mirerə (257) who has taken and brought up a younger man Sikamimpə (254) to be her husband. Unlike the avuncular adoption this action does not have social approval, but the disapproval takes the form of tolerant amusement rather than overt condemnation.

Avuncular adoption has been interpreted as a man's earliest claim as recompense for the loss of his sister. There are difficulties in the way of unquestioned acceptance of such an interpretation of the Trio practice. In the first place the mother's brother frequently has a wife and the sister's young daughter is a second wife, which eliminates any idea of urgency. Secondly, the young girl is not necessarily taken as a wife; this is implicit in the term *arimikane*, and is also revealed by the statements of informants when they said that a sister's young daughter is not an *emerimpə*. Finally there does not appear to be any explicit understanding of such an element of exchange with regard to this institution. However, the idea of exchange is so well developed in the Trio system of marriage that one cannot dismiss it from possibly being the principle underlying the practice of avuncular adoption. Unfortunately the number of examples and the lack of detail in the case histories I collected do not permit the depth of examination which the institution deserves. In particular it is uncertain to what extent, when the man is a husband as well as an *arimikane*, the union is a polygamous one. In example 4 Orininapə had no other wife, but in example 5 Mooso did have another older wife, although in this case Mooso's role seems to have been simply that of *arimikane*. The important thing to note is that in the majority of polygamous unions there is no difference in role or age between the wives, and that sister's daughter marriage does not only occur as a secondary marriage form as some authors assume (cf. Lévi-Strauss, 1948).

Three out of these four types of secondary marriage are logical extensions of the primary form, and each stresses some particular element of it. The polygamous union, because it frequently appears in sororal form, confirms that sisters tend to marry in the same place. The marriage of father and son to the same woman or to sisters expresses the persistence of the opposition of wife-givers and wife-takers. Avuncular adoption demonstrates the crudest form of the system of direct exchange which is inherent if not always obvious in all Trio marriages. The fourth type, that in which a man marries a woman and her daughter, is an interesting example of behaviour which is inspired by sentiment but which is structurally unsound—a case in which social convention and approval support structure not sentiment, and one of the few instances in Trio society where they are in disagreement.

Several references have been made to the principle of exchange in Trio marriage, and it is intended to finish this section by a brief discussion of this subject. Direct exchange is implicit in the Trio relationship terminology and is a part of most marriages, as has been indicated by the examples of marriages between related partners which have already been given. Below are listed a few more examples in which the exchange aspect is very pronounced.

1   Eoyari (62) married Tawiruye (61) and gave his half-sister Siwapun (53) to his wife's brother Iyakɔpo (52).

2   Korokoro (300) married Ukɔre (307) and gave her brother Naraeyiyi (310) his daughter Minori (306).

3   Pisikiki (312) had been married to Pasopo (554) who has recently died. Two of Pisikiki's younger sisters have been taken by his wife's father and brother.

4   Arensu (73) married Sipare's (89) half-sister Marere (124), and Sipare took Arensu's sister Pisekane (88).

5   Amasina took as his wife Wɔrimuku (216), and gave to Wɔrimuku's full brother Mĭtĭipĭ (59) his classificatory sister (MZD) Wɔripena (58).

However, the exchange of women which is a feature of so many Trio marriages is not an isolated event, and the alliance is merely the start of a continuous flow of obligations and prestations between the two families which lasts not only through the duration of the alliance but may be renewed by a further exchange of women in the following generation. These affinal exchanges are so important in every sphere of Trio life that marriage, which brings them into being, can be said to be the generative force in Trio society. Before turning to consider the nature and the range of this affinal behaviour, a brief description of the process of marriage and divorce is given.

V

There are two Trio words for 'to marry': *ipïhta* used by men, which literally means 'to wife' (*ipï* = wife, *hta* is a verbalizer), and *inyohta* used by women, which literally means 'to husband' (*inyo* = husband, *hta* is the verbalizer). Conventionally, however, a man marries a woman, although exceptions to this do occur; for example, Mairupə (110) forced Rorï (173) into marrying her. The reason which the Trio always give when asked why they marry is that they want children who may grow up and marry so that their children-in-law may look after them in their old age.

The following description of a marriage arrangement is a synthesis of a number of examples recounted to me, and it is unlikely that all, or even any, of the stages are gone through in a particular case. The assumption here is that the marriage is of a conventionally acceptable form and that the participants are fairly closely related or acquainted.

A man goes to a girl, once or several times taking her a gift of game, and says, 'I want you to be my wife'. The girl then goes and tells her mother, who, if she approves, says 'Fine, but it is up to you. Feed him.' So the girl takes the man cooked food and drink and they eat together, after which the man will tell the girl to take the pots and baskets back to her mother. This may happen several times, and then the man says to his future mother-in-law 'I want your daughter as a wife'. Then the girl takes her hammock and hangs it beneath that of her husband. There is no further ceremony or ritual attached to the start of co-habitation. When there are no young children who normally sleep in their mother's hammock, husband and wife will often share the same hammock. A woman can refuse to allow her daughter to marry, and it is said that Kumarau (152) had for a long time resisted the marriage of her daughter Maposi (168) to Makïpə (169).

The affair becomes more complicated when a man wishes to

take a wife from a distant village. In such cases the arranging of the marriage is likely to take place with the girl's father or other senior male relative, and involves bargaining with a ceremonial dialogue. It is not intended to describe in any detail Trio ceremonial dialogues and their functions, but further comment on this subject will be found in Chapter X. It will suffice to say here that it is a formal mechanism for use between strangers in situations which are likely to give rise to conflict. It is conducted in difficult and archaic speech of which few young men have a competent command. In the arranging of marriage it is used for deciding such features as bride-price and the question of post-marital residence. This helps to explain why there is a tendency towards matrilocal residence when marriage occurs between strangers.

Bride-price seems to have been a poorly developed institution among the Trio, and only to have been paid when a man took an unrelated woman. I have a record of only two instances in which bride-price was paid. Korokoro (300) took as his first wife a woman who lived in a village at some distance from his own. He paid her father with beads, salt, an axe, and a knife. This contrasts with his second marriage which is with a classificatory sister's (FBD) daughter. Korokoro claims that he did not want to marry this girl but that his father persuaded him to because she is a close relative. No bride-price was paid in this instance.

Tɔmeta (482) claims that he had given many goods, without being specific, to Apari's (360) mother; her father was dead. I am not certain that Tɔmeta was making a clear distinction between bride-price and bride-service; this latter institution existing among the Trio.

Marriages do not take place entirely on the initiative of future spouses, and are sometimes arranged by the relatives of one or other party. There is the example just given in which Korokoro was urged by his father to marry his sister's daughter. Eoyari (62) persuaded his half-sister Siwapun (53) to marry his wife's brother Iyakɔpo (52). Asikiri (170) had tentatively arranged that his sister's son Rorï (173) should marry his young daughter.

While there is actual encouragement for a man to marry a closely related person, there are also well defined sanctions to discourage the outsider from poaching on the community's female resources. The absence of bride-price in the marriage with a close relative affords but one example of this.

Men normally marry when they are between 15 and 20 years old, and women at a slightly younger age, 14 to 16 years. The younger married men are hardly more than boys who have not reached full economic maturity. For the first few years of their married life they depend to some extent on outside assistance which is usually provided by either their father or father-in-law. A young woman, by reason of the nature of her upbringing, is more suited to take on the economic burden of marriage than is her husband.

Pre-marital sexual intercourse occurs, and considerable freedom is allowed for early sexual experiment, and although such activities should conventionally be confined to an *emerimpɔ*, such limitations are sometimes ignored. If a girl becomes pregnant her mother may try to make the man responsible marry her but there is no obligation upon him to do so. Men think that it is bad for a woman to bear a child out of wedlock, but women do not mind and say that after one has given birth to a child there is no difficulty in obtaining a husband. Three mechanical methods of procuring a miscarriage are known but the single means of contraception is magical.

Extra-marital sexual intercourse occurs to a considerable extent, but this depends more on opportunity than on any socially licensed freedom. In general, individuals while gossiping about another's sexual exploits do not condemn them unless their own wife is involved. A man has some right to the sexual services of his brother's wife. While adultery is the cause of most social friction and conflict, the woman is not held to blame unless she has actually provoked the affair. A woman is thought unable to deny the sexual demands of any man, but this is not promiscuity but the culturally conditioned submissiveness of women in such matters. Accordingly infidelity is not adequate cause for separation or divorce.

Divorce, like marriage, can be expressed in male and female terms, and the actual process involves no more than unknotting the hammock from the house posts to which that of the spouse is tied. This action may be taken by either partner.

It has been noted that divorce frequently occurs when a

man takes a second wife, and this is the reason which women normally give for leaving a man. However, on the other side of the coin, a man often takes a second wife because of the inadequacies of the first. Inadequacy is either barrenness or failure, of either spouse, to fulfil their duties in the economic partnership of marriage.

Tasi (252) said that she had left her husband Təpepuru (245) because he had taken a second wife. Təpepuru, on the other hand, said that she is lazy. I can vouch for this from my own experience, and add that she is a slut and that her bread is repulsive.

Another example is Koi (390), who left his young nubile wife Wĭwĭ (393) and their baby daughter, and instead married an older barren woman, Parososo (385), who has had several former husbands and is only recently separated from her previous one, Pisere (381). This is an interesting case because Koi left Wĭwĭ because she was casual about providing his food and drink—a socially acceptable reason. However his marriage to Parososo has earned him the society's disapprobation because she is barren, although an excellent house-keeper. If Koi had taken another child-bearing woman in place of Wĭwĭ, no comment would have been made.

Husbands also send their wives away if they are scolds; Pesaipə (93) divorced Mĭkĭpə (20) for this reason, and Kəsəpə (139) put away Wəripena (58) because she fought with his other wives. Marriages also seem to have broken up as the result of men returning from a long absence to find their place usurped or because they have taken another wife on their travels.

A divorced woman will return to her family, or, if her parents are dead, go and live with a brother. Such behaviour is conventionally recognized. Tasi (252) made the journey back to her family at Alalaparu after leaving Təpepuru (245). Makarepən (434) went to live in her brother's household, and Wĭwĭ (393) in her brother's. Siwapun (53) said she would go and live with her half-brother Eoyari (62) in the event of her husband's death or of their separation.

It is not possible to judge what proportion of marriages end in divorce, but it is probable that these unions are more stable than the impression of numerous marriages by some individuals gives. It must be remembered that the low expectancy of life means that any person who has a life longer than average is likely to outlive a number of spouses. This is more pronounced with men since old men are more likely to remarry than are old women.

The end of a marriage is more likely to be brought about by the death of one or other of the partners than by their separation. At the moment there is a rather high proportion of broken marriages as a result of the disruption of some polygamous unions following the arrival of Christianity. There are among the Surinam Trio both surviving partners of twenty-one broken marriages; of these, eight are attributable to a greater or lesser degree to the influence of Christian teaching. This suggests a divorce rate in the region of 15 per cent of the marriages.

In the preceding chapters have been described the ways in which the Trio are brought into relationship with one another—the factors involved are descent, residence, and marriage. In the following chapters is described how the individuals thus brought together interact among themselves.

PART THREE

TRIO SOCIETY—CONTENT AND MEANING

In this third part there are two aims. First, to show how the daily and yearly events and interactions of Trio life fit within the framework already described. This is more obviously attempted in Chapters VIII and IX than in later chapters, and in these first two chapters I am concerned to reintegrate the system of terminology with the system of attitudes. Among the Trio there can be shown to exist a high degree of coincidence between these two levels, but this does not mean that I assume that this is always the case, nor that, even among the Trio, such correlation is complete and static. Indeed, the ambiguous status of the category *manhko* seems a good example of the dialectical way in which Lévi-Strauss considers the relationship between terminology and attitude to change (1958, p. 343). At the end of both these chapters I reach some conclusions about the principles which underlie both the form and the content of Trio society.

Until this point the emphasis has been on intra-village action, but in Chapters X and XI the same principles and associated values are sought in inter-village relationships—in political institutions and the dance festival. In Chapter XII, with the aid of various myths, an attempt is made to show that all Trio institutions carry a similar message because the principle on which each operates is the same.

VIII

LIFE'S DULL ROUND

i—Co-operating Kin

Two DIFFERENT levels of approach are used in this chapter: first, conventionally expected attitudes and behaviour, and secondly, actual behaviour between different relationship categories. The treatment of this subject may appear old-fashioned, because a start is made by describing behaviour in terms of simple dyadic relationships; this is no more than a preliminary step, of certain expository value, towards providing a total schematic layout. Further, if in these chapters it appears that relationship categories have become confused with genealogical specifications, it must be remembered that we are now concerned with actual events and not statistical abstractions, and that, with communities averaging thirty inhabitants, virtually all action involves individuals related by descent, residence, and/or marriage. A question which arises from this is 'Does relationship category imply status?' The full answer to this will be found at the end of the chapter, but it may be noted here that to some extent it does, but it may be modified by other considerations such as age, residence, and marriage.

I

Before embarking upon this subject, there is one point which requires clarification; this concerns the distinction between kin and affines. It will have been noticed that in Chapter IV little attention was paid to the affinal specifications of the relationship terms mentioned there. Furthermore, the terms in Appendix A which have affinal connotation only (Nos. 18–22 inclusive) have so far been ignored. The difference between these two sets of terms, those which have genealogical and affinal specifications and those which have affinal specifications only, is identical to the distinction made by Dumont (1957) between 'genealogical' and 'immediate' affines. However, among the

Trio this distinction is not particularly useful but instead can be replaced by another which distinguishes between what I shall call 'related' and 'unrelated' affines. Related affines are those related by genealogy and/or residence as well as marriage; unrelated affines are those allied by marriage but otherwise unrelated. For the present purpose these two classes can be considered to be terminologically and behaviourally distinct although, as will be shown in the next chapter, there are gradations between them. The terms 18–22 in Appendix A are only fully applicable to unrelated affines and the absence of direct address forms for these terms is a logical corollary of the fact that such people do not talk to each other. Related affines may continue to refer to and to address each other by the terms they used prior to marriage. This differentiation between two types of affines has far greater social consequences than the distinction between kin and affines. Indeed, within the village setting, that distinction tends to disappear, and at the level of attitudes and behaviour the inhabitants tend to appear as an undifferentiated group of consanguineously related individuals, with only the unrelated affines as exceptions. For this reason, in this chapter all the relationships are discussed as if they are kin ones, even if they contain a potential affinal content.

Within the group regarded as *itïpïme*, whether the qualification be genealogical or residential, the Trio recognize only a single clearly defined conventional attitude. A Trio divides his society into those with whom he can joke (even obscenely) and be familiar, and those with whom his behaviour must be more restrained. The Trio verb for this is *enəpï*, which means 'to joke', and in its negative form, *inenəsewa*, 'to respect' or 'to restrain one's behaviour'. The best defined boundary between these two divisions is that between the sexes; a man may joke with men but not with women. The exceptions to this rule are that a man may joke with women who are his *emerimpə*, and that he is expected to be restrained with his related male affines.[1] In a less clear cut way, although more obvious among men than among women, the same respect attitude is associated with difference in age. In this sphere it is expressed in terms of

---

[1] Restraint between related affines must not be confused with avoidance between unrelated affines, which subject will be discussed in the next chapter.

relationship categories, and thus in terms of genealogical level; a man is expected to respect members of categories from ascending genealogical levels and can expect to be respected by members of categories of descending genealogical levels. In spite of this it is readily admitted that age overrides convention in this matter, and when faced with a situation in which age and genealogical level do not coincide a Trio will adjust his behaviour to coincide with age, and explain it through age-grade terms.

These terms, which are listed in Appendix A, Nos. 23–31 inclusive, are applied on the criteria of age and number of children, and stratify the community into stages of wisdom and maturity which are the basis of respect. *Emu* and *epa* are a baby boy and girl respectively, and these terms are applied until the child is about three to four years old. At this age children become less fully dependent on adult care, and a boy will start spending his days with his age mates. The next stage is *musere* and *papoti*, boy and girl. The upper age limit for a *musere* is difficult to define but it is approximately twelve years old, the age at which he should start participating in mannish rather than boyish activities and begin to take an interest in girls, which is indicated by studious attention to his appearance. The next stage is that of *kirïmuku*, a word derived from *kïrï*, 'a man', and *muku*, 'a child'. This term continues to be applied to a man until he is the father of at least one child.

A girl is described as *papoti* until her first menstruation, after which she becomes a *wərimuku* (*wəri*, 'a woman', and *muku*, 'a child'). She continues to be a *wərimuku* until she has had at least one child and her breasts have begun to sag as a result of suckling it. An elderly but childless woman may still be referred to as a *wərimuku*.

The next stage is *kïrï*, 'a man', and *wəri*, 'a woman'. These are the main terms for distinguishing between the sexes, and an Indian will spend almost the whole of his or her adult life under these labels. It has already been mentioned that these terms can refer to younger siblings but that their usage is relatively rare.

Yumme, which literally means 'ripe' but has the connotation wise or mature, applies equally to men and women, and the criteria for its application are the number, age, and marital status of a person's children. *Yumme* also covers the terms *tamutupə* and *notipə* which as well as distinguishing between the sexes carry the explicit indication of the existence of grandchildren. For a woman there is the further qualification of the onset of the menopause.

These terms, because they are not ego-centred but rather denote a status which has the same value for every member of the community, are employed to overcome any contradictions between age and genealogy by cutting across the relationship terminology in terms of which conventional attitudes are ideally expressed. However, it must be added that it is more difficult to be definite about the attitude dependent on age difference than about that on sex difference. This is mainly because the latter is an absolute distinction and the former a relative one without any hard and fast divisions. This is not helped by the Trio language which lacks grammatical forms for comparatives,[1] which means that when one is involved with shades of difference other than polar opposites, one has to fall back on an impressionistic view.

Bearing in mind the conventional attitudes based on sex and age, a detailed examination of the conventional and empirical behaviour between the various relationship categories will now be made.

II

i. *tamu/ipa*: the age of the member of the second descending genealogical level is an important factor in this relationship. The behaviour between a grandfather and a young grandchild is very free and easy, much more so than between father and child. Men will spend much time playing and fondling their young grandchildren while it is unusual to see a man doing this with his own offspring. The arrival of a grandchild means for a

---

[1] Comparison is achieved by varying the emphasis on different syllables in the word. The first syllable is lengthened, and in words of more than two syllables the pitch of the voice is raised sharply for the second and gradually dropped for the final syllable or syllables, e.g., *kutuma*, painful; *ku-u-u'tuma*, more painful or very painful. There are also two emphatic suffixes, *-sa* used on adjectives, and *-imə* on nouns. This latter suffix is used in a slightly different way—to distinguish a separate and larger class of objects and not just a particularly large one. For example, a canoe is *kanawa*, a big canoe is *mono kanawa*, not *kanawaimə* which means an aeroplane. The suffix *-sa* is allied to physical size—*piya*, small; *piyasa*, very small.

man enhanced respect in the community. As has just been mentioned, the term for grandfather, *tamu*, reappears in the word for old man, *tamutupɔ*, and also in the term for village leader, *itamu*, all of which terms carry the connotation of respect due to old age and the wisdom which comes with it. Thus with the increasing years of the members of both these categories, the early familiarity gives way to respect of the junior level for the senior one. Consistent with this is the potential father-in-law role of a *tamu*.

ii. *nosi/ipa*: a grandmother will frequently substitute for the mother, either temporarily while the mother does her work or travels with her husband, or permanently if the mother dies at an early age. The following examples illustrate this:

1. Koruyari (195) and Konopo (198) went on an extended journey and their two sons were left in the charge of Isĩnaoi (201), Konopo's mother.

2. Aranre (229) and Pĩpuru (230) both died, leaving two young children who are being brought up by Sine (82), Pĩpuru's mother.

3. Paruparu (24) brought up her son's daughter Mĩkɔripɔ (30) whose mother had died when she was very young. In this case the substitution has become identification since Mĩkɔripɔ regards Paruparu as her mother and calls her such.

4. Surake (744) lives with his dead wife's mother who looks after the three young daughters of the late marriage.

5. Pĩtĩ's (494) mother died when he was very young, so he was brought up by Pĩropi (499), his mother's mother.

Such duty seems to fall indiscriminately to paternal or maternal grandmother, and the main qualification in the above examples is existence, since in four out of the five cases the only surviving grandmother is involved.

The practice of women calling their brothers' children by the same term as that used to those of the second descending genealogical level means that there may not be an age difference between the members of these two categories. In such cases it is not possible to distinguish a difference in behaviour from that obtaining between brother and sister. This would seem logical because, except for the age factor, there is a broad similarity in the relationship between a man and either a *nosi* or a *wɔi*—both

13

are potential mothers-in-law and are also women with whom marriage is forbidden.

iii. *ipapa/imuku:* There is no clearly expressed convention, other than that resulting from age difference, about the attitude between the members of these two categories, but there does appear to be an underlying ambivalence in the relationship. This may arise from the system of marriage whereby the father and son are, at least in theory, in competition for the same woman. The Trio possess a version of the Oedipus myth in which the sons kill their father in order to obtain his wives. Only one obvious case of discord between father and son was observed. An old man Təpepuru (245) and his son Ipanapə (655) are married to sisters and, according to Təmeta (482), a normally reliable witness, the father had previously been married to both but had surrendered the eldest in the face of his son's jealousy. I could find no further confirmation of this, although there is certainly some trouble within the family. In theory, competition for women will be between father and son or brother and brother, and since in practice all cases of violence concern disputes over women or dogs, an undertone of hostility can be expected to mark such relationships. In fact such open dissension is mainly restricted to strangers.

The father will often take a hand in looking after his son when the child is old enough not to need his mother the whole time but too young to join in the village play-pack, but from the age of five until early adolescence the contact between father and son is limited. The father will make his son's first toy bow and arrows, and when he reaches the age of ten will take him on hunting trips; Kəsəpə (139) often goes hunting accompanied by his eldest son, 12-year-old Tunahkana (142), and Ororinapə (155) by his son, 10-year-old Pirome (158). Most of a young boy's life is spent in educational play with his age mates—learning to swim, to climb, to hunt, and to fish. Any boy is at the beck and call of any adult male who can send a child to run an errand for him, but final authority and responsibility for a child's behaviour appears to rest with the father. This was clearly demonstrated at Alalaparu when the community would not accept Anaore (178) as a Church Elder because he did not control his unruly son. How far this is a new

value injected by Christian teaching and how far a traditional
view it is impossible to tell, and the whole question of jural
authority is discussed below. The degree to which a father
disciplines his son varies from moderately severe to the down-
right permissive, the tendency being not to force a child to do
something which it really docs not want to do. For example, a
6-year-old boy, Sinïkə (657), was suffering from a severe
swelling of the jaw, and the opportunity arose for him to be
flown to hospital in Paramaribo. Although his family tried
every means of persuading him, the boy refused and was
finally allowed his own way.

If the father of a young boy is dead, his place is taken by
another older male, either a father's brother or mother's
brother (which, exactly, the Trio judge to be unimportant).

The practice of father and son hunting together continues
when the son is full grown and married; for example Koi (390)
frequently accompanies his step-father, Poiye (405), and
Matatə (31) his father, Asapə (43). However, relatively few
grown men have surviving fathers or ones who still hunt,
and the tendency, especially at Alalaparu, is for men to hunt
alone. At Paloemeu, where greater use is made of canoes,
groups of relatives (composed of all possible combinations of
relationships) go out hunting together. Co-operation at other
levels does occur; Sipi (23) and Pepu (22) share a field, as do
Siparc (89) and Kamapə (83).

Social intercourse between father and son is slight and their
attitude to each other is marked more by restraint than
familiarity. However the father has definite affection for his
son, and greatly mourns the death of one. Eoyari (62), who has
lost all his children save a young boy whom he cherishes, still
feels his loss. The son's affection (this may be no more than
conventional) for his father is displayed by the unwillingness
of the bereaved son to see his dead father's belongings.

Concern for a living son can also be detected in these two
examples. Toropəti (305) made a trip to Brazil lasting several
months and while he was away I went fishing one day up the
Paloemeu with his father Korokoro (300). When we turned for
home, Korokoro paused on his paddle and for a while gazed
back upstream in the direction of Brazil. When I asked what
he sought, he replied that he wanted to see his son. When,

however, his son finally returned no sign of affection was to be observed between them.

The other example involves the old man Tɔpepuru who lives at Paloemeu but one of whose sons is married and lives at Alalaparu. When I moved to Paloemeu from Alalaparu Tɔpepuru came often to me to ask about his son's welfare.

The relationship between father and son is marked by a restraint which seems to conceal an underlying affection, but there is one further facet which requires attention. It is an element difficult to define since it lies on the border between mutuality and reciprocity. An example of what is meant will help to clarify the situation. When the twelve batteries of my tape recorder became too weak for their purpose but still retained enough charge for use in a torch, I gave them all to Amasi (476), partly because he had been playing his flute for me to record and partly because he is the only Indian at Paloemeu who regularly hunts at night. Soon after I had given the batteries to Amasi, Sanɔpɔ (343) came in, saw the batteries and helped himself to four of them. When I asked why he did this, Sanɔpɔ replied '*yipapame iweike*' ('he is my father'; in fact, father's brother).

The brusqueness of this behaviour is exceptional (although not for Sanɔpɔ) but the reason given for his action is not. Within a certain degree of relatedness it is considered reasonable to ask for something which another has (especially if he has more than one), and unreasonable to refuse such a request. Such demands, however, are occasional and lack the essential reciprocity which marks the exchanges between affines, although both types overlap at the point where it becomes a duty to provide certain unsolicited gifts or services. Between kin a request is made directly and the right to ask is implicit in the relationship. A request from an affine is made through the mediation of the third person whose marriage not only has brought into being the affinity but also represents cause and part of the reciprocal obligations which accompany it. Exchanges between affines are the result of an earlier exchange; rights and obligations between father and son are only preceded by birth.

iv. *ipapa/emi:* This relationship is mainly an affective one, although contact between father and daughter is for the most part slight. An exception to this is Asapɔ (43), who is often accompanied around the village by his young daughter who prefers her father's company to that of her mother. It was explicitly stated by several informants that they would grieve if their daughter married a stranger and went to live in another village. When Susuku (1) was injured by a tree falling upon him, his daughter was greatly concerned about him and his welfare, while his wife left the scene of the accident, saying her husband was dead,[1] and evinced no interest in him until it was obvious that he would survive.

A girl may provide some food and drink for her father, but this is unimportant compared with her role as link between her parents and her husband, who holds a key economic position in the life of her parents.

The important question of whether or not the father has authority over his daughter to give or refuse her in marriage cannot be answered simply. In some cases the authority does lie with the father but in others the mother is concerned. In the absence of the father, jural authority over the girl may be exercised by a brother or mother's brother. It should also be remembered that a young girl may pass temporarily or permanently into the care of a mother's brother.

v. *lĭ/imuku:* This is potentially a restrained relationship since it contains the latent affinal specifications of ZH/WB and WF/DH, but no difference in behaviour to that between father and son is conventionally understood or empirically observable. The idea of taking or asking because 'he is my father' is equally acceptable in the form 'he is my mother's brother'.

Korokoro (300) stated that the sons of both brothers and sisters should be treated with reserve, and Tɔmeta (482) said that one should not joke or play with a sister's son, but his behaviour belies his word since he carries on a very free and easy relationship with Simuru (511), who calls him *yetĭ*.

The lack of terminological distinction between own or

---

[1] The Trio regard any person who is either seriously ill or unconscious (even semi-conscious) as at least socially dead. The same word is used as in actual death, *watese*, which is formed from the negative *wa* and the eternal form of the verb 'to be', *tese*; *watese* is 'not being', i.e. dead (cf. Rivers, 1926, pp. 36–50).

brother's child and sister's child repeats itself here through the absence of behavioural differences. For the moment the potential affinal character of this relationship can be disregarded. An individual looks on his mother's brothers as kin since in the absence of formality the concept of wife giving or taking only reaches realization in the actual event. Accordingly affines are individually, not categorically, defined.

vi. *tĭ/emi:* Since the sister's daughter is a potential wife, certain features of this relationship are reserved for discussion later in this chapter.

The practice of a young girl of under ten years passing into her mother's brother's care has already been mentioned, and it is worth repeating that one informant at least did not regard his sisters' young daughters as potential wives.

It is also possible to distinguish between the jural authority which a man exercises over his daughter and the right which a mother's brother has over his sister's daughter. In certain circumstances these different aspects seem to coalesce. For example, when Matatə (31) wished to marry Numepə (29) her father Sipi (23) was away, so he asked Kinini (79) whom Numepə calls *yetĭ*. Again, when Papopə (154) was maltreated by her husband Piwara (156), it was her mother's brother Asikiri (170) who intervened.

vii *imama/imuku:* The dependence of a boy on his mother normally lasts well beyond early childhood. The age at which a child is weaned depends on a number of factors including how soon the mother next gives birth. Boys of four or five years old will frequently return to their mother's breasts in search of satisfaction if not nourishment. The mother is the primary supplier of food, and when the young boy begins to catch fish or shoot small birds and animals, he gives his catch to his mother who prepares it for him. Thus even before a young boy is ten years old the idea of economic interdependence with a woman is realized. All his life an Indian will give his game to some woman; first it will be to his mother, but this economic partnership will sooner or later through death or delegation be replaced by one between brother and sister, and in due course by that between husband and wife.

The mother is more concerned with the discipline of her young children than is the father and, although the majority are permissive, the severity of the punishment which some mothers inflict on their children far exceeds that administered by any father. There is undoubted affection between mother and son, and on a statistical level it has been shown that children of the same mother but different father are more likely to live together than are those of the same father but different mother. This affection receives little overt expression since the conventional restraint between the opposite sexes is further reinforced by that between proximate generations. However, I have a number of records of women showing concern about young and adult sons when they have failed to return to the village at the expected time. Once again, on their appearance there is no obvious sign of affection or delight at the safe return.

viii. *imama/emi:* Together with that between sisters, this relationship is the most obviously close one since it receives continuous expression in economic co-operation. Almost all the female subsistence activities are carried out in working parties which consist of mother and daughters or a group of sisters.

The life of a young girl is very different from that of her brother, and no sooner is she capable of looking after herself than she is given the task of looking after her younger siblings. She will rarely leave her mother's side, and from about the age of five upwards will begin to imitate her mother's everyday chores—carrying small gourds of water or baskets of firewood. By the age of ten her efforts begin to play a substantial part in the subsistence of her family. A girl will normally be married by the time she is fifteen and will before then be fully occupied with the tasks which she will continue to perform for the rest of her life. A number of young girls pass into the care of their mother's brother, but this does not necessarily mean that they will be separated from their mother.

For much of a woman's adult life her household duties are completed with the help and companionship of her daughter; they will go together to the creek to wash or collect water, into the forest to fetch firewood, or to the fields for cassava and other produce. These tasks are all ones which, although more pleasant when done in company so that there is relief from the dullness of the routine, are also ones which it is considered improper for a solitary woman to do, since they are socially recognized opportunities for extra-marital affairs. The various processes in the preparation of the cassava are also jobs which are lightened by co-operative efforts since they allow the chance for a quiet gossip.

A woman may substitute for her daughter when the latter is unable to fill her normal role because of pregnancy or menstruation, and as she becomes older the mother will take on the duty of minding the grandchildren while their mother is working.

The work party of mother and daughter reflects itself in the layout of the villages; for example houses 18E, 19E, and 22E contain a mother and three daughters who regularly form a working party, and so do 15E, 16E, and 21E (see Fig. 13, p. 135).

This relationship is not a purely economic one and there is also a strong affective tie between mother and daughter which finds overt expression in infantile behaviour throughout life. For example one day, during the period of half an hour I was talking to her, Atu (80) who is over 30 years old and has an adolescent daughter of her own was sitting in her mother's hammock and fondling her mother's breasts. Again when Sere (9) went on a journey to Brazil, his wife's mother moved into his house at night in order to keep her daughter company.

Of the four possible relationships between parent and child that between mother and daughter is strongest, both in economic and emotive content. The father/daughter and mother/son relationships suffer from the double restraint of different sex and generation, and the latent antagonism between father and son is absent between mother and daughter. The mother/son relationship has, however, a theme of economic reliance. Thus the statistical tendency revealed in Chapter VI of half-siblings of the same mother staying together more often than those of the same father finds tenuous reaffirmation in the form of economic reliance and affection.

There is one further way in which the parent/child relationship must be viewed—that is to consider which side of the family the offspring of any union are regarded as belonging to. As might be expected from what has already been written, this often depends on circumstances, and the criterion of descent is frequently overriden by that of locality. This is clearly shown in the case of mixed Trio/Waiyana marriages. There are eight such marriages with issue: in five cases the father is Trio, and in three the mother is. The Trio consider all the children of these marriages to be Trio. The children from four out of these eight marriages are old enough to be identifiable as one or the other; two are entirely Trio and unable to speak Waiyana, one of these has a Trio father and the other a Trio mother. The other two are bi-lingual and have other Waiyana traits—once again the father of one is Trio, as is the mother of the other. Both these families had lived in Waiyana villages, which no doubt accounts for the difference, but since they now live in the large Trio village at Paloemeu they will probably grow up as Trio.

The other occasions on which this question is brought into the open are when either the parents separate or one of them dies. Some examples of what happens in such cases are now considered.

1. Asoro (435) and Makarepən (434) separated; their son Yemisi (622), aged four to five, stayed with his father but is mainly cared for by his father's mother. Their daughter, Peti (623), aged two or three, stayed with her mother who lives with her brother.

2. Aretlna (98), a boy about ten years old, lived with his mother, Pipa (99), when I first knew him. His father, Pesami (97), is dead. During my stay at Alalaparu, he left his mother's house and went to live in that of his father's brother, Pesaipə (93).

3. Koi (390) left his wife, Wïwï (393), who retained the custody of their two- to three-year-old daughter.

4. Atu (80) left her husband, Kamapə (83), when he took her younger sister Mori (87) as a second wife. She remarried but has no children by her second husband, but her three children by Kamapə—a girl of fourteen years, and two boys aged ten and six—live with her in a relatively spacious house. Her former husband has a son by his second wife and they live in a small house with two other families. The elder of Atu's sons frequently eats with his father's parents who are also related to Atu, Kamapə's mother being Atu's father's sister.

5. Papopə (154) has an eight-year-old son and a seven-year-

old daughter by Ororinapə (155), whom she had left to marry Piwara (156), who in turn left her, but not before he had had a daughter by her. Papopə is now married to Itiimare (153), and Piwara's baby remains completely in the care of the mother, but the two older children divide their time between the parents, although the boy is more with his father who takes him hunting.

If there is a conclusion to be drawn from these examples it is that young children of either sex will tend to stay with their mother on whom they rely for food and care. That this is not always so is attested by the case of the young boy being looked after by the father's family. Among older children, girls stay with their mother or her family, but boys do sometimes go with their fathers, although it must be remembered that such a move has been made much easier by the growth of the large villages. However, the mother consistently emerges as the important figure, and the question of who exercises jural authority over the children depends on her fate. This cannot be really understood until the content of the relationship between siblings, particularly brother and sister, has been described.

ix. *wəi/akəmi:* It is natural to move from the mother/daughter relationship to this one, since in substance they are very similar, and the latter is a continuation of the former in the next generation. This relationship is more obvious still than the mother/daughter one, since there are relatively few surviving mothers with adult daughters but there are numerous groups of female siblings.

To repeat what has already been said, sisters frequently marry in the same place. Most cases of polygamy are of the sororal type, and there are examples of the marriage of a father and his son to sisters, or two brothers to two sisters. The separation of two sisters who have been co-wives does not necessarily stop the pre-existing co-operative efforts. Two good examples of this can be given. Toropə (107) was married to two sisters, Sore (109) and Mairupə (110), and they all lived in house 17E. He was ambitious to become a Church Elder for which monogamy is an essential qualification. His efforts to rid himself of Mairupə were successful and she persuaded a young Indian, Rori (173), to marry her. This couple then went to live in house 33G which was empty at the time because the inhabitants were away on a prolonged journey. From then on there was a constant procession formed by the two sisters and their children walking backwards and forwards between the two houses, and all routine tasks continued to be done together.

A similar continual movement could be discerned between 9D and 37G; the sisters, Ikəri (46) and Papopə (154), had previously both been married to Ororinapə (155), but Papopə had left him and after a number of vicissitudes has settled down with Itïimare (153). The break-up of the polygamous union has not affected the relationship between the sisters who continue to co-operate in daily activities.

However, conflict does occur between sisters, and there are several examples of marriages breaking up as a result of a man taking his wife's sister as a second wife. An example of this is Kamapə (83) who had been married to Atu (80) for a number of years and they had three children ranging in age from five to fourteen. Kamapə then took as a second wife Mori (87), who is Atu's half-sister (they have the same father, although Mori is also the daughter of another of Atu's half-sisters by the same mother; the sister relationship is dominant). Atu immediately left her husband and is now married to Asonko (78). There is no observable antagonism between Atu and Mori.

This is a suitable point to give an example of sisters staying together while brothers separate—an occurrence which is statistically more probable. Among the group of Indians who arrived at Alalaparu in November 1963 were three married couples who are interrelated thus:

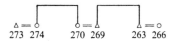

The sisters 274 and 270 are only half-sisters since they have different fathers. The brothers 269 and 263 are full siblings. The sisters however stayed together, for the couples 273 = 274 and 269 = 270 went to live in 11D, and the couple 263 = 266 in 2D.

In summary it should be noted that the very apparent economic and affective ties between mother and daughter, and sister and sister are important in the routine of everyday affairs, but their obviousness must not mislead one into regarding this relationship as the key one in the social organization of the Trio. The overwhelming impression which initially confronts the observer is false and merely superficial evidence of the nature of the division of labour and of those tasks performed by the women. The work-group to which a woman belongs is fixed at an early age, and the Trio system of marriage and post-marital residence does little to disturb this.

x. *ipipi/akǝmi*: This is the sibling group which one is least likely to find living together although statistically only half of them will be separated. This has been accounted for in the previous chapter in these terms; it is normal and conventional for a man to find himself a wife (not a woman a husband) and while there is social pressure to marry within the community, the lack of a suitable spouse will drive men outside their immediate social and residential sphere in order to find one. Since it is usual for those who marry outside to live with their wife's relatives, this gives rise to the underlying hint of matrilocal residence.

It is difficult to be too affirmative about the relationship between brothers. It is not as obvious as that between sisters but few of the male economic activities require co-operative effort, and in many tasks the place of co-operating relatives is taken by obligated affines. It can be quickly mentioned that the mass of affinal obligations, prestations, and services are exchanged by men.

Brothers, however, do work together and many cases of joint effort were observed. The following examples give some idea of their range: Sipi (23) helped Iyakǝpo (52) thatch his new house, Sǝisǝi (457) gave Pesoro (602) a hand in the construction of his house, and Pisikĭkĭ (312) joined Naraeyiyi (310) in the same task. This last pair hunt together, as do Kǝsǝpǝ (139) and Muyopǝ (32) on occasion. Brother frequently helps brother with his field but this evidence cannot be taken as entirely reliable since the nature of such working parties has been obscured by missionary activity in encouraging co-operative effort. However, a feature of the tasks in which men co-operate is their temporary nature when compared with the unending routine of female co-operative work.

However there is little display of affection between brothers, and there were few occasions on which I observed full brothers chatting and laughing together. A man does show concern for his brother's safety and, for example, will worry if he has not returned to the village by nightfall and will go to the edge of the clearing and call for him.

By elimination, joking behaviour should reach its most highly developed form among brothers. This is a difficult thing to judge, for although such behaviour conventionally exists the number of occasions on which I heard any form of obscene joking was very few. It is possible that it has been suppressed by the Waiwai missionaries. There is also the question of intimate behaviour among men such as holding hands or entwining arms round each others' necks or waists. The main criteria for such behaviour are friendship and a similarity of age, not specific relationship, and, of course, it also depends on the character of the individuals concerned. Young men, married or unmarried, are more likely to behave in this way than older men. Such behaviour is banned between affines.

Theoretically there is latent competition between brothers for the same woman but I could not find an example in which this occurred between closely related brothers. It would be going too far to say that a man has socially recognized access to the sexual services of his brother's wife because no informant ever explicitly expressed this opinion. There is a hint of this in the fact that a number of Indians when asked who were their *emerimpə* only indicated their brothers' wives. This notion is supported by the behaviour of Wïsiwa (555) and Minori (306), his elder brother's wife, who when found together in a hammock showed no sign of guilt or even of disturbing themselves (cf. Lévi-Strauss, 1961, p. 352).

xi. *ipipi/wəri* and *wəi/kïrï:* To begin this section it is useful to recapitulate briefly some aspects of Trio ideology concerning the role of women in the society. It has been mentioned that women are the most important single possession in the culture, that subsistence and survival depend on the co-operation of both sexes, and thus the smallest viable economic unit is the male/female partnership. The conventional division of labour and the strict adherence to certain aspects of it means that men and women do not join in the same tasks but that their joint and independent efforts achieve a whole, which no unisexual co-operation can. For a Trio, both as a boy and man, this partnership can be with his sister.

Initially, of course, the mother is the dominant female figure but for reasons already given this relationship may well fade early in the boy's life. If this does happen the mother's role may be accepted by a woman of the second ascending genealogical level (theoretically this may include a father's sister), by the mother's sister, or by an elder female sibling.

The example has already been given of a girl brought up by her father's mother who now identifies her as mother; when an informant was asked if this could happen with respect to an elder sister no example could be given, but it was considered possible although thought that such a mistake would be corrected by the sister.

Regardless of whether the mother is alive or not, in a large family a boy will spend much time during his early years in the care of an elder sister who may carry him in a sling from her forehead, balance him on her hip, and later walk hand-in-hand with him. From an early age, therefore, an affective relationship grows up between brother and sister, and in later life develops into an economic interdependence which is most apparent when neither is married and is least obvious when both are married. It has already been shown statistically that 80 per cent of the brother/sister pairs live together.

A large number of examples of this behaviour between brothers and sisters can be given, but a limited sample will indicate its range and nature.

1. The three-year-old boy Musoro (358) is looked after most of the time by his six-year-old sister Sïrəwi (357).

2. Natətə (534), a young married girl, looks after her younger brother Kowərina (553), who lives in the same house as his sister and her husband.

3. A young widow, Arena (462), looks after her younger brother, eight-year-old Sipo (685), who is about the same age as her own children.

4. When Makarepən (434) was deserted by her husband, she went to live with her brother Pareya (430).

5. Tawiruye (61), now her husband has left her, is provided

with meat by her brothers Iyakapo (52) and Sipi (23), and she gives them bread and drink.

6. Siwapun (53) declared that if she lost her husband she would go and live with her half-brother, Eoyari (62).

Two longer examples will illustrate this behaviour most clearly, and they are also ones of which I have considerable first-hand experience since they involve the families with which I lived at Alalaparu and at Paloemeu.

At Alalaparu I lived in house 22E. When I first arrived the residents consisted of Susuku (1), his wife Mïkuri (3), and her son by a former marriage, Morime (7). Morime, about 30 years old, is now unmarried although he previously had been married to a woman who must have been much older than himself. In the neighbouring house 18E lives his full sister Tarara (8), her husband and two young sons, and in 19E his half-sister Pakiri (6) (being the daughter of Susuku and Mïkuri), her husband and young daughter.

Morime when he hunted gave his game to his mother or sisters, who prepared it for him and fed him. Morime had also cut a field, the only unmarried man at Alalaparu to do so, which he claims to be for the use of his mother and sisters. After I had been living with this family for a few weeks Susuku suffered a serious injury and stayed hammock-bound for some time. During this period Morime was looked after almost entirely by Tarara, since his mother was busy caring for her husband.

Nearly two months after this, a second full sister of Morime, Tasi (252), arrived at Alalaparu from Brazil because she had been deserted by her husband. Tasi came to live in 22E and took over much of the household work from her mother, and, in particular, the care of her brother Morime. Morime's life also underwent a change since in partnership with Tasi he began to play a far more normal role in the usual economic activities. Morime and Tasi frequently went hunting together and on one occasion went off for a week on a fishing expedition. When Morime went hunting alone he handed his game to Tasi who gave him drink and prepared his food, although he still received some food from his mother and other sisters.

At Paloemeu I lived in house 16A with Korokoro (300), his

wife Ukǝre (307), and her two brothers, an elder one Pisikĭkĭ (312) recently a widower, and a younger one Wĭsiwa (555). Ukǝre does not go hunting with her brothers because she is married and goes out instead with her husband. Her brothers hand their game to her (or sometimes to their other two sisters who live in 7A), and Ukǝre prepares and gives them their food. This is supplemented with food and drink from the other two sisters who provide all the food if Ukǝre is away. This behaviour was extended to me (I called Ukǝre elder sister, and the other two younger sister), and when everybody in my house was away one of my two younger sisters would regularly bring food across to me.

As well as preparing food for her brothers Ukǝre also performed a number of other routine little services such as stripping back their hammock covers each morning and re-arranging them in the evening.

Besides such full-time services and interdependence between brothers and sisters, many casual and intermittent exchanges take place. These mainly consist of small gifts of food; meat normally passing from brother to sister, and drink from sister to brother. Korokoro (300) who claims to have many sisters (they are mainly the daughters of his father's *imoitĭ*) carries on, to a greater or lesser degree, such an interchange with all of them. After a successful fishing expedition Korokoro sends presents of the catch to all his sisters. He, in return, receives little presents of cooked food and drink. His closest tie is with his half-sister Napanakĭ (313), who is a widow, and Korokoro completes for her most of the tasks, such as making various basketwork items, which a husband normally does. Exchanges of one sort or another are almost a daily affair between these two, and although Napanakĭ lives with her adult, married son he does little more than supply his mother with some meat.

In summary it can be said that a man finds in his sister one possible solution to an economic system which requires a male/ female partnership. A man's relationship with his sister may begin when he is very small and his sister substitutes for his mother. Economic interdependence may be realized any time after adolescence, but the degree to which it develops at any particular age will depend on the marital status of the partners. It is least developed and least obvious when both brother and sister are married; it is most intense when neither is married, in which case their relationship bears many similarities to that between husband and wife. It is, however, the differences which prevent the brother/sister relationship becoming total. The restraint between brother and sister which is conventionally claimed is also observable in their behaviour. Little affection is shown between a brother and sister, and it is almost rare to see them talking to each other and certainly not conversationally. Morime (7) took little notice when his sister Tasi (252) arrived from Brazil, although her mother and sisters expressed both excitement and pleasure. Although they do not show it, men dislike the idea of being separated from their sisters.

xii. *inyo/ipĭ:* This relationship, as just stated, has similarities to that between brother and sister. The most important difference is the contrast in behaviour between the restraint between brother and sister and the familiarity between husband and wife. A man may conventionally joke with an *emerimpǝ*, and with his wife this behaviour is extended to public acts of physical intimacy such as standing or walking with their arms around each other's waist or shoulder. Another feature which marks the behaviour of husband and wife is their practice of going to defecate together; behaviour otherwise confined to pairs of related women, usually sisters. I believe also, although I admit some doubt on this point, that only a wife is allowed to paint the complicated body designs on her husband (cf. Huxley, 1963, p. 167).

The man is expected to be the authoritative partner in the marriage, and Pisere (381) was considered unsuitable to be a Church Elder because his wife's talk was a little stronger than his. However, a husband is not expected to dominate or maltreat his wife, and Pesoro (602) was blamed when his son fell seriously ill, since he had recently beaten his wife for infidelity. Genuine affection exists between many married couples, and a man greatly mourns the loss of a wife. It is said that Ororinapǝ (155) wept when his wife Papopǝ (154) left him. Pisikĭkĭ (312) had certainly not completely recovered his composure six months after the death of his wife.

By marriage a man combines in a single woman all the functions which are otherwise only obtainable from separate

14

women; a wife conjoins the functions of sister and *emerimpə*. The relationship between brother and sister is that of economic partnership in which intimacy and familiarity are forbidden. The relationship between *emerimpə* is intimate and familiar but lacks economic content. The relationship between husband and wife is both an economic and sexual partnership, and thus marriage can be seen as the joining of two separate roles.

Marriage does not eliminate the tie between the brother and sister, and, although the economic interdependence appears to diminish when both are married, this is mainly an illusion caused by the creation of affinal ties. The cessation of marriage sees the re-emergence of old ties, and as has already been stated the conventional behaviour for a widow or deserted wife is to return to her family, and in particular to her brother.

This completes the description of the various dyadic relationships—this has been a prolonged business but it will be shown to have been of real analytic value. Before considering what this might be, it is useful to look at a more diffuse interrelational aspect—jural authority. From what has been written it is obvious that there are no firm rules about the exercising of jural authority, that control over children is not invested in any specific person, but that the offspring of a marriage belong equally to both sides of the family. Furthermore, at a general level, any older person exercises such authority over any younger one. To be more specific the father controls his children, but in his absence this authority may pass to someone else, and who this is will depend on the fate of the mother, with whom young children tend to remain. A woman, widowed or separated from her husband, often returns to her family and in particular to her brother—in this case the jural authority will be in the hands of the mother's brother, a fact which throws new light on the institution of avuncular adoption. Alternatively a woman may remarry, and conventionally this would be to a brother of her late husband, and in this circumstance the jural authority will remain in the hands of someone in the relationship of father. These variations, and examples of them have been given, explain why informants could only describe particular cases when questioned on the subject. However, from these variations one can deduce a pattern of behaviour—jural authority over young children rests with the man with whom the mother is living in a state of economic interdependence. It should not be overlooked that a woman also exercises as much if not more control over young children of both sexes than a man. A mother's control over her son diminishes as he grows, but to a large extent she maintains it over her daughters, where it is supported by co-operation and affection.

Control over women is most obviously expressed in the giving in marriage and, as has been shown, father, mother, mother's brother or the girl's elder brother may all exercise this right. An adult woman has considerable freedom of action, and control over women only becomes important when strangers form a potential threat to the female resources of a community. This subject is treated in detail in the next chapter; it is merely interesting to note that any older male member of the community has some authority over the younger, unmarried women of the community.

III

The next step is to try to find some form in the inter-relationships described, and in doing this I wish to take as my starting point the statement of Leach.

The principles of classification which I have assumed to be relevant are those of sex, age and place of residence, but I would now argue . . . that in certain cases the essential key to understanding is to perceive that a particular relationship 'p' is *the opposite of* another relationship 'q' (1961, p. 28).

The significant words in this sentence are 'in certain cases' since it immediately gives rise to the questions 'Which cases?' and 'How are they to be recognized?' Twelve dyadic relationships have been described in this chapter, which means when they are combined there are 66 sets of possible opposed relationships. In the first place it has been quite adequately demonstrated that sex, age, and place of residence are some of the qualifications in deciding which relationship category an individual belongs to, and that genealogical relationships will override all these criteria. However, genealogical relationship is not the same as descent, which has a central role in Leach's discussion, but the concept of which is lacking among the Trio.

If we are to find Leach's certain cases, I think that as far as the Trio are concerned we must start with an opposition more fundamental than that between any pair of relationship categories—the opposition between male and female. In Durkheimian terms the male/female relationship is an organic one, and this contrasts with the unisexual relationship which is a mechanical one. Furthermore this distinction is maintained by the conventional reserve between men and women. I will come to the exception to this in a minute, but first let me see how far the relationship between certain categories supports this thesis. Firstly, only two conventional attitudes are expressly understood by the Trio—one relates to the difference in sex, and the other to a difference in age. Unisexual relationships are characterized by co-operation and differentiated by an inequality based on age difference, although the former is more obvious among women and the latter among men. For example, compare the brother/brother relationship with the father/son one, or the sister/sister relationship with the mother/daughter one. There is no opposition here, and what difference there is is of degree, and not of kind. The difference in content, i.e., in the extent to which they co-operate, being directly related to the economic duties of the respective sexes. Furthermore, using conventional attitudes as a yardstick, it is not possible to distinguish between the mother's brother/sister's son relationship (in its kin role) from the father/son one, although why the kin aspect of this relationship has been divorced from its affinal side was explained at the beginning of this chapter.

If one examines the opposition between an all-male relationship, such as brother/brother, and an all-female one, such as sister/sister, the result is more fruitful since some contrast does appear. Indeed the greater the age difference in one relationship and the less it is in the other, the more obvious the contrast becomes. There is also a contrast between short-lived and long-term co-operation, but even so the solution does not lie here because the relationships on both sides are still mechanical, and in terms of the culture are non-viable units.

The third possibility is the opposition of relationships which are unisexual on one side and mixed on the other; for example, brother/brother or sister/sister compared with brother/sister. Here opposition emerges in the forms co-operation:interdependence and sex difference:age difference. In this latter opposition the sex difference is absolute but the age difference is relative, or to put it in behavioural terms there is always restraint in the male/female relationship but in the unisexual one this is a corollary of age difference. Opposition of such categories are merely particular cases of the wider male/female opposition.

The final possibility is the opposition of two mixed relationships, and this reaches its best development in the form brother/sister:*emerimpə/emerimpə*. These relationships are directly opposed to each other in sexual and economic content, and also in terms of stability. Furthermore it can also be clearly identified as a male/female opposition. The brother/sister relationship epitomizes the relationship of man to woman in its chaste form. On the other hand there is much in the form and content of the *emerimpə* relationship which is similar to that between men of the same age—joking, familiarity, no economic interdependence, but short-lived co-operation for a specific purpose. Sexual relations, in their active and destructive aspect, are undoubtedly a male concern, but I will return to this point later. Of more immediate concern is the role of the husband/wife relationship which stands in a mediating position. This relationship can be equated with the brother/sister one in its economic content but distinguished in the sexual aspect, and *vice versa* with the *emerimpə* relationship. The husband/wife relationship also holds a middle position in terms of stability—it is a far more stable relationship than that between *emerimpə* but lacks the perdurable tie which exists between brother and sister. Thus, at a different level of analysis, Trio marriage has emerged as a fundamental institution—in the earlier chapters it appeared as the life-giving force in an otherwise inert structure, and here it creates a relationship which conjoins otherwise disparate conceptual units.

No further progress can be made until the relationship between those who exchange women is taken into account, and this is the subject of the next chapter. To close this chapter it will be helpful to give a summary of the main conclusions reached in it.

There are two conceptual units, male and female; in both, behaviour and attitudes are characterized by co-operation and modified by age differences. The former is more obvious in the female unit, and the latter in the male unit. The two units are separated by restraint in the attitude of the members towards each other, but are linked by an interdependence on which the society's and the individual's survival rests. This link is realized in the husband/wife relationship.

A model constructed on the basis of conventional attitudes is not a contradiction of that created from the analysis of the relationship terminology, but is complementary to it. The dominant criterion in deciding relationship category is genealogy, and one can combine with this the qualification of co-residence. Where these factors are missing, age plays an important part, but when considering behaviour age is of far greater significance. This leads to a paradox that where horizontal boundaries between categories are most clearly drawn, the behavioural boundaries are most indistinct. In behavioural terms it would not be possible to distinguish between a man called father and another called elder brother who is the same age. However, conventional attitudes are expressed in terms of sex and genealogical connexion, i.e., category, since this is the only way which the Trio has of locating himself in the social matrix.[1] In any particular instance age will determine to what degree behaviour and convention coincide, and when they do relationship category implies status. For the purpose of model building one can assume that they always do.

----

[1] It is worth comparing this situation with that among the Mbuti pygmies as described by Turnbull: '. . . the network of consanguineal and affinal interpersonal relationships is recognized to link all members, so that the terminology, while referring to age levels regardless of actual or fictive kinship, still has the same affective qualities of kinship terminology . . .' (1965, p. 283). Thus among the Mbuti age is the primary factor and it overrides other considerations, while, in contrast, among the Trio category is determined by consanguinity which in behavioural terms may be overruled by age.

IX

LIFE'S DULL ROUND

ii—Obligated Affines

At the beginning of the last chapter it was noted that, among the Trio, consanguinity is stronger than affinity, and the contents of the chapter were concerned with the conventional attitudes and empirical behaviour between members of categories determined by genealogy, residence, or age. It is now time to introduce the factor of marriage and affinity, which is done in this chapter. The same procedure as in the last chapter is followed; a start is made with a discussion of the conventional attitudes between affines, and then the empirical behaviour between them is described. In the final part of the chapter Trio inter-relationships are considered as a totality. First, however, it may prove useful to the reader if a description of the 'immediate affine' terms (Nos. 18–22 inclusive in Appendix A) is provided. They are:

18. *yau*: the spouse's father.

19. *yuupï*: the spouse's mother.

20. *konoka*: This term refers to the brother-in-law, either the wife's brother or sister's husband. It is also extended to include step-fathers, and even in some circumstances the husband of a father's sister. This rather complex application is considered below. At Paloemeu there is said to be a direct address term for use between *konoka* which is *kono*; I never heard this term used and it is identical to the reciprocal term used by Waiyana male cross-cousins.

The female equivalent to *konoka* is *kori* or *koko* by which names a woman refers to her sister-in-law. There is no difference in usage between the terms and a woman will use them indiscriminately in referring to another. The terms are used both for reference and address for brother's wife or husband's sister. A common feature of their usage is the lengthening of the words by the suffix *-mpǝ* which means 'former'. When I queried

this addition it was explained to me that one did not previously speak to a *kori* or *koko*,[1] but now one does talk so they
are 'former *kori* (or *koko*)'. The implication is that the
direct address usage of these terms has only recently been
adopted.

21. *ipaeye:* the son's wife. For a woman it also covers the
sister-in-law, and thus overlaps the terms *kori* and *koko*.

22. *ipamĭ:* the daughter's husband.

As has already been stated these terms have reference forms
only and apply to 'immediate affines' only. They come into
being as a result of marriage and do not exist as categories of
inherited affinity. However, it has already been pointed out
that the distinction between immediate and genealogical
affines is not particularly useful in understanding Trio society,
and one between related and unrelated affines has greater
value in the Trio context.

I

The conventional attitudes between affines are clearly and
precisely understood, and explicitly stated in terms of avoidance.

Avoidance in Trio is expressed simply by the negative of the
verb 'to talk', i.e., *inyompaiwa*, and that affines do not talk to
each other is logically portrayed in the absence of direct address
terms for affines. However, of greater interest is the reason
given for this avoidance; to talk, for example, to one's wife's
mother is *kutuma*, or one does not talk to her because it is
kutuma. This word has more than one meaning and in certain
contexts it means pain—to have a palm thorn in one's foot is
kutuma, to have a headache or fever is *kutuma*—but it is also
used to describe something which is potentially painful—the
ears of an electric eel are *kutuma* even if one does not touch
them.[2] In the sense of pain the word is often and precisely used,
and when I first came across the word in the context of affinal
avoidance my immediate reaction was to ask where it hurt
when one talked to one's mother-in-law. This was considered a

---

[1] There are indications of the collapse of affinal avoidance as a result of
unification in large villages and because of Christian teaching.

[2] The Trio, and also the Macusi, believe that the ears of the electric eel
are the source of the shock which this creature can give.

terrific joke, and my informant never forgot it and mentioned it on frequent occasions thereafter. This seems sufficient
evidence to indicate that there is at least no overt recognition
of a connexion between the meanings used in the different
contexts.

Attempts were made to see if the word, in its two senses,
could be brought into the same general sphere of meaning, and
partial success in this was achieved, although the result is
perhaps a slightly forced one. A female informant remarked that
she was very sad when her child married a stranger, and that
her grief had been *kutuma*. This statement was cross-checked as
far as it was possible with other informants, and it emerged that
it is grievous for a child to marry a stranger, and such grief is
painful—a tentative link.

There is also in the Trio language a verb of which the stem is
ikutuma; the exact meaning of this word has eluded me, but
there is no doubt about its general area of meaning. It has the
sense of 'to answer in anger', but can also mean 'to avoid
scolding in case the person concerned becomes angry and re-
fuses to answer', and thus a natural extension of this is the simple
sense of 'to not answer'. To refuse to answer someone who
speaks to you is an advanced form of anger among the Trio,
who have many words to describe this emotion, but few to
describe amity. If one relates *ikutuma* to the practice of the
person related to both parties acting as a go-between for the
avoiding affines—for example, a man will make a request
of his son-in-law through the medium of his daughter—the
verb takes on an added significance and could perhaps be
understood to mean 'not asking directly in case of angry
refusal'.

Thus the *kutuma* relationship can, in one way, be interpreted
as a device to reduce friction within the community by
preventing direct demands for services between affines, and
also ensures, by the use of a mediator who is affectively connected to both sides, that even indirect demands do not become too burdensome. This, however, is only one aspect of
the *kutuma* relationship, and to understand it further we must
turn to a point which has already been mentioned. Not all
those related by marriage avoid each other, and indeed it
would be perplexing if this were so since in the case of close

relatives it would call for a drastic deterioration in attitude [1] to an individual from the moment of taking their sister or daughter in marriage. An informant when asked 'Do you talk to your sister after you have married her daughter?', replied 'Yes, because she is my sister'. Although this claim, and other cases, were substantiated by observation, it must not be assumed that the relationship remains entirely unmodified, especially as far as closely related male affines are concerned. While such individuals are frequently seen talking to each other, it is said that if one wants something from the other the request should be made through the mediating spouse—a fact which seems to indicate that the conventional restraint between such categories hardens following marriage. However, this does not invalidate the distinction between those related by both descent and marriage, and those allied by marriage only, since affines who are *kutuma* are clearly distinguished, by attitude and behaviour, from those who are not. This does not mean that there is a simple dichotomy, because there are innumerable gradations between the two classes but, in the main, the extent to which avoidance is observed depends on the closeness of relationship prior to marriage—both genealogical connexion and residence being determinants of the closeness.

Marriage with someone who is *itïpïme* does not involve *kutuma*; on this point there is unanimous agreement among all informants. This application is useful since it helps to demonstrate who is *itïpïme*. When ego's son marries ego's sister's daughter the avoidance is hardly discernible since the marriage is between two people who are almost equally *itïpïme*. If, however, ego's sister's daughter marries a distant or classificatory brother's son, the avoidance with this man is practised since he is an outsider, or *itïpïmeta*, in comparison with the sister's daughter. Marriages between people who are both *itïpïme* are considered good.

Co-residence is nearly as effective in reducing the degree of avoidance; it has already been explained that one's *imoitï*

---

[1] In some societies a complete change in attitude following marriage does occur (cf. Firth, 1964, p. 105). However, among the Tikopia marriages between close relatives are generally frowned upon because, Firth suggests, it disrupts traditional attitudes. In contrast, the Trio favour marriage between close relatives, and such unions are not accompanied by any great adjustment in attitudes.

become merged with kin, and it is explicitly claimed to be *kutuna* (i.e., without *kutuma*) to take the sister of one's *imoitĭ* as wife. This situation is to some extent qualified by length of co-residence although little distinction is made in the Trio mind between those with whom one lives and those to whom one is related.

Hypothetical cases are not easy to explain to the Trio and it is difficult to get a precise answer to a question unless an informant can think of an actual example. It appears, however, that if a person who is closely related to ego, but is little known because he has spent his life in a distant village, returns and marries ego's daughter he will be only slightly *kutuma*. One of the obstacles in the way of posing such a question is the difficulty for the Trio to understand the concept of somebody being closely related but little known and living far away.

One can diagnose a pattern of avoidance which is most weakly developed when marriage takes place between closely related people who live in the same village, and at its most intense when between a person closely related to ego and an unrelated stranger. Between these two extremes there are all grades of behaviour, depending on the important factors already mentioned and also on the personality of the individuals concerned. Therefore even in such a universally accepted convention as affinal avoidance there is no rigid rule of application, but each individual case is ordered according to the circumstances obtaining. Examples of this are given below, but first it is necessary to make a brief digression to consider all the potential *kutuma* relations.

Where avoidance is not practised, or practised only on certain occasions, the affine terms of reference are hardly applicable. A man who has married the daughter of his mother's actual brother will call his father-in-law *yetĭ* as he did prior to the marriage. If he is asked what the relationship is he will probably say *yetĭ* although he will recognize that the man is also his *yau*. In cases of less closely related people, there is an equal chance of the relationship being regarded as *tĭ* or *yau*. Finally, there is the case where only the affinal relationship term is recognized, no direct address term used and perhaps one not even known. For example Iyakɔpo (52) has never used a direct address term to Asapɔ (43), his sister's husband,

and could not even suggest one. He only thinks of him as a *konoka*.

Furthermore the extension of avoidance to other members of the same category varies according to the circumstances of a particular situation, and in extreme cases a man does not speak to all those in the community whom his wife calls *pahko*, *manhko*, *pihko*, or *kami*. The same degree of avoidance is not enforced through the whole range, although its potential existence is recognized.

There are, as well as affines, other relatives with whom avoidance is practised. Step-parents are avoided although the same rules apply here as in the case of affines. If, for example, an outsider marries ego's mother he is avoided, but if the father's brother marries the mother this does not apply. It was also suggested that this is the case with a step-mother, but since for a male ego she is an *emerimpə*, if not closely related to the mother, I am suspicious of this since I have no example of it and only heard of such behaviour from one informant. The opposite occurs with a woman who avoids her step-mother but not her step-father. Examples of this can be given. Susuku (1) had married Mïkuri (3) and her adult son by an earlier marriage regards Susuku as his *konoka*. Aiyatu (28) declared that she did not talk to Mïkəripə (30) because she is her step-daughter.

A further application which initially appears anomalous but was verified by several informants is that the husband of an *emerimpə* may be avoided. This case provides a useful key to the understanding of one of the institution's functions.

Avoidance, in one role, can be interpreted as an institution which reserves for the community its human resources (especially female ones) by acting as a deterrent against strangers. This function is clearly understood by the Trio,[1] and finds

[1] This function of avoidance and the Trio's awareness of it suggest that avoidance and sister's daughter marriage can be employed for the same purpose. Although I cannot state emphatically that this is why this type of marriage is well developed among the Trio, its function in this respect is recognized among Carib-speaking people. I am grateful to Dr. Audrey Butt for the following unpublished example from her field notes which she made during her investigations among the Akawaio Indians of Guyana in 1952. I quote: 'He (Abel, the first Hallelujah prophet) enjoined that men should not move around so much and leave Amokokupai (village) for

expression in the idea that now the Trio live together there need not be any *kutuma*. Certainly the deterring effect of intensely applied avoidance which may last a lifetime is not to be underestimated. It has already been explained that there exists in Trio thought a correlation between not speaking and anger or hostility, which emotions the Trio consider to be similar.

It is now intended to provide two examples which illustrate how avoidance is applied, and how this application varies according to circumstances.

At Alalaparu there is an extended family which in the senior generation consists of Paruparu (24) and her half-sister Mïkuri (3). Paruparu's family consists of two sons Sipi (23) and Iyakəpo (52), and two daughters Tawiruye (61) and Nuwimpə (44), and various grandchildren, some of whom are married. Mïkuri's family consists of her son and two daughters by an earlier marriage, and a daughter by her present marriage to Susuku (1). Both Susuku and Nuwimpə's husband Asapə (43) are regarded as strangers and avoided by all the men mentioned above.

Asapə came from somewhere in the east and only he knew the names of his father and mother, who had never been seen by other members of the family. In spite of having been married for at least twenty years (the couple are listed together in Schmidt's census), neither Iyakəpo nor Sipi has anything to do with him, or as little as is possible in a community of this size. They do not eat together, they would not hunt or fish together, they do not talk to each other except in cases of absolute necessity, and then only a few mumbled words with their faces averted.

So much care is taken to avoid each other that examples of their behaviour *vis-à-vis* each other were difficult to observe. The following good illustration was recorded. One day while I was sitting taking to Iyakəpo, Asapə came to me with a bowl of

---

marrying. He stated that it was bad to move around as it led to fighting. A man would live with his wife's father, and at that place he might die. Then his kin might think that his wife's father's village had killed him— and that would lead to trouble and fighting. The means of avoiding marrying out was partly to marry a girl in one's own village and partly for a girl to marry a mother's brother. In this way Abel had stated that this was the way to remain in the village.'

drink (the purpose of his visit being to ask to borrow my shotgun). I drank about three-quarters of the bowl and returned it to Asapə with the conventional *naka*, enough. Asapə was then obviously in a quandary about what he should do with the rest of the drink—in the case of non-avoiding people the bowl would have been passed to Iyakəpo who would also have drunk and said *naka*. However, it is conventionally wrong for Asapə to offer his wife's brother drink, and care is usually taken to avoid such embarrassing situations.[1] Asapə hesitated before offering the bowl to Iyakəpo, which action he completed half turned away, and it was received in like manner by Iyakəpo who, when he had drunk, returned the bowl without a glance and merely a grunt of acknowledgment.

A similar example can be quoted in reference to Susuku. Once again I was talking to Iyakəpo, this time in Susuku's house, when Susuku, who was busy about something else in the house, was given a large bowl of drink by his wife. Susuku came across and offered me the bowl, and after I had drunk I passed it directly to Iyakəpo who, after he had drunk and finished the contents, returned it to me so that I could give it to Susuku, although they were nearer each other than I was to either of them. Iyakəpo, prior to Susuku's marriage with his mother's half-sister, had called him brother, but now regards him as a *konoka* and step-father. Susuku's life history indicates a very unsettled existence in which he wandered from village to village without anybody asking him to stay. The men are also inclined to gossip about Asapə and say that he is a great teller of fisherman's stories (same idiom in Trio as in English), and that while good during the day, he is bad at night. I never discovered exactly what is meant by this accusation, but believe that it hints at sorcery. The attitude towards these men contrasts curiously with that towards other men who have married women of the family, such as Eoyari (62), who was until recently married to Tawiruye (61), while his half-sister is married to Iyakəpo (52), his wife's brother. Avoidance in this group is not recognized, and the attitude is no different to the conventional restraint between proximate generations, as has been described in Chapter VIII.

---

[1] I once observed a woman bring her brother food and, finding him absent and only her brother's wife present, take it away again.

Finally, in Paruparu's family there are the marriages of the generation below—her grandchildren. Sipi's daughter Numepɔ (29) is married to her father's half-sister's son, and since both partners are considered *itĭpĭme*, there is no *kutuma* in their relationship with the spouse's parents on either side. This case is interesting since Matatɔ (31) is *itĭpĭme* because he is a sister's son, and in spite of the fact that his father is a complete outsider. Sipi's other daughter, Mĭkɔripɔ (30), is married to Muyopɔ (32), who is Sipi's mother's half-brother's son, but the relationship is actually traced through Muyopɔ's mother, whom Sipi called sister; thus Sipi regards Muyopɔ as his sister's son and Muyopɔ calls him *yetĭ*. There is a slight avoidance between these two men which is possibly based upon difference of residence, since Muyopɔ comes from the village of Okoimɔ and Sipi from Panapipa. It is said of this relationship that while they do not joke, and will not willingly chat with each other, they do talk. It is also said that if Sipi wanted some arrow canes from Muyopɔ it would be conventionally correct to make the request through the mediation of the daughter/wife, but if she were not present the demand could be made direct. On the other hand it is stated that on no account would the formalities be waived in the case of Asapɔ and Susuku.

This example shows very clearly the different modes of behaviour which may be found. A further example can be taken from the Paloemen village.

Korokoro (300) lives among a group of kin who have practised, with remarkable regularity over a number of generations, marriage with a sister's daughter. An inspection of Sheet 1 of the Genealogical Table will show how inter-married this family has become. Of the present surviving members there are Korokoro, who is married to his father's brother's daughter's daughter, and his wife's brother Naraeyiyi (310), who is married to Korokoro's daughter Minori (306). The relationship between Korokoro and Naraeyiyi, whose age difference is nearly twenty years, is marked by restraint but certainly not avoidance. Korokoro denied that it is *kutuma* for them to talk to each other, but said it is wrong for them to be too familiar together, because they stand in the relationship mother's brother/sister's son.

Korokoro's wife, Ukɔre (307), always provides the food for

her unmarried brothers who are sometimes joined at meals by Naraeyiyi. Korokoro's behaviour varies—on occasions he eats with his brothers-in-law and at other times he waits until they are finished and then eats in company with his wife.

Korokoro's behaviour in respect of his sister's sons (which is the way he thinks of them, not as wife's brothers or daughter's husband) as compared with that to his own son Toropəti (305) was very striking on one occasion. Toropəti, Naraeyiyi, and Pisikĭkĭ (312) had all been in a group which had made a journey into Brazil. On the evening of their return, no contact was observed between Korokoro and his son, but he sat up late into the night listening to the news from his sister's sons.

Toropəti also said that he does not joke but does talk with Naraeyiyi, whom he calls *yetĭ*. Toropəti has married a woman, Mĭnaiye (354), who only marginally belongs to the central core of this family and is the one person whom Korokoro thinks and speaks of in affinal terms; he regards her as his *ipaeye*.[1] While Toropəti was away he left behind his wife and children, and Korokoro regularly received gifts of food from his son's wife, but they were always brought by his son's daughter. This is an interesting case because Mĭnaiye (354), while under an obligation to give food to her husband's father, cannot do it directly for two reasons. Firstly, they are *kutuma*, and secondly she is also an *emerimpə*, and thus presents of food have a sexually suggestive connotation.

This raises the question of the *kutuma* relationship between women, and men and women. There are no cases of women carrying avoidance to the extreme which it attains among men, although this does not mean to say that it is absent. Its function between women is undoubtedly that of restricting conflict in a group which is traditionally co-operative. The other function is not really involved because they are women, and they are exchanged by men.

There are two cross-sex affinal relationships: son's wife/husband's father and daughter's husband/wife's mother. There are two ways of looking at these relationships. First there is an economic aspect. The main reason given by the Trio for

---

[1] Korokoro also regards my wife, whom he has not met, as his *ipaeye*. He does so because he calls me *yimuku*, my child, and I call him *yetĭ*. We are also *imoitĭ*.

marriage is the advantage of having sons-in-law and daughters-in-law to provide for their old age. There are therefore clearly defined economic obligations implicit in this relationship, and with it the possibility of exploitation and potential conflict arising out of it. In the case of the DH/WM relationship there is also a sexual aspect. A man's mother-in-law conventionally belongs to one of the categories which are prohibited. Among close relatives this prohibition is adequately expressed in the actual relationship, but in a wider society this interdiction collapses, since all unrelated women are potential sex partners, and in this situation the traditional ban is reinforced by the more powerful sanction of avoidance.

Although the reason Korokoro gave for his son's wife not giving him food directly suggests perhaps a similar interpretation in the case of SW/HF, there are some additional factors which must be considered. In a truly matrilocal society the son's wife and husband's father will have little contact, and the formalities surrounding the relationship are likely to be little developed. The Trio admittedly are not truly matrilocal, although there is a slight tendency towards this form of post-marital residence. Indeed, if the present pattern results from a development of marriage with the sister's daughter, any previous system of post-marital residence must have been matrilocal since a patrilocal form would have remained unaffected by such a process. Furthermore, the matrilateral cross-cousin is not involved in this because the son's wife is then two genealogical levels removed from the husband's father. The problem centres on ego's patrilateral cross-cousin (his father's ZD) as is the case with Korokoro and his son's wife. This is because such a woman is a potential spouse of both men. In the absence of any incest ban (and, indeed, in the presence of exactly the opposite—a conventional sex partnership) some form of limitation needs to be placed on the content of the relationship, regardless of how close it might be, if conflict between father and son is to be averted. Accordingly in this relationship also avoidance is used as a means of marking off important structural boundaries.

A summary of the function of affinal avoidance among the Trio can now be attempted.

i. Duties exist between all categories of affines, and avoidance is practised in those cases in which the demand for their fulfil-

15

ment could cause friction and conflict between the two parties. In cases of marriage between close relatives or near neighbours this avoidance does not differ in form and expression from the conventional degrees of respect and restraint, or the obligations differ from those which already obtain between such categories of relatives. Since conflict is most likely to occur between strangers, the avoidance is most highly developed in such marriages.

ii. Avoidance also acts as a prohibition on sexual behaviour in the circumstances where the incest ban weakens or disappears and where such behaviour would prove socially disruptive. In these situations, as in i. above, avoidance acts as a marker between the divisions of the social structure.

iii. Avoidance represents a method of deterring strangers who are a danger to the community and in particular to its female resources. This form of avoidance is most intense among men since they are the members of the community who exchange women. To lose a woman to a stranger greatly reduces the chance of receiving another in her place, and this is particularly so in a society which lacks any precise rule of residence, and where women are the society's main assets.

II

Although a man who marries a close relative is not bound by the avoidance which attaches itself to a stranger, such a marriage does not free a man from obligations to his wife's kin. This is important to note, for elsewhere in South America the marriage with a sister's daughter has been interpreted as a means of eliminating bride-service (cf. Kirchhoff, 1932, p. 58; Gillin, 1936, p. 96, and 1963, pp. 849–50; Fock, 1963, p. 201; Métraux, 1963, p. 111). Among the Trio to distinguish bride-service *per se* is to make an artificial distinction in the complete system of affinal exchange. The Trio have only a single word for such actions; in verb form, of which the stem is *ekehka*, it literally means 'to work for someone', but as a noun, *ekehkato*, it can also mean 'something owing to someone' or 'an obligation'. I do not include bride-price in this broad category of affinal exchange because it has already been described as an exotic rarity, an exception rather than the rule. What is to be demonstrated in this section is that interchanges among affines are not

simply a single exchange of women and short-lived bride-
service, but a continuous exchange of gifts and services which
last through life and after death, and may even, as has been
shown in Chapter VII, find reaffirmation by a further exchange of women in the next generation.

Before embarking upon a description of the exchanges which
take place between affines, there is a further point which requires clarification. There are obligations between all categories
of affines, but those between brothers-in-law appear to receive
the most formal recognition. The term for brother-in-law is
konoka, and although it is a reciprocal term it does not necessarily mean that both aspects of the brother-in-law relationship,
wife's brother and sister's husband, coincide in the same individual. The reason for this is that the sister's husband is
sometimes the wife's father, and the wife's brother the daughter's
husband. In such situations the term *konoka* is always used in
preference to the father-in-law or son-in-law term. My tentative
interpretation of this situation is that the male/female relationship of interdependence is epitomized in the brother/sister
relationship and the removal of a sister from an unmarried
man destroys his economic independence and thus there is a
primary obligation to replace her. In some cases, age and/or
previous relationship category appear to influence the use of
the term, but there are not enough examples to make any
positive confirmation of this. However, one good example is
Susuku (1), whom Iyakəpo (52) called younger brother until
he married Iyakəpo's mother's sister Mikuri (3), since when
they have regarded each other as *konoka*.

This is not to say that the other affinal relationships are
unimportant, and indeed in everyday affairs they are more
important. It must be remembered that the Trio give as the
main reason for marriage the advantages of having sons-in-law
and daughters-in-law. The content of these relationships is
mainly routine; a son-in-law is conventionally expected to
provide meat for his wife's parents, make basketwork, bows
and arrows, weave hammocks, cut a field and build a house. A
daughter-in-law is expected to bake bread, make drink, cut
firewood, and prepare other foods. The extent to which such
duties are demanded and performed depends very much on the
individuals involved. The routine services are normally only

performed for a spouse's parents, but it is said that a dead man's brother or a dead woman's sister may sometimes expect such services to be done for them, but this will depend as much on their rapport with the mediator as on their relationship to the spouse. Minor, more sporadic services may be demanded by more distant relatives of the spouse's parents.

During discussion on this topic I suggested to my informants that certain of the younger married men, such as Matatə (31) and Amasina (215), were too immature and unskilled to carry out some of these tasks. This was agreed, and it was said that they would learn and in the meantime they would be provided for by their wife's parents. In the future, when the wife's parents had grown old, their daughter's husband would look after them. Coupled to this is the absence of any such tests of a bridegroom's ability to support his wife and her family as are reported from many Carib-speaking peoples (R. Schomburgk, 1847, b, p. 316; im Thurn, 1883, p. 221; Crevaux, 1883, p. 307; de Goeje, 1910, p. 18; Farabee, 1924, p. 76).

In everyday affairs exchanges between *konoka* are not basically different from those between other classes of affines, and a start will be made by describing the nature of these regular interchanges. Towards the end of this chapter and in Chapter XI will be described occasions on which the exchange between *konoka* takes on greater importance. In the meantime, and purely for expository purposes, two types of the more universal obligations are recognized; these are (a) sporadic services for which actual demands have to be made, and (b) routine services which occur automatically.

Sporadic services cover many aspects of Trio life as these first three examples show:

i. Susuku (1) wanted his daughter's husband, Sere (9), to make a journey to Paloemeu in order to obtain some metal cooking pots for him.

ii. Sere through the agency of his wife used to borrow his father-in-law's hunting dogs.

iii. When Tamori (273) was ill she asked her brother Susuku to get his wife to cut her firewood and to provide hot water (for medical not hygienic reasons).

However, sporadic services are best developed in the case of housebuilding, and here are a few examples of this.

i. When Iyakɔpo (52) built his new house he asked his sister Nuwimpɔ (44), to ask her husband, Asapɔ (43), to fetch leaves for thatch, and his mother's sister Mĭkuri (3) to ask her husband, Susuku (1), to help with the thatching. Iyakɔpo regards both these men as *konoka*. Although Iyakɔpo did much of the work himself, he was assisted at odd times by his brother Sipi (23)— only once as far as I have record—and by Matatɔ (31) who is his ZS and BDH, while the most help came from Susuku and Epoika (210), a man without relatives or wife but who is looked after by Tawiruye (61), Iyakɔpo's sister. It was also noticeable that both Sipi and Matatɔ actually assisted Iyakɔpo, while Susuku, Asapɔ, and Epoika worked regardless of whether Iyakɔpo was there or not.

ii. Susuku's house was built by his daughter's husband.

iii. Sareyuna's (470) house was built by her daughter's husband, Amasi (476), who regards his wife's mother as a younger sister.

iv. Pesoro (602) was helped in building his house both by his brothers and by Pokĭi (556) who is his WMH and also his ZH and they regard each other as *konoka*.

v. Kĭsi (616) built Pikiri's (367) house because he regards her Waiyana husband as his *konoka*, a brother of his own Waiyana wife.

There are exceptions to this rule, and Sapɔ (151) built a house for his wife's sister Isĭnaio (201) although her daughter's husband was at hand. This may be accounted for by the fact that her son-in-law is young, and inexperienced in such tasks.

The other clearly defined obligation is cutting a field, but on this subject it is not possible to be very precise since the traditional behaviour in this activity has been disrupted both by the development of large settlements, and, at Alalaparu, by the missionary organizing the Indians into a weekly routine and giving them considerable verbal encouragement to follow it. Emphasis is also placed on the total co-operation of all members of the community which has obscured the traditional composition of working parties.

With allowance for the distortion resulting from these factors, the composition of a number of working parties was noted on some occasions when it was known that no active encouragement had taken place. Their composition was invariably an equal mixture of kin and affines as this example shows.

Sepĭ's (74) field, which had nearly been completely planted by a vast working party, was finished by a group consisting of Sepĭ himself, Kinini (79) his half-brother, Asonko (78) his sister's husband, Kamapə (83) a half-sister's husband, and Pesaipə (93) his father's half-brother.

It was also decided to examine the relationships to the owner of those who use his field. A distinction must be made between the main crop, cassava, and the supplementary produce. The subject of cassava is considered first.

i. Sere (9) said that his wife and his wife's mother would use his field. Susuku (1), who had been ill through much of the field-cutting period and accordingly had not cut a field of his own, claimed that this field was in fact his.

ii. Morime (7), whose field has already been mentioned as being the only one cut by an unmarried man, said that his mother, his sister Tasi (252), and his married sister Tarara (8) would collect their cassava from his field. In the case of Tarara, Morime's work might be thought a service rendered for the sister's husband, Mono (14), who suffers from bouts of giddiness and is not very active, but Morime stressed that the field was for his mother and sisters.

iii. Muyopə (32) said that as well as his own wife, the wives of the following men would take cassava from his field: Sipi (23) his wife's father, Iyakəpo (52) his wife's father's brother, Matatə (31) his wife's sister's husband, Pepu (22) his wife's brother, and Kəsəpə (139) his elder brother.

iv. Kinini (79) cut a field which was shared by his wife and his wife's mother although the latter appeared to regard the field as her own.

v. Mĭtĭipĭ (59) cut a field which was to be used by his wife, his married sister whose young husband had not cut a field, and his widowed mother and grandmother.

It is not possible to draw examples from Paloemeu because at this village a single huge field had been cut and planted by the co-operative effort of the whole village. The question as to which particular part an Indian considered to be his received such variable answers on different askings that one assumes the field to be a communal one, although no confirmation of this impression could be gained from the Indians themselves. However, communal ownership of fields does appear when one turns to the question of supplementary crops. The owner of a field does not have exclusive rights to the use of the ground, and a number of people plant crops, other than cassava, in somebody else's field. Ownership of these plants—usually bananas, sugar-cane, yams, and sweet potatoes—is known and respected. Before planting in another's field, one is expected to ask the owner's permission. Iyakəpo (52) planted bananas in Anaore's (178) field, and asked his permission through the agency of Arami (179), who is his mother's brother's daughter and considered more closely related than is Anaore.

The right to plant in another's field does not rely on any specific relationship, and Mono (14), who planted some bananas in his wife's brother's field, put some others in the field of a totally unrelated person. The general rule seems to be that one plants anywhere it is considered to be convenient, in the case of sugar-cane, for example, in fields close to the main paths leading out of the village because it is at hand to cut when leaving the village to spend a day in the forest.

It is difficult to make any firm assumptions about the traditional system from observations made in the present situation. It seems probable that a traditional village would have only a single field which would be co-operatively maintained by all the inhabitants of the village. The community would cut one field each year and the area would be divided out among the inhabitants. This much is agreed by Eoyari (62) who said that when he was leader of Panapipa he decided when and where the field should be cut and would divide it among the people.

This may have happened at the larger villages, but it cannot always have been arranged like this since there is a strong tradition of people preparing their own fields which recurs in the tasks of secondary clearing and planting. One must also relate this to the practice of Indians moving from village to village within the agglomeration, which means that either they owned a field at each settlement or, which is more likely, they had a right to food from another's field, a right which can only have been based on kinship. It is valueless to try to reach any conclusions beyond this since there are no facts to substantiate any conjectures. Fortunately, however, while recent developments have upset behavioural patterns of agricultural activity, this is not so in the other main subsistence occupation, that of hunting and fishing. This is demonstrated by the coincidence of claimed conventional behaviour and observable practice. However, the distribution of game belongs to the second class of affinal obligation since it invariably takes place without request, although minor variations occur from time to time.

In Chapter VIII it was noted that an unmarried man or a widower gives his game either to his mother or to his sister. This behaviour, in purely quantitative terms, is insignificant since there are few men who hunt regularly but are not married. A married man does not keep the game he brings home, or at least not all of it, and often none of it. The husband gives it to his wife who, in turn, hands it over to her parents or brother. Not only does the game change hands, but also the ownership of it in terms of rights over its further distribution. This does not mean to say that a man does not eat the meat he kills, because a portion is handed back.

A man returning from a successful day's hunting walks through the village carrying his game on his back but taking no notice of anybody and ignoring all comments.[1] He drops his load outside his hut and goes and sits in his hammock where he is soon brought a bowl of drink by his wife. His wife takes the game and gives it to her parents. A slightly different pattern occurs at Paloemeu, where canoes are used; here the man leaves his game in the canoe and his wife goes and collects it from there. The parents-in-law butcher and prepare the meat, and, while retaining some for their own use, will return some to their daughter, distribute some other pieces, and provide a communal meal with the remainder.[2] This is the ideal, but while observation shows that practice follows this pattern, variations occur according to circumstances. For example the

[1] This contrasts with the behaviour of the unsuccessful hunter who waits for semi-darkness and then takes the shortest route from the forest to his house.

[2] Normally, at a communal meal, a man does not eat meat which he himself has killed. It is said that he does not eat because he has meat in his house, but this does not stop the person to whom the meat has been passed from eating and he has far more meat than the hunter. This behaviour is the everyday realization of a practice which receives more overt expression on ceremonial occasions. I return to this subject in the next chapter.

size of the catch will have an important bearing in any particular instance. In Table 33 are listed twenty Indians from Alalaparu, and the person to whom an informant considered they should give their game. A note is added as to whether or not this practice was observed, and cases where further comment is required are marked with an asterisk and considered below.

TABLE 33

Relatives to whom men pass their game.

Hunter	Recipient	Relation-ship	Ob-served
1. Iyakəpo (52)	Eoyari (62)	ZH/WB	Yes*
2. Sipi (23)	Muyopə (32)	WF/DII	Yes
3. Eoyari (6a)	Tïnaiye (70)	DH/WM	Yes
4. Kamapə (83)	Piriuta (77)	ZH/WB	No*
5. Pepu (22)	Sere (9)	ZH/WB	No
6. Sipare (89)	Mori (87)	HF/SW	No
7. Kəsəpə (139)	Anaore (178)	ZH/WB	Yes
8. Muse (182)	Asikiri (170)	ZDH/WMB	No*
9. Pesaipə (93)	Kïwaipipi (63)	DH/WM	Yes*
10. Toropə (107)	Sere (9)	ZH/WB	Yes
11. Rorï (173)	Sere (9)	ZH/WB	No*
12. Apirosi (161)	Anaore (178)	ZH/WB	Yes
13. Asonko (78)	Tïnaiye (70)	DH/WM	Yes
14. Piriuta (77)	Mono (14)	DH/WF	Yes
15. Waraka (116)	Mono (14)	DH/WF	No*
16. Ororinapə (155)	Pesaipə (93)	*Imoitï*	Yes*
17. Orosisi (126)	Pesaipə (93)	*Imoitï*	No*
18. Sere (9)	Susuku (1)	DH/WF	Yes
19. Mono (14)	Mïkuri (3)	DH/WM	Yes
20. Muyopə (32)	Sipi (23)	DH/WF	Yes

Before commenting on any particular case it can be seen from Table 33 as a whole that eight out of the twenty examples involve the passage of meat from son-in-law to wife's parent, and two in the reverse direction, from a man to his child's spouse. Seven cases are between brothers-in-law, and the other three are outside both these classifications and are explained below. In none of the cases where meat passes between brothers-in-law is there a surviving parent of the wife, but in the majority of cases where the wife's parent is the recipient there are existing brothers-in-law. The wife's parents thus seem to have a prior right to the game which is brought in by their daughter's husband. However, one must not lose sight of the fact that the daughter's husband has a right to the game shot by his wife's father. The two examples of this in Table 33, cases 2. and 6., both deserve brief comment. Sipi's (23) wife has no close relatives at Alalaparu but it is not because of this that his meat goes to his son-in-law Muyopə (32). Sipi confirmed that his game went to Muyopə both because Muyopə is his daughter's husband and because he, Sipi, is the recipient of Muyopə's game.

In case 6., Mori (87), who is Kamapə's (83) wife, is the daughter-in-law of Sipare (89), and is the recipient of her father-in-law's catch in preference to Pesaipə (93), who is Sipare's wife's half-brother, but also his brother's son. Although there are only two instances in Table 33, others do occur; for example, Susuku's catch was always passed to Sere (9), his daughter's husband. This behaviour definitely involves a two-way flow, although the system is best developed in the movement from DH to WF because few men whose daughters are married still hunt regularly and there are, accordingly, far fewer occasions on which game passes in the direction of WF to DH. However, the obligation is conventionally and empirically practised, and therefore it is wrong to regard the transfer of game as a form of bride-service.

Cases 16. and 17. require an explanation since the relationship of *imoiti* is the reason given for this transfer of game. The Trio explain it in this way: Pesaipə (93) is the recognized leader of the Alalaparu village and as such is the controller of the communal meals, in which capacity he holds the status of *sipari entu*, or the owner of the basket.[1] The food for communal meals is placed in front of him in the *anna*, he distributes it, and he is the person to whom *naka* is said at the end of the meal because he is regarded as the provider or source of the food. There are close parallels between this explanation and the formal type of exchange to be described later, and it gives a hint of political allegiance expressed in the same form as affinal

[1] Bread and meat are served on basketwork mats the largest types of which are used at communal meals.

obligations. This point will be considered again in the discussion on political organization and social control, but it will be useful to include here some additional information. This cannot be done in the case of Orosisi (126) whom I met only briefly and about whom I know very little. Ororinapə (155), however, does give game to people other than Pesaipə, for example to his widowed half-sister, Misita (134). It is necessary to look further to understand why the informant stressed the transfer of game between Ororinapə and Pesaipə. In terms of kinship Ororinapə belongs to section G of the Alalaparu village (see Figure 13), but his house 36G faces away from those of his kin and towards that of Pesaipə, house 26F. To all intents and purposes, when both Indians are sitting outside their houses they form a single group. There are no genealogical or affinal ties between Ororinapə and Pesaipə, and the former, having turned his back on his own family, has allied himself to the latter; thus although this is a political, not a marital, alliance it is overtly expressed in the same manner. The information which is lacking is Ororinapə's motive for forming this association, but this alliance is obviously of sufficient importance for the informant to refer to it rather than any other.

The other exceptional case is 8.; Asikiri (170) keeps a very close relationship with his sisters' daughters, who are, first, Muse's (182) wife, who is the daughter of Asikiri's father's brother's daughter, and also Papopə (154) and Ikərl (46), who are the daughters of his half-sister. These three are regularly to be found in Asikiri's house where they work together and form a co-operative group. Asikiri undoubtedly exercises some jural authority over these women and it has already been mentioned that he intervened when Papopə (154) was maltreated by her ex-husband Piwara (156). This is a valuable case since it demonstrates an extension of *itĭpĭme* so that the sister's children are not only called by the same term, but a similar pattern of behaviour surrounds them as surrounds a man's own children. This explains why Muse passes his game to Asikiri.

In all the other cases in Table 33 which are marked with an asterisk alternative patterns of behaviour were either stated or observed. These are described below:

Case 1. Iyakəpo (52) and his brother Sipi (23) both said

that they also gave meat to their elder sister Tawiruye (61) who had recently been deserted by her husband, and this behaviour was observed on a number of occasions. Iyakɔpo also receives a regular supply of game from his son-in-law Mïtïipï (59), but my notes lack any reference to a reverse movement of meat although I can recollect it happening on one occasion.

Case 4. Kamapɔ (83) is also said to give his meat to Sepï (74), the half-brother of his wife. On one occasion Kamapɔ's game passed to Pesaipɔ who is his mother's half-brother and his father's brother's son, although the former relationship is the one respected.

Case 9. Pesaipɔ (93) also gives meat to his elder half-sister Pisekane (88).

Case 11. I never observed any game caught by Rorï (173) go to Sere (9) although his wife, Sere's sister, used to take him cooked food from time to time. On one occasion when Rorï brought home a pig it was passed to Itïimare (153), his sister's husband.

Case 15. Waraka (116) is a Waiwai who has married a Trio woman; I have no evidence that he conformed to Trio practices in this matter but the Trio informant considered that he should.

While convention stresses the affinal character of these exchanges, in practice there is also a kin element especially marked by that between brother and sister. This pattern must not be considered as too rigid a system of behaviour, and an individual's actions vary from day to day and from circumstance to circumstance. For example, Piwara (156) and his wife who both lack relatives in the village sometimes give their meat to Pesaipɔ (93), which is presumably a similar expression of political allegiance to that just described, sometimes to Sipare (89), with whom they have recently formed a fictive kinship, and on other occasions keep the whole bag for themselves. Only rarely is all the game given away if it consists of more than one item, but that which is given away the hunter loses all rights over, and ownership passes to the recipient. Two personal examples will illustrate this. I played my part in the subsistence of my family at Alalaparu by lending a gun and cartridges to various Indians in return for meat—a system which worked well but which I modified when I moved to Paloemeu so that my behaviour coincided more with Trio lines of obligation.[1] I noticed immediately that the meat I received in exchange for the use of the gun rarely came from the Indian to whom I had lent it. One simple illustration will be enough to explain. One day I lent my gun to Piriuta (77) and that evening received half a bush-turkey from the hand of Tarara (8). Traced from Piriuta the bird had followed this route, Piriuta—W—WF—WFW—myself.

On another occasion Sepĭ (74) came and asked me for some salt, which I gave him, and in return he brought me some meat. Since I knew that Sepĭ had not been hunting that day I asked whose game it was. It turned out that it had been shot by Asonko (78), Sepĭ's sister's husband.

It has also been noted that the transfer of meat does not stop after one movement; some is returned to the hunter unless he has kept some back, some is sent for a communal village meal, some is retained by the first recipient, and some is distributed along further lines of obligation. No rigid pattern for this further distribution can be recognized and, as the following examples show, it is distributed through a network of relationships which are based on either consanguinity or affinity.

i. Mono (14) arrived back from a day's hunting with a land turtle and an armadillo. The turtle was kept by Mono, and his wife, Tarara (8), took the armadillo to her mother, Mĭkuri (3), who passed it to her husband, Susuku (1). Susuku butchered the animal and gave a piece to his sister Tamori (270) who, in turn, kept some for herself and husband, and gave the rest to her half-sister Sipakari (274). Sipakari's husband, Mooso (273), handed over part of this (not much more than a mouthful by now) to his widowed sister Misita (134).

ii. Muyopɔ (32) came back from hunting with a pig and a small monkey. Both these animals were passed to his wife's father, Sipi (23), who kept the pig and sent the monkey across to his elder sister Tawiruye (61). Tawiruye prepared the meat

---

[1] The simplest and most obvious way of doing this is by integrating oneself into the system of relationships. Once I had people whom I called *wƏi*, *yetí*, or whatever appropriate term, the mutual obligations immediately appeared. I was fed by my sisters, or asked for something because of my relationship to the person making the request, and, in turn, made demands in the same way.

and some was given to her other brother, Iyakɔpo (52), and some to her mother, Paruparu (24). The remainder she kept to feed herself, her son's son Panesi (36), and Epoika (210), for whom she cares.

iii. Amasi (476), who regularly hunts by night, brought home two labba. They both passed through his wife to his wife's mother, Sareyuna (470), and then one of them was taken by Sareyuna's younger sister Arena (462) and given to their older brother, Korokoro (300). This animal was prepared by Korokoro and his wife; part of the meat was sent for the communal meal and the rest eaten in the family which includes Korokoro's wife's brothers and sisters.

The initial transfer of meat is almost always between affines, but after this the distribution may equally be to kin or affines with considerable emphasis on the brother/sister relationship. It has already been noted that this is the conventional and actual behaviour among unmarried brothers and sisters, and it is now obvious that it continues after marriage. In the light of such practice the advantages of marrying a sister's daughter become obvious. In such a marriage the sister takes on the role of the wife's mother, and there is no disruption in the previous pattern of interdependence but merely that a third and middle party is introduced into the system. Services, duties, and obligations continue to flow along pre-existing lines. Nor does this contradict any statement made about affinal obligation because implicit in such a marriage are the equations $ZH = WF$ and $WB = DH$, and every individual relationship is duplicated so that no realignment of social or economic obligations is required. This point is a valuable one in the understanding of Trio social organization.

This discussion of the distribution of meat has mainly been confined to Alalaparu. The system is ordered along identical lines at Paloemeu, but its distribution in any particular case is normally more limited. The first movement, that from hunter to wife's kin, invariably occurs, but only rarely does it move further than this. The reason for this is a simple one; the hunting is much better than at Alalaparu and accordingly most households at Paloemeu are well provided with meat. This can also be seen at Alalaparu by the practice of unrelated people soliciting for meat, behaviour never observed at

Paloemeu, where the distribution of meat is confined to members of the family. This leads one to suspect that the extended lines of distribution are the result of the large settlement units, and that in the small traditional-sized villages the close degree of relatedness of the inhabitants would make the behaviour similar to that observed at Paloemeu.

Attempts were also made to see if any specific relative had any particular right to any part of an animal. Although informants willingly described how different animals are divided among their relatives, observation revealed that such claims bear no resemblance to practice, and it was concluded that informants were merely describing actual incidents and not conventionally recognized behaviour. However, some interesting points did emerge from this approach; the Trio consider the liver and skin the poorest part of an animal, and it is observable that the unrelated people who ask for meat are normally fobbed off with one or other of these. The stomach of the animal is kept by the first recipient but this is an important ingredient in the making of the gravy which, it has already been noted, is almost public property. A piece of leg bone may be kept by the hunter, particularly if his wife is pregnant or if he has a very young child, since it may be needed in certain couvade rituals if the infant falls ill and the spirit of the dead animal is diagnosed as the cause. The only other bone part which is regularly kept is the lower jaw of the pig, which is an essential tool in the making of a bow. At Alalaparu the head of a pig is nearly always sent to the *anna* for the communal meal. Pesaipə (93), the usual *sipari entu*, always keeps this part for himself, but neither he nor any other informant could advance any reason for this other than that he likes it. Interestingly enough, the same thing does not happen to the head of a pig at Paloemeu. Except for these minor parts, the bulk of any animal is not distributed in a set way, and individual taste seems the important factor save in the universal preference for fat meat.

These examples will suffice to illustrate how an alliance created by the exchange of women is daily reaffirmed in a multitude of ways. So far only exchanges between the living have been considered but it has been stated that affinal obligations continue after death—this fact is to be seen in the Trio institution of inheritance.

Property inheritance is a poorly developed institution among the Trio because of the lack of inheritable wealth. In the traditional culture most material objects can be made by any male/female unit. At death, the conventional practice is to destroy all the dead person's property, although, in fact, often only a token destruction takes place. The items which are spared are those which it is difficult to replace or require considerable time and effort to do so. For example, one informant told me that at the death of a woman her sieve, cassava squeezer, and pots would be broken, but not her baking plate because the younger women do not know how to make one.

Trade with the Bush Negroes introduced into the society many items which are irreplaceable by Trio techniques or out of the resources of the environment, and thus possess an intrinsic value which does not belong to traditional objects. Although these new possessions have not changed the basic pattern, since at a man's death objects such as his knife may still be destroyed, the greatly increased amounts of wealth in exotic goods which an individual can accumulate through trading has had a number of consequences, not least of which is the strengthening of the system of inheritance.

The number of cases in which wealth has been inherited are still few but they are sufficient to allow a comparison between conventional and actual behaviour.

A basic feature of inheritance is that it is sex-linked since, as the Trio point out, a man has no use for a woman's things, and *vice versa*. This is not quite true since knives and beads are things which both men and women use and want.

It is said that a man does not inherit his father's property nor a woman her mother's because in their grief they do not want to see their parents' belongings. It is considered that a man's property should pass to his *konoka*, and a woman's to one who called her *nosi* but who is also her *ipaeye*, and thus probably refers to the brother's daughter who conventionally belongs to the class of son's wife. However, women own far less inheritable wealth so that there is some doubt about female practices.

The following case histories illustrate the extent to which this ideal is followed.

  i. When Kumupï (301) died, his possessions were taken by

Pekaraipo (315), whom he called *pito* but who was also his *ipami* or *konoka* since he was his daughter's husband. On Pekaraipo's death his son, Inəsi (317), inherited his goods which, it was said, were very few.

ii. When Koita (661) died, Pantapə (340) inherited because Koita's wife was his classificatory sister.

iii. Sonə (681) inherited Tanari's (444) possessions; Sonə called Tanari *yeti* although the actual connexion traceable in the Genealogical Table is MHWSWF (this can be reduced thus: MHW = M; MHWS = MS = B; MHWSW = BW and MHWSWF = BWF = WF who can be expected to be *ti* in 54 per cent of Trio marriages).

iv. When Simore (463) died, Surekore (471), who was both his daughter's husband and wife's brother, inherited his belongings. At Surekore's death, however, Enapere (263) seized them. Enapere called Surekore father, because his own father called Surekore younger brother.

v. The hereditaments of the brothers Sariku (472) and Kararemən (308) went to Retipə (359), as he was the husband of their younger sister Aminu (540) and their *konoka*.

vi. Musere's (535) goods went to Wiwiki (634), who was husband of his sister Nantawi (635).

vii. Amakiriki's (500) possessions went to his classificatory younger brother Pakoti (726), but the informant, Amakiriki's son, said that there were very few.

viii. Amasi (476) said that when his brother Paiye (344) died, everybody seized his belongings.

ix. Asanri (451) said that all his father's goods were destroyed at death and the same with his mother's except for a few balls of spun cotton which he took himself (presumably for his wife).

This handful of examples was all that it was possible to collect, and most Indians either did not know what had happened to their father's things, or said there had been none, or that they had been destroyed. A summary of these case histories does reveal an agreement with the conventional mode of behaviour described by informants:

i. DH: S.
ii. WB.

16

iii. ZS (perhaps DH).
iv. WB/DH: BS.
v. ZH: ZH.
vi. ZH.
vii. yB.
viii. Inconclusive.
ix. S, but probably for SW/BD.

The affinal character of inheritance, and particularly the *konoka* relationship, is very pronounced, but it must be noted that in the absence of any means of enforcing such a system opportunity must play a large part in deciding exactly which affine will inherit. There is, however, one outstanding exception to this system of inheritance and it involves the shaman's rattle and its accompanying spirits. Unlike other objects this is an item which is never destroyed at its owner's death because, the Trio say, this would allow the spirits to go free. Instead the rattle should pass straight into the ownership of another person since there is great fear of unowned and uncontrolled spirits. A shaman's rattle is conventionally inherited by his son, and this practice is almost unerringly followed.

i. Sipare (89) inherited his rattle from his father, Pia (90), who had previously obtained it from his father.

ii. Susuku (1) inherited his rattle from his father Tuhori (2).

iii. Makampɔ's (710) rattle was jointly owned by his wife Rekewa (700) and her eldest son (by a different husband), Atipa (707).

iv. Kusene (756) inherited a shaman's rattle from his father Pisure (671). It was stated by one informant that Pisure's sister, Wiripɔ (785), had been a shaman but there was uncertainty about what had happened to her rattle. One person suggested that it had been buried with her but the general consensus of opinion was that this would have been far too dangerous.

v. Sirai's (466) rattle had been inherited by his son Natara (732).

vi. Makara's (196) rattle; this example is not too clear. The rattle apparently passed to his wife, Wiwi (197), and at her death it was seized by Pisekane (88) who gave it to her husband (89) (this is not the same rattle as example i.). Mooso (273), who had been married to Wiwi when she died, was considered to have some claim to it.

It is clear from these examples that the son of a shaman normally inherits his father's rattle, but this does not mean that he assumes the status of shaman although it seems to give an impetus in that direction. More important is the fact that the Trio believe it to be dangerous for a rattle to lack an owner; a system of patrilineal inheritance is the society's solution of this dilemma.

III

At this point it is possible to correlate the more important conclusions from this chapter with those from the last one, and thus form an over-all picture of Trio inter-personal relationships.

In discussing kin, it was concluded that any attitude between categories was simply a particular instance of a much wider set of attitudes which involve respect arising from age difference, and restraint arising from sex difference. In dealing with affines a distinction was drawn between those genealogically or residentially related, and those unrelated except by marriage. When one compares the empirical behaviour and conventional attitudes between categories of kin and related affines one is struck by the similarities. This is most clearly seen in the case of the sister to whom a man's obligations and attitude remain virtually unaltered after he has married her daughter. This is the most obvious example, but when one considers other categories of related affines it is possible to see also that the conventional attitude between individuals in their role as kin is closely matched by that in their affinal status. Associated with this is the feature of the Trio kinship terminology which places only siblings at ego's genealogical level and removes to the first ascending or descending level his wife's or mother's agnatic kin (i.e., his potential male affines). It has been explained that the conventional attitude of respect which exists between members of proximate generations is verbally expressed through the relationship terms, but that the extent to which it is realized depends on relative age. When obligations involve the exchange of women, no disruption in the basic pattern occurs, since the ties of consanguinity are duplicated by those of affinity.

Avoidance has no place in such marriages because its presence would be superfluous—the pre-existing attitudes, implicit in the old relationship, suffice to order the new status. Among unrelated affines this cannot happen, and thus formalized avoidance is called upon to do duty in place of the attitudes which are intrinsic in the close relationships. However, it has been shown that there is no sharp division between related and unrelated affines, but that infinitely variable gradations exist between them. This is made possible by a basic similarity in the type of attitude, restraint and avoidance, and also by similar sets of obligations. The relationship between affines, whether related or unrelated, is characterized by organic interdependency which is typical of the male/female relationship, and which contrasts with the mechanical co-operation between those of the same sex. This interdependency between all affines emerges in the Trio reason for marriage—an alliance which, in due course, will create sons-in-law and daughters-in-law on whom the couple can depend in old age. It has been shown that it is wrong to regard this as asymmetric bride service but, because it is a symmetrical relationship, it implies interdependency.

One needs to be careful in drawing too close a parallel between the male/female relationship and the affinal one, since in so doing one tends to emphasize the similarities of content, and to obscure basic differences of form by identifying the conventional attitude of joking/non-joking with that of talking/non-talking. The first set of attitudes forms the guide lines for behaviour within the known social world, and the second set divides the known from the unknown. This distinction is obvious if we think about it in the context of strangers; strange women are welcomed as *emerimpɔ*, but strange men are feared as potentially hostile. This situation, almost a mirror image of that among friends, can be remedied by incorporating its representatives in the inside world, a process which is achieved through the agreement on relationship terms. Thus for a Trio to say that he does not talk to a man because 'they had not measured each other' is simply saying that he is still an outsider, and the expected attitude towards him is the same as that toward an unrelated affine,[1] i.e., they do not (cannot?) talk to each other.

There is another way in which it is useful to look at this situation, and that is through the *pito* relationship. A *pito* is neither kin nor affine nor stranger, although he is also a bit of each. It is a relationship marked by restraint rather than either familiarity or avoidance, and spasmodic but enduring interdependency rather than short-term co-operation or long-term interdependency.[2] The *pito* relationship stands in a position between the relationship obtaining between brothers and that obtaining between unrelated affines. In the last chapter the opposition between the relationships brother/sister and *emerimpə/emerimpə* was demonstrated, and that the husband/wife relationship plays a mediating role between them. A *pito* relationship stands between kin and affines in the same way as the husband/wife mediates between the male and female conceptual units, although it should be remembered that in a very obvious way spouses also mediate between kin and affines.

As has already been stated, the Trio lack terms for kin and affines; in one context affinity becomes merged with consanguinity, and in the other the opposition between these two classes is expressed in other ways. As related/unrelated (*itï-pïme/itïpïmeta*), resident/stranger (*imoitï/mano*), measured/unmeasured (*ikuhtu/ikuhtuna*), talk/avoid (*iyompu/inyompauwa*), and painful/painless (*kutuma/kutuna*). However, the Trio do not fully perceive the implications of these distinctions which are so explicit at the level of conventional attitudes and so observable in everyday behaviour. These distinctions, which belong to the systems of attitude and behaviour, correlate with the system of terminology as presented in the appetitive model; the Trio see and explain their society in terms of their conscious model. To the observer the disparity between ideal and practice is obvious as is the problem contained in it. Related affines are a way to individual security, but unrelated affines can assure the

---

[1] See p. 101.

[2] The relationship between trading partners, *ipawana*, is traditionally that of *pito*. Such partnerships, which mainly involve the transfer of hunting dogs and manufactured goods, once formed appear to be almost permanent although exchange may occur only infrequently.

society's welfare;[1] marriage with close kin strengthens the opposition between the known and the unknown, unrelated affines afford a way to the resolution of this opposition. In Chapter XII an attempt is made to fit these conceptual oppositions into a broader framework, but first it is necessary to consider the form and nature of relationships between Trio villages.

---

[1] Some Trio are aware of this problem. For example, Korokoro (300), who possesses great sociological awareness, stated that a man should marry *mano* (a far one) since in this way there were people with whom one could trade (and marry again). He himself, however, had married a closely related woman (his FBDD).

X

INSIDE AND OUT

THE ECONOMIC and social aspects of the traditional settlement pattern have already been explored; now it is the turn of the political organization to be examined. In some ways this is the most difficult part to deal with, since, in the absence of any formalized arrangements on one hand, and the mobility of population and the temporary nature of villages on the other, it is hard to describe what is in fact a very fluid situation without making it appear too rigid.

The autonomous political unit is the village, but this must not be taken as a dogmatic statement since it is obvious that, with a mobile population which assembles and disperses again either at will or at need, the system must permit wide variations. A small village only a few hours walk away from a larger one may have little contact with it, or it may consider itself politically subordinate to it. If the inhabitants of two such settlements were formerly all of one village, the attitude will mainly depend upon whether the separation was in anger or amity. Whichever it is at any one time this will not be a permanent state, for the relationship between any two villages may go through cycles of friendship and hostility. Thus over a period of years the single village is the autonomous unit, since any external affiliations are short-lived. However, before considering how relations between villages are ordered, it is vital to consider the mechanisms of social control within the village.

In the first place it must be remembered that the average size of a traditional Trio village is thirty people, all of whom are likely to be inter-related, either consanguineously or affinally. Thus the internal political organization, if it can be called that, is little more than a reflection of the kinship system. However, there are recognized ways both for asking for intrinsic obligations to be fulfilled and for sanctioning unacceptable behaviour. The positive encouragement is less well developed, and an Indian, in order to muster co-operative help from his kin for such tasks as clearing or planting a field, does so either by providing drink in the *anna* and asking publicly, or by taking drink round to each house and asking individually. In fact, there is very rarely any need to do this since co-operation in such economic duties is normally readily forthcoming.

Among the negative sanctions, that most frequently employed is gossip. It is difficult to tell exactly what force gossip might have had in the sphere of the small village, but it is undoubtedly an effective control in the larger settlements. To some extent the influence of gossip will vary in any individual case, but most Indians do not like being gossiped about. Pikume (365), an ambitious and independent man, whose attentions to other people's wives were considered excessive, said it was bad for him that his brothers should talk about him. On the other hand, Yapi (339), who had virtually given up all traditional occupations to work full time on the Paloemeu airstrip, seemed to be completely indifferent to the open sneering directed at him. Gossip in its most virulent form becomes an accusation of sorcery,[1] which is a powerful sanction acting towards social conformity. In the sphere of the village it is doubtful if gossip ever develops this far, and one informant declared that no one would curse another member of the same village. This seems reasonable if one considers what disruption cursing or the accusation of its practice could have in such small communities. Even in the setting of the new large villages I heard no accusations made; no one at Alalaparu accused anybody of that village of cursing, although Təmeta (482) was mentioned as a curser. The same is true of Paloemeu, and here Təmeta accused both Kəsəpə (139) and Emopiripə (165) of being powerful and persistent cursers. However one must be careful here to distinguish between ideal and practice, and all the more because they are very close together. An accusation of cursing in a village would result in its division or alternatively it may follow on the division of a village; either way practice falls in line with the ideal.

If gossip is the most moderate method of expressing popular disapproval, violence is the most extreme. Presumably violence sometimes occurs between close relatives or co-residents but I have no record of such happenings. The majority of cases of

---

[1] I use this term interchangeably with cursing.

violence involve either women or dogs, which is a corollary of the Lévi-Straussian idea of war as trade gone wrong (cf. Lévi-Strauss, 1943a). The similarity between trade and marriage occurs in Trio thought and practice, as will be seen when the subject of ceremonial dialogue is introduced later in this chapter.

The individual, assuming that he is not supported by popular sentiment, has limited recourse for the reparation of a wrong—sorcery or violence, including poisoning, being an extreme form of self-help, the use of which will expose the practitioner to revenge cursing[1] and further violence. There is a practice whereby a man can declaim his complaint in a loud voice. Since I have only a description of such an action, I have no knowledge of the actual content of such a declamation. One of the cases described involved an axe stolen from Kɔsɔpɔ (139), who went out into the anna and exclaimed for a long time in a loud and angry voice what had happened. The other case involved Keriya's (346) adultery with Sini's (566) wife, and Sini spoke his piece in a field which was being cleared. One thing which is definite is that these speeches do not involve cursing since no Trio would dare admit openly to such practice. However, one must assume that, as well as affording a certain emotional release, it does contain the threat of cursing and in the case of theft the possibility of reparation.[2] I do not know if Kɔsɔpɔ received back his axe, but since he is a shaman it seems probable that the thief would have taken an opportunity to return it.

Finally, in the case of disagreement it is possible for the dissenting individual or group to leave the village and go to live elsewhere. However, not all population movements arise from conflict, and some have purely social or economic causes and take place without dissension. It is also true that conflict is

---

[1] The majority of informants professed to know the method of revenge cursing (even if they did not, it was necessary to do so for self-defence) but denied the knowledge to curse. The single description of cursing which I collected showed the technique to be the same as in revenge cursing. This is logical since cursing and revenge cursing are not two parts of a complete action but merely two events in an endless series.

[2] This accords with the Trio degrees of anger; shouting is high on the scale but silence is the worst form and implies more than simply the threat of cursing.

likely to be expressed in social or economic terms—thus the shortage of game, and an associated unwillingness to fulfil social obligations, will give rise to discontent.

These sanctions, however, are the exception, and normally the maintenance of social order within the context of the village setting simply relies on the smooth functioning of the reciprocal obligations intrinsic to the kinship ties. Indeed, it is only within this network of relationships that the role of the village leader can be understood. The village leader (*itamu*) [1] has no formally invested authority, but depends, for what influence he can exert, on his place in the network of village relationships. However, while a strategic position in the system of relationships is an important qualification and a fundamental one in gaining and maintaining the co-operation of the inhabitants, a leader's success or failure will ultimately depend on his competence in mediating disputes and ordering everyday affairs, such as the selection of good garden sites and the organization of fruitful hunting and fishing expeditions. Since any man can found his own village, of which he will then be the leader, the system allows wide scope for the politically ambitious, but at the same time requires proven ability for anyone to become politically successful. The incompetent leader will find the size of his village dwindling until it consists

---

[1] Also *pata entu*, literally 'owner of the place'. *Pata*, although used for village, means place as opposed to *itu*, forest or 'without a place'. Villages are known both by the name of the locality, invariably that of a stream or river, and by the name of the owner.

The distinction between forest and village receives daily recognition in simple rites of passage. Although I was unable to discover any traditional act, under the present Christian régime most Indians stop at the edge of the village clearing to say a prayer before entering the forest. Before returning to the village from the forest, although not from nearby fields, the Indians invariably wash before reaching the village clearing. This may not seem worthy of comment except that at Alalaparu a much used trail crosses a small stream just before the surrounding fields are reached. In the wet season there is plenty of water and it is reasonable that one should bathe there. However, in the dry season there is only a muddy trickle, but the Indians continue to insist on washing there rather than enter the village unwashed and swim in the deep, clear Alalaparu creek which they do at other times. No Indian could provide an explanation for this behaviour, but it seems likely that it is to avoid bringing the aura of the forest into the village. Certainly such an interpretation fits with Trio ideas both about the adhesive quality of spirits and the cleansing of some polluted states by washing.

of a small core of kin, perhaps simply his nuclear family. A good and strong leader will tend to attract people to his village, and Eoyari's (62) village of Panapipa was given as an example of this. However, there is even fluidity here and successful leaders are not necessarily tied to their village. For example, Kanre (202), at the death of a son, left his village at Paikarakapo and founded a new one at Aro, and Eoyari temporarily deserted Panapipa and built a new village at Matïtïkiri. He gave two reasons for doing this—the death of a son and because he wanted Brazil nuts; the former would seem to be the reason for leaving Panapipa, the latter for building his new village at Matïtïkiri, an area containing many Brazil nut trees.

While a man can become a leader by founding his own village, he may alternatively inherit an existing village. Frikel (1960) claims that village leadership passes from father to son but the following examples, drawn partly from ethnographic sources and partly from information which I collected, do not completely support this statement.

i. Village of Panapipa: Eoyari (62) had succeeded his father, Anapi (296). Eoyari, now an oldish man, said that Pesaipə (93), who is his WDH, had taken over the leadership in the more energetic economic activities before the village was abandoned at the time of the move to Alalaparu.

ii. Village of Okoimə: Kuruwaka (91) was succeeded by Pika (39) although the former was still alive (Schmidt, 1942, p. 19). Pika was Kuruwaka's sister's husband.

iii. Village of Paikarakapo: Tuna (187), an old man, was succeeded while still alive by Kanre (202) (Schmidt, 1942, p. 33). Kanre was Tuna's daughter's husband. Sometime after Schmidt's visit, Kanre, at the death of a son, went to live in the village of Aro, and Tunareka (166) became leader at Paikarakapo. At Tunareka's death he was succeeded by his son Anaore (178).

iv. Village of Alapite: Schmidt observed the death of the leader, Alapite, and assumed that the son Apoeka would succeed him (1942, p. 27).

v. Village of Koepipanompə: Təmeta (482) became leader of this village at the death of Arupi (382) in which it is rumoured Təmeta had been involved; there was no relationship.

In those examples where the leadership changes hands during lifetime the successor is an affine; when it takes place at death the son succeeds. This difference does not appear to be recognized by the Trio who have no conventional rule of succession. Indeed, taking into account the absence of an office to which to succeed, the tendency of a village to be deserted at the death of its leader, the importance of the personal abilities of the successor, and the fluidity of the population, it would be a curious anomaly to find any definite rule of succession.[1]

In summary, it can be said that the control over the members of the community which a Trio leader can exert depends on his ability, his experience, and his influence from holding a central position in the intra-village network of relationships. The power available to him is different in strength but not in kind from that which any individual can exercise. If the composition of the village is simply that of an extended family, a man's role as head of the family and leader of the village are identical. But even when strangers are present it is difficult (perhaps ridiculous to try) to distinguish between political allegiance and familiar duty since the former is expressed by the means of affinal prestations. This behaviour parallels the need for a stranger to be incorporated, by the adoption of a suitable relationship term, into the kinship system before social intercourse is possible.

The leader, as owner of the village, can refuse to allow a stranger to settle in it, and it is as the village's representative in dealings with other villages, strange visitors, and the outside physical world that the leader achieves his most important role. This introduces the question of relationship between villages, but before turning to this it is vital to say a brief word about the Trio shaman (*piai*). Whatever might have been the case in the past, Trio shamanism is now of a low order, and is being further weakened by missionary influence. There is only one renowned shaman, Tǝmeta (482), and his reputation has spread beyond the Trio and his power is feared by the Waiyana. Tǝmeta himself has little respect for other Trio who regard

---

[1] It is uncertain to what extent a man takes over full leadership while his predecessor is still alive. There is no suggestion in Eoyari's case that he had completely relinquished his leadership, and Pesaipǝ's role is more that of heir apparent than leader.

themselves as shaman, and some undoubtedly aspire to such office merely through the possession of a rattle which they have inherited from their father.

It would be difficult simply by observation of normal routine to identify a Trio shaman. There are certain restrictions on his behaviour and he will own the important shamanistic accoutrements, the rattle and its contents, but apart from this he will appear to participate fully in social and economic activities, not be obviously richer, nor necessarily have more wives. The shaman may be a village leader, but is not always so, and Eoyari (62), who is recognized as a good and powerful leader, is not. The important distinction is the attitude of laymen towards the shaman. This is basically one of respect, perhaps awe at his ability to communicate with the spirit world, but the actual attitude of any individual depends on where he stands in relation to any particular shaman. The more closely acquainted one is with a shaman the more beneficent he appears, while the unknown shaman is feared. Within the village the shaman is a medico-religious adviser and complements the leader as the village representative in dealings with the supernatural unknown; thus it is the task of the village leader to oppose unwelcome visitors, but that of the shaman to combat the curses they leave behind. The known shaman is a focus around which the community coheres, but the unknown shaman is an equally powerful means of expressing social solidarity through opposition. The importance of the assumed existence of unknown shaman in Trio ideas concerning the causation of misfortunes will be returned to below.

The relationship between neighbouring villages is to some degree controlled along similar lines to those within a village. The links of kinship still exist but the further one moves away the weaker and fewer these ties become. Gossip is ineffective in this wider social environment, and the proclamation of injuries or wrongs more difficult to implement. Cursing becomes a potent force in controlling behaviour but its practice or its threat is of little value in the ordering of face-to-face contact between strangers or the slightly acquainted. For this purpose use is made of ceremonial dialogue. This institution has previously been mentioned, and it is now intended to describe it more fully. For greater detail and certain comparative aspects of ceremonial dialogue one can refer to Fock's work on the *oho* chant among the Waiwai Indians (Fock, 1963, pp. 216–30). The Trio practice is very similar, and, where dissimilarities do exist, they would appear to correlate with the differences in social structure of the respective groups.

There are three forms of Trio ceremonial dialogue, and they are graded by their intensity or strength. The Trio use the word *karime* which has the meaning of strong and well, in contrast to weak and sick. Talk can be described by this term, and when applied to ceremonial dialogue it also has the connotation of length. So a person whose dialogue is *karime* can talk forcibly for a long time; this introduces the basically competitive aspect of the institution in which, to be successful, one's talk must be both long and strong.[1]

The weakest form of ceremonial dialogue is called *tesəmïken*, and its use involves little formality. It may take place between two or more people, often closely related, and is sometimes used between those who conventionally should not speak to each other. Its purpose is to make a welcome, to pass news, give a plan of intent, or, less frequently, persuade someone to do something.

The second grade of ceremonial dialogue is called *sipəsipəman*. This is normally only used by men, although it is said that some of the older women know it. This dialogue is made between two men, but it is not used between those who are closely related. For example Eoyari (62) said that he used to speak *sipəsipəman* when he visited the village of Aro, which is in a different agglomeration to his own village. The uses of this talk are similar to those for *tesəmïken* but it also has a competitive or bargaining side and is used for trading or for obtaining a wife.

The third and strongest talk is *nokato*. It is similar in form and usage to *sipəsipəman*, but only the older men are fluent in it. This talk is used between strangers—Eoyari said that he would use *nokato* if he visited a village on the Marapi.

Ignoring the *tesəmïken* of which both the form and function differ from the other two, both *nokato* and *sipəsipəman* are

---

[1] In this context one can note the correlation between the stool of which the use in ceremonial dialogue is essential, stone out of which the first stool was carved, and hardness and permanency which the stone symbolizes and which are the necessary attributes for success in ceremonial dialogue.

carried on between two Indians sitting on their stools facing each other. The participants take it in turn to speak for about five, ten, or fifteen minutes, while the adversary grunts acknowledgment. The dialogue is constructed on the repetition of a single rhyme-word at the end of each short sentence, but the sentences themselves consist of words and phrases not used in everyday speech. Many of the younger men and most of the women do not understand large parts of these conversations. The older men are considered to know these dialogues best and accordingly to have the strongest talk. When I asked who were the strongest talkers of *nokato*, the oldest men's names were always mentioned.[1] Between two experienced men the ceremonial dialogue can continue for twelve hours or more. When one of the participants finally gives in, he says *kone*, an emphatic expression of agreement, picks up his stool and leaves.

The basic pattern of usage of ceremonial dialogue is that its intensity increases outwards from any particular centre, and in this it parallels other Trio institutions such as affinal avoidance. However, the external limitation is coterminous with the distribution of the Trio. The Indians themselves say that they do not use these forms of speech with non-Trio, and their specialized linguistic features strongly supports this claim. Thus the ceremonial dialogue defines a unit within which there is a recognized and institutionalized method of dealing with situations which involve potential conflict. Its use both in settling a marriage and in trading is logically allied to such an interpretation. The importance of these activities in Trio culture has already been stressed, and while existing bonds reduce the possibility of disagreement among those closely related, a more formal system is necessary to order the exchange between strangers. For this reason there is no competitive element in *tesəmiken*, but this talk does share with the two stronger forms the common purpose of making a welcome on one side and a formal announcement of arrival on the other. In this aspect of the ceremonial dialogues the outstanding feature is the em-

---

[1] It was this fact that made me query the extent to which Pesaipə (93) had superseded Eoyari (62) as leader of Panapipa since Pesaipə is not regarded as an experience talker of *nokato*. This is an important qualification for a good leader who must speak for his village in ceremonial dialogue with strangers.

phasis from both sides of their respective goodness, their lack of colds and sickness, the absence of evil intent, and that they are not cursers. These claims are reiterated on both sides, and this repetition in the dialogue means that these assertions become intermingled and barely indistinguishable. To understand what this means it is necessary to consider Trio beliefs on the subject of causation of sickness and death, which in turn cannot be separated from ideas about cursing.

The role of sorcery as a social regulator in the setting of the single community has already been mentioned, as has the fact that, conventionally, people do not curse their own *imoitĭ*. Sorcery, however, plays an important part in the ordering of inter-village relationships and attitudes. It was explicitly stated by a number of informants that the Trio live far apart from each other because they are frightened of each other and fear strangers as cursers. They do not like visiting strange villages because of this, and when they go to an unknown village, they say on arrival, 'I am not a curser, I am good, look at my baggage. Now you be good and do not curse me.' When visitors come to their village they give them food and drink, and are open and laughing because the only safeguard against being cursed is openness and expression of good intent—a description of behaviour which closely matches the overture of the ceremonial dialogues.

There appear to be two attitudes of anxiety surrounding the stranger; the stranger as the bringer of colds and the stranger as a curser. In fact these are two ways of looking at the same thing, and in Trio thought they are but one. For the Trio sickness and death are classed together and are not considered to be natural phenomena; death is merely a more violent form of sickness. The Trio sicken or die as a result of being cursed, and this can come about in one of two ways. An Indian may be cursed by a layman, or shot by a spirit, who acts either of its own free will (the more infrequent occurrence), or at the instigation of its controlling shaman. Most people are considered to die as the result of a shaman's cursing which is considered powerful enough to destroy all the inhabitants of a village. It is noticeable that although the Trio think of their spirits' behaviour as ambivalent, it is the human agency which is considered ultimately harmful.

A curser is not necessarily a Trio, but while a shaman can curse from a distance, a layman needs some contact with his victim if only in the form of a footprint.[1] It is also recognized that cursing is more powerful if direct contact, such as blowing on the intended victim, is involved. Sickness and death following close on the heels of a visit by strangers (as so often happens), brings inevitable accusations of sorcery against them. Strangers are feared for the sickness which they bring, and because of Trio beliefs concerning the causation of sickness, the stranger is in turn feared as a curser.

This fear exists on both sides—the traveller fearing the inhabitants of an unknown village and the inhabitants fearing the powers of the strange visitor. This allows for a tradition of hospitality which, even if offered as an indication of beneficence, is in fact a prophylactic against witchcraft. The desire to trade or the need to seek a wife are the two main reasons for travel, and their urgency is strong enough to overcome the dangers involved. It is logical that the ceremonial dialogue, the only formal method which the Trio possess for ordering relationships, should be best developed for cases of contact, trade, and marriage when unrelated, potentially hostile, and anxious parties meet.

Some Trio, but usually as young men, have travelled widely and visited all parts of the Trio territory. Eoyari (62) described how he, as a young man, had visited villages on the Anamu, Marapi, and Paloemeu Rivers. On one journey he came to a village and the inhabitants refused him food, and they stayed in their houses and said, 'Previously you cursed us when you were here, and now we are going to kill you.' After he got home, Eoyari said that he travelled no more but stayed in his village, and was fierce to visitors. I do not know how typical this case history is since I have no other examples

[1] The Trio distinguish between death caused by a shaman and death caused by a layman. In the former case the injury is done by spirits which are sent by the shaman who is in touch with the supernatural world. The shaman can therefore kill from a distance, but the layman who has no contact with the spirit world must rely on some contact with his victim. The diagnostic feature is the absence of a spirit's weapon in the body of the deceased killed by a layman's curse, and its presence when death is caused by a spirit acting either on its own volition or at the instigation of a shaman. Spirits are thought of as hunters who shoot people for meat, which is logically related to the dominant part played by carnivores in Trio beliefs.

17

except that of an Indian who said that one became more frightened (*narike*) and thus fiercer (*əire*) as one grew older.

However, comparatively few people seem to have travelled far, and the picture of the Trio living in small, scattered villages with limited communication between them is basically correct. Admittedly Indians move around freely within their own agglomeration but even so, and as has already been mentioned, there is sometimes no contact between neighbouring villages whose inhabitants are at enmity. For example, a missionary informant told me that when he arrived the inhabitants of the two Trio villages near the mouth of the Paloemeu, which are less than an hour's downstream paddling from each other, had virtually no contact and were in a state of hostility. He also added that they only got together to dance. The Trio dance festival is the subject of the next chapter but some comments on the political aspects of this institution are pertinent at this point. The dance festival is a period during which enmity is suspended, and it thus allows members of different villages to unite in an atmosphere in which hostility is replaced by community for the expression of common values. However, this unity contains the seeds of its own disintegration, for while such gatherings give the chance for the reparation of old wrongs and the formation of new bonds, they are by their very nature the source of much new ill feeling. The congregation of the inhabitants from a number of villages allows plenty of opportunity for the spreading of any sickness in the area, and accusations of sorcery will follow. Furthermore the mildly orgiastic nature of the dance festival, drunkenness and sexual licence, lead to allegations of adultery and wife-stealing. This and the associated pattern of cyclical shifting alliances revealed in attendance at drink parties have been well described for the Cubeo of the North-West Amazon area (Goldman, 1963, pp. 202–18), and it seems likely that in their traditional setting the Trio behaved similarly.

To put this in another way, while the Trio dance festival is an institutionalized way of bringing the outside inside, it also contains the means of restoring things to their normal, if re-patterned, state. Indeed it would appear that the scheme of events in the dance festival provides symbolic recognition of this feature, and this is the subject of the next chapter.

XI

DANCING AND DISTRUSTING

IT MIGHT be thought that the contents of this chapter deserve an earlier and greater prominence, but for one good reason a different order cannot be justified. The facets of Trio social organization already described were available for observation; this is not the case with the features considered in this chapter which, by the time my investigations had begun, had virtually disappeared under the influence of external contacts. This is particularly true of the dance festival, a ceremony which I unfortunately never observed because the Trio of Surinam have given up dancing. However, one aspect of the dance festival which involves an affinal prestation and is perhaps its central theme lingers on although isolated from its full setting. Indeed, so attentuated is its form that I had recorded three such prestations before my questions elicited the fact that they had anything to do with dance festivals. The best approach to the subject would seem to be to start on the firmest ground, and to describe an event actually observed, add some details from other occasions, and then try to relate these activities to the descriptions of the traditional dance festival as given by various informants and as they exist in the ethnography. The incident which I describe is the return of an earlier prestation which I had seen but had not fully understood, and whose salient features I had failed to notice.

One evening at about 6.0 p.m., about thirty minutes before sunset, Aiyatu (28) placed in the *anna* four pots of drink—two pots together to the north side of the *anna* and the other two together on the southern side.[1] Sipi (23), Aiyatu's husband, who was painted and wearing some feather decorations, left his house, taking with him his stool. He went and said a single word to Susuku (1), his mother's sister's husband, whom he

---

[1] The compass points are used merely as terms of reference to describe the situation. They are not important for the understanding of the ceremony. The Trio have words for east and west which are derived from the verbs for sunrise and sunset, but none for north and south.

regards as a *konoka* so that they do not talk to each other. Sipi then went to the *anna* and sat down to north-west of the more northerly pair of pots, and faced slightly away from them.

Susuku finished what he had been doing, dressed himself in a clean lap, painted his face and put on some strings of beads.[1] His wife Mïkuri (3) also put on beads, which is unusual for her, and she and Susuku both went into the *anna*. In the meantime (about twenty minutes) Sipi had been sitting alone on his stool, taking no notice of anybody and in turn ignored by everyone. Susuku placed his stool to the east (and left) of Sipi, and directly in front of the northern pair of pots where he sat facing them. Mïkuri sat on a bark mat near the southern pots facing more or less towards her husband. Aiyatu took up her position on the ground to the right of her husband. Susuku then called everyone to come and drink. The men congregated around Susuku and drank from the two pots in front of him, and the women settled around Mïkuri and drank from those two pots. Little intermingling of the sexes occurred but within these groups the pots of drink were passed around in either direction and handed from neighbour to neighbour without formality.[2] As the pots were emptied they were refilled by Aiyatu who otherwise stayed near her husband; neither of them drank anything and for the most part remained aloof from everyone.[3] The main body of the people sat or stood around talking and drinking, their behaviour being in no way exceptional. The party lasted for nearly four hours and then people began to disperse. *Naka* (enough) was said to Susuku, and Sipi was entirely ignored. When the last person had gone Susuku and

---

[1] Paint and decoration are a sign of amity or at least of good intent. Members of a war party wear neither paint nor decorations. Kayser recounts that his Trio guides covered him with urucu before they reached a strange village (Kayser, 1912, p. 44).

[2] This contrasts with the Waiwai who, according to the missionary Claude Leavitt, always pass their drink in a clockwise direction and the pot has to be returned to the originator. The only hint of this in Trio behaviour is their insistence on receiving from the actual hands of the owner any object which they borrow and their care in returning it into the hands of the owner.

[3] This isolation and that before the party began can be compared with that of the successful hunter on his return, and the failure to join in the drinking with the refusal of the hunter to eat his own meat at a communal meal.

Mīkuri retired to their house, and only then did Sipi and Aiyatu gather up the pots and leave the *anna*.

The following day when I asked Susuku who had been the owner of the drink he replied that he had been.[1] The drink, however, was made by Aiyatu who was helped by Tawiruye (61), Siwapun (53), Tarara (8), and Sipi's two daughters.

Two months earlier I had noted the first part of this exchange, although at the time it had meant little to me. I did record that a huge quantity of drink had been consumed in the *anna*, and that Susuku and his wife had supervised the provision of drink, but that Sipi had been considered the 'owner'.

There is also a slightly more complex example of which I saw only one part. Towards the end of November, when the rivers are getting low, is the time which the Trio favour for fish poisoning. In 1963 the Indians at Alalaparu planned a grand-scale poisoning of the Kuruni River, and the organization of this was in the hands of Asapɔ (43). The venture was a great success, and when the Indians returned from it, the largest proportion of their catch was given to Asapɔ who with the help of his wife Nuwimpɔ (44) placed it, on palm leaves, in the *anna*. Sipare (89) and his wife Pisekane (88) then came and distributed the catch among the villagers. Three days later a party, almost identical in form to that described above, took place, with Asapɔ and his wife providing food as well as drink on this occasion, and Sipare and his wife taking the role of 'owner'.

Sipare is Asapɔ's wife's brother and they regard each other as *konoka* and do not talk. My enquiries as to whether this was the first or second part of the exchange failed to get a satis-factory answer, and I was left with a strong impression that it is not thought of as a double and reciprocal act, but merely as

[1] The Trio word for owner in this context is *entu*; the nearest English equivalent is 'source' although this is not quite adequate. A man is said to be the *entu* of his house, and a tree root the *entu* of the tree. But an orphan such as Mupi (69) is said to be *entuna*, without *entu*. The word also crops up in Trio beliefs since the *kapu entu*, the source of the sky, or *tuna entu*, the source of water, are the same place, i.e. the horizon, and it is the *kapu* or *tuna entuhtao* in which departed souls exist and thus also the source of soul matter. Water is undoubtedly a feminine symbol, and, indeed, the first woman was a fish. The sky is not so obviously a masculine symbol but it is true in general that Trio feminine symbols are more apparent than mascu-line ones.

a single transaction in a whole series of interchanges. The reason given for these gifts is simply stated, 'because they are *konoka*', implicit in such a comment being the fact that the relationship has previously been brought into existence by either an exchange or a transfer of women. It was also said that such affairs take place when either the cassava is ripe, when fish are poisoned, or when the spider monkeys are fat. These events cover a period from the end of November until the beginning of April, which coincides with the time of Trio dance festivals as reported by other ethnographers (Farabee, 1924, p. 204; Figueiredo, 1961, p. 2; Schmidt, 1942, pp. 20–22).

It is to the descriptions provided by these three ethnographers[1] that it is most useful to turn next in order to continue the examination of the Trio dance festival. These accounts are far from satisfactory, but at least they provide a general scheme of the event which my more detailed but fragmentary evidence does not. However, my information has expository value, and is thus reserved for use in the analysis of my own and others' observations. The descriptions by Farabee and Schmidt are reproduced below in their entirety, but Figueiredo's account is too long for this, so instead relevant passages are provided.

Farabee observed a Trio dance festival near the Anamu/Kutari divide, and wrote,

We sat about the plaza or dance ground for a long time. Then the women brought two large drink pots holding about three gallons each and placed them in the centre of the plaza. After another long wait the master of ceremonies, who was not the chief, walked to the centre and gave several loud inarticulate yells. A man came and sat on the north side of one of the bowls of drink and a woman came and sat facing him on the other side of the bowl. Each assisted the other in holding the bowl for a drink. In like manner another man and woman came to the other bowl, the man this time on the south side. Seven women came and stood around the second pot. Three men carrying a pole twenty feet long now came in from the north and rushed around the plaza with yells and shrill whistles, stopped at

[1] The lengthy description of a dance festival associated with puberty rites that is given by de Goeje (1908, pp. 1089–93) refers to the Waiyana, and not, unfortunately, to the Trio as Roth claims in his translation (1929, p. 90).

the north and turned the other way singing while the leader kept time with a small gourd rattle. Another man joined the group carrying a ceremonial club on his shoulder and smoking a cigarette fifteen inches long. The other two men carried clubs as staffs and sang accentuating the rhythm with a heavy thump of the right foot on the ground. They advanced, then retreated with side-steps and advanced again. While they were dancing men and women came to drink, the two guardians of the bowl holding it up for them. The dancers would advance toward the drink and retreat, at last the leader would go with the end of the pole to the bowl and drink while the others sang and drank in turn. When both bowls were empty the dance stopped until they were filled again from the reserve supply stored in the troughs. Next time four men holding the pole rushed around the plaza and were joined by two more men and seven women; the men holding with the left hand, the women with the right.[1] Then a large man appeared, smoking a long cigarette and carrying a staff. He acted as a clown and followed behind the dancers with the pole. At intervals the leader would turn quickly with the pole and chase the clown. The men assisted the leader, while the women tried to protect the clown. The long pole with the women holding on one side made quick movements rather difficult, and the clown was never caught; yet he had many narrow and noisy escapes. The leader appeared very thirsty and would often advance to the pots for a drink, but rush away after the clown before he or the women could drink. Then he would rush into a house, the clown always following; if they found nothing to drink they soon backed out and rushed away at the clown, the drink pots or into another house. Once they found some drink and the women were able to pass some back to the clown before the leader could prevent it. Once when the leader charged the clown and was on the point of catching him two women caught hold of the leader but were dragged loose as he rushed. Occasionally the dancers would cross or dance on the sounding board. The leader carried a gourd rattle for keeping time to the music and the dance. The men and women all sang while they were dancing and while standing at the drink bowls. The women all wore the bell nut aprons which assisted in keeping the rhythm

---

[1] Which means that the men were on the right, the women on the left. Right and left are not absolute terms in the Trio language. The words used are *yapɔitun* and *yapɔiyano* which both derive from the verb *apɔi*, to seize or catch, and literally mean 'the one (i.e., arm) caught by' and 'the one (i.e., arm) not caught by'. This refers to picking up the just born baby from the floor—an action by which its human status is recognized. The *yapɔitun* arm is the strong and skilled one, but this may be the left or right arm.

and added to the music. The men wore the same kind of feather headdress and other ornaments as we found the Waiwais wearing in their dances. In another half hour the drink in the bowls was exhausted, and the dance stopped. Neither the clown nor the group of women joined in the third dance but stood together near the drink. About ten-thirty the leader, showing weariness, stopped the dance and all retired for the night. As we had no interpreter we could not understand the whole performance. (Farabee, 1924, pp. 204–5.)

Schmidt emphasizes different features of the dance festival which he observed, but his account is complementary rather than contradictory to that given by Farabee.

It is almost half past ten in the morning when Pike[1] stands up and says, 'come'. We go outside the hut and now I also hear in the far distance the sound of bark horns. These horns are made from strips of woodbark twisted in spiral form. They are 20–40 cms. in length and of various tones.

Two youths immediately go and fetch a calabash of red *koesoewe* paint and smear themselves with it all over. Each takes an arrow with a broad bamboo point in his hand, the type of arrow which is used for settling disputes with neighbouring tribes.

Outside in the middle of the village is a hole of which the dimensions are 1 meter deep and 60 cms. in diameter. This is covered by a plank of 1½ meters' width cut out of the root of *manbarklak*.

The two youths now stand on the plank over the hole. In the left hand they hold the arrows so that for one the bamboo tip points upwards and for the other downwards, the signs of hostility and friendship respectively. They now stamp vigorously with their feet on the plank. This produces a dull but penetrating sound that can be heard from afar. The returning Indians reply to this noise on the bark horns.

Pike now comes out of the hut with a stool and sits down solemnly at some distance from the two youths who continue to stamp and make the noise. He has only brought with him a big cigarette rolled in the paper thin bark of the *ingipipa* tree, which is also well known to the coastal Indians. During the feast he smokes practically non-stop.

Now there appear in the village square the two women previously mentioned[2] who have in one hand a leafy sugar-cane stock and in the other a branch of cotton bush. They begin to dance

[1] In the Index to the Genealogical Table, Pika (39).
[2] When Schmidt arrived at the village on the previous evening he had found only Pika, two women, and three youths in residence (p. 20).

around the two youths, moving around the plank and bowing rhythmically at each step. This continues for some time, and then they place the sugar-cane and cotton branches on a plank in front of the village leader.

They disappear again but shortly return with a piece of cassava bread on a basketwork fan which is put down in front of the leader next to the sugar-cane and cotton. Once again the women begin dancing around the two stamping youths and singing loudly, while the returning group answer, but not now with their horns but by imitating the noise of the Spider monkey, their most valued game.

Then from the forest appear ten women with four adolescent girls among them. All the women carry heavily laden baskets on their backs. They go straight to the two stamping youths and dance with their loads around them.

After this seven men and two youths emerge from the forest blowing on horns. They carry nothing else but their bows and arrows. They join the women dancing round the youths.

Next the women leave the circle and take their carrying baskets to their huts. Three entire baskets full of smoked meat and fish are placed in the village square in front of the sugar-cane, cotton, and cassava bread with which they form a triangle, inside which a small fire is lit.

The men now give up dancing and leave their horns on the three baskets filled with meat. Then they also disappear.

It is not long before both men and women reappear in the square and renew the dancing and loud singing around the two youths who have continued incessantly to produce the dull penetrating sound.

Throughout this time Pike has remained sitting gravely on his stool, smoking his cigarette.

Once again the ten women leave the dance ring. The other two only now come back, and solemnly take from the hand of Pike both pieces of cassava bread on their basketwork fans, which they offer in turn to the dancing men who each break off a small piece and eat it. Then the two women fetch a calabash of kasiri, a fermented drink which the Indians prepare from cassava, and let all the men drink.

Then they fetch the sugar-cane and cotton and, after dancing once more around, disappear.

The leader then stands up and goes over to the dancing men. One by one as they pass him he blows cigarette smoke over them from top to bottom. In the same way among the Indians the sick are fumigated to cure them. This ends the first part of the ceremony.

* * * *

Meanwhile it has become dark and I seek my hammock. At 9.0 p.m. the festival begins again in the big hut and lasts until 1.0 a.m. but I remain in my hammock (Schmidt, 1942, pp. 20–22).[1]

As stated earlier, the account of a dance festival given by Napoleão Figueiredo is too long to reproduce in its entirety, but the following relevant passages have been extracted.[2]

The feast of the collectors (*wanano*)[3] among the Aramagoto[4] is one of the interesting aspects of their culture. Taking place during those periods in which there is an abundance of food (vegetable, fruit, fish, and game), it is basically a collective manifestation to commemorate a gathering economy which is made by groups of families who move away from the village to a distant locality with the aim of practising such a mode of subsistence in spite of owning fields of cassava, sugar-cane, and bananas. . . . At the more or less suitable time the village divides itself into groups; those that are going to participate in the collection (*kuriya-entu*),[5] those who are going to look after the preparation of the cassava products (*dou-entu*),[6] and finally an uninterested element which does not want to participate in these activities (p. 2).

The collectors stay away for two weeks or so, and during this period those left in the village prepare cassava products, including kasiri,

[and] begin what we can call the 'early preparations' for the feast. The members of the *dou-entu* group begin to dance, and intone songs suitable for the encouragement of good collecting, fishing or hunting. Groups of five or more men perform this in the centre of the village over a drum dug in the ground, beating rhythmically with their feet, and always accompanying it with a song. Almost all smoke rolled cigarettes . . . (p. 4).

The collectors almost always arrive back in the afternoon. . . . Their return is announced by them with the sound of horns (*kura*).

[1] My own translation.
[2] My own translation is used for all excerpts.
[3] I am unable to identify this Trio word.
[4] A Trio sub-group (see p. 22).
[5] Literally 'owner or source of the land turtle'.
[6] I do not recognize the word *dou*, and private correspondence and conversation with Professor Figueiredo has failed to elicit further information. Allowing for the difference in phonetic spelling, the nearest and most obvious equivalent which I can suggest is *uru*, bread (the Trio often slurr over an initial vowel), but it could possibly be *rui*, a species of bamboo, but also the word for the flute or pan-pipes made from this wood. This possibility is discussed below.

The sound emitted can be heard at a great distance, and is replied to by those who remained in the village. When this alarm is heard, the number of dancers increases, and various men attend to the drum. The first songs of the feast are sung, while the women and children go to the river bank to await the arrival of the collectors. The latter disembark from their canoes and unload what they have obtained during their trip; land turtles (*kuriya*), fish (*kana*), already smoked, wild honey (*wane*), the game and various types of wild fruit (*eperu*). They are received with signs of pleasure; little bamboo flutes (*kuira-kuhtu*) [1] sound at the same tempo as the horns, while the collected produce is piled near the drum and covered with palm leaves and the land turtles are firmly secured so that they cannot run away (p. 5).

The author then goes on to describe the dress of the Indians and their various decorations before returning to the events of the dance.

After dancing, the collectors reunite in front of one of the houses. This is the moment at which the women give food, bread, and smoked fish to the men. During this act there is no singing, but only the sound from the horns and little flutes. After this the men change places with the women, whom they now serve.

At the end of the eating ceremony they continue to dance round the drum. The women, almost attaining a run, seize smoked fish from the hands of the men grouped round the drum and immediately flee. Then the men chase them to try to recapture the fish. This ludicrous act is repeated by the children who run several times round the village and then hide the fish under the drum. It is truly a farce; some pretend that it is to procure food and when they find it they run in a circle eating it.

The land turtles, which, covered with leaves, are tied near the drum, are the centre of interest in this feast. It is around them that the dance is performed and the participants place themselves in circles; the men occupying the outside and the women the inside. . . . The leader of the *dou-entu* plays the drum (pp. 7–8).

When night descends, all the villagers, including those who have not taken part in either the *dou-entu* or the *kuriya-entu* group, reunite for a communal meal. . . . The leader of the group which did not participate in the collection presides over the meal. It is he who

[1] Probably *kiira*, a bird whose spirit is a guardian of the cassava.

divides the bread and fish among those present while the women distribute the drink[1] (p. 8).

The description continues with the statement that the dance continues, with reduced enthusiasm, for several days, and several variants are observable and 'in one of which women only participate. They carry in one hand a long branch of cassava . . . When the rhythm . . . changes the women make a half turn and pass the stick of cassava to the other hand' (p. 9).

The tempo of the feast increases again as it nears its close, which is brought about by the diminishing supply of food and drink. On the last day—

In the afternoon the number of dancers increases. In a short time everyone from the village is in the square. Even those who do not belong to either of the groups who made the feast join in. The turtles are fixed to a long rod which are carried by men who run, shouting, first in circles and then backwards and forwards. Those who are not carrying the turtles also run, some blowing little flutes of bamboo and others bark horns.

The dances and songs finish with the general slaughter of the land turtles. After they are removed from the rods, they are placed on the earth to receive from the men ceremonial blows made with a machete on the undershell. Then the women finish the killing, open the shell and remove the viscera. The meat, separated from the shell, is then cooked.

While the women prepare the land turtles, the men reunite around the drum and start a form of physical competition which is part of the ceremony. Each one picks up a companion by the waistband, carries him for some metres and deposits him on the ground. Initially, the contender offers a fictitious resistance which appears to us to be simply ritualistic and which everyone performs in the same way. The contestants take turns and even the children compete.

After this the men scatter themselves about the square, sitting on stools carved out of wood or on turtle shells. Then the final communal meal begins. The women eat after the men. . . . When finished, boys and girls arrive carrying pots of wild honey which is

[1] There is a footnote in the text which reads 'The president of the meal is separate from the tribal political organisation. The feast which we attended was presided over by the headman Ionare, because he was also the leader of the *dou-entu*. In the case of the headman not being leader of the *dou-entu* it is the actual leader of this group who presides over the meal, the other being merely a normal participant of the feast.'

served on pieces of wood with a peculiar nap raised on the tip. This point is stuck in the pot, mixed with honey and then sucked (pp. 10–11).

Figueiredo's conclusion is that 'this feast . . . is the commemoration of the type of economy which is directly related to a ceremonial mythology and a system of division of labour. Although the main source of food is cultivation, the Aramagoto, like all the Trio, are also collectors, and collecting, hunting and fishing are the important factors in the subsistence of the group' (p. 13).

Although there are discrepancies between these accounts, and between them and the attentuated festivals I observed, and as will shortly be seen between both of them and the descriptions of dance festivals given to me by various informants, there are many features which can be identified as being common to all of them. Whilst the longest and most recent description, Figueiredo's, is the most disjointed, the author does stumble, perhaps unwittingly, on what would appear to be one of the fundamental messages being conveyed in the dance rituals—an opposition in Trio society which is most clearly recognizable in the division of labour. In the analysis which follows, I wish to highlight some other oppositions which are discernible. I am fully aware that by present standards this analysis is hopelessly superficial, and indeed there are many aspects of the accounts for which I can offer no certain explanation, but the choice was either to do what was possible or to do nothing. In every way the former course is preferable since what can be extracted gives further evidential strength to features already outlined.

Firstly there is a series of oppositions running through the dance festival which deserve attention. This is most obvious in that of the sexes—from my own observation men stand around and drink from one pot, the women from another.[1] In Farabee's account the distinction is observed in the method of holding the pole and the women's assistance of the clown. A roughly similar act can be seen in Figueiredo's account of women snatching food from men who then chase after them, but even more obvious is the pattern of dancing with women

[1] When the missionaries first started holding church services for the Trio, men and women sat apart. Under the influence of the mission teaching this pattern disappeared and members of a family started to sit together.

on the inside and the men on the outside. However, I received an important variation on this pattern from two informants, Korokoro (300) and one of the missionaries, who both said that the men formed the inner circle and the women the outer circle, and to which the missionary added that the men moved anti-clockwise and women in the opposite direction.[1] I cannot offer an explanation of this although attention should be drawn to a definite case of role reversal. Figueiredo describes how men are fed by women and that they then change places, and an identical event was described to me by a Trio informant, Eoyari (62). A photograph which accompanies Figueiredo's article (p. 16) shows that this is not simply a casual event but a ritual one, as the emphasis placed on it by the Indian informant suggests. This is merely to stress that role reversal does occur in Trio dance festivals although, without additional evidence which is lacking, this cannot be taken to explain why men sometimes dance on the outside and at other times on the inside.

To return to surer ground there is no difficulty in recognizing, at least at a material level, the distinction between hunting and cultivating, between forest and village. In the first place this is obvious in the activities of the two groups, and the contrast appears as strongly in Schmidt's account as in that of Figueiredo. As well as the purely economic activities this opposition is also symbolized in other ways; it is excellently portrayed by the musical instruments associated with the two places—the deep throated horns with the forest, and the drum with the village. However, I was told that the drum is used only at dances which concern the *itamu* of game animals and not played at those connected with the *itamu* of cultivated plants. The smaller bamboo flutes are the musical instruments associated with the latter, including the pan-pipes which, de Goeje says, are played in conjunction with the tortoise-shell harp (1906, p. 24). This may have some relevance for the names of the two groups described by Figueiredo; it has already been mentioned that the term *dou* has not been identified exactly, but that it may possibly mean pan-pipes. This would help to explain why the hunting group is called *kuriya-entu*, because the land turtle is

[1] A photographic illustration of Figueiredo's article (p. 17) shows both Indian men and women dancing in an anti-clockwise direction.

not particularly prized as game although it is appreciated as a way of preserving fresh meat.[1] This is not a solution but it does fit with the more comprehensive meaning of the *kuriya* suggested at the end of the chapter.

More important than this for the understanding of Trio social organization is how the groups which represent male and female, hunters and cultivators, forest and village, are related to each other. The first clue to this lies in the relationship to each other of the people sitting round the bowls of drink in the middle of the *anna*. Farabee is the only ethnographer who appears to have noted this feature, and, while in many respects my observations agree with his description, there is one important aspect on which we differ. Farabee states that a man and a woman sit opposite each other and help each other to drink, and this layout is the same as that described to me by a missionary and an Indian informant, Korokoro (300), although these last two both said that three men sit opposite three women. The missionary added that this pattern only lasted a short time, and while his numerical estimation can be accepted at face value it is necessary to be cautious about Trio figures since *aerao* means a few rather than the exact number three. However, I received from both these informants two accounts, and in both cases the second account is distinctly different from the first. This is particularly curious in the case of the missionary, who had attended only one dance festival. In his second account the missionary said that there were two men and two women in the centre of the *anna*, and that the men sat facing each other and sharing a bowl of drink, and the women did likewise. Korokoro's description is more helpful and very close to my own observations. He said that the maker of the drink gives it to his *konoka*, and he stressed this relationship above all other affinal ones. The drink, he said, is prepared by the maker's wife, and then the maker gives it to his sister who, in turn, hands it

[1] The *kuriya* does not figure in any Trio myth which I have heard, but it is a central character in the Waiwai origin myth. The *wayam* (i.e., Waiwai for land turtle) woman is the mother of the culture hero Mawari, and she is hacked to death by the jaguar men (Fock, 1963, pp. 38–48), an incident which brings to mind Figueiredo's description of the fate of the *kuriya*, which he considers a ritual act. A further aspect of the *wayam* among the Waiwai must also be mentioned; the term *wayamnu* which literally means 'my land turtle' is their equivalent of the Trio *emerimpə*. The Trio *kuriya* lacks such overt sexual connotation, although possessing similar medial value.

to her husband. In the *anna* the maker sits opposite the owner, and his wife sits beside him and opposite the wife of the owner who is also her sister-in-law, her husband's sister. The maker of the drink does not drink.

A similar account was received from Təmeta (482) who said that at a dance the drink is made by one man but the owner is another, the former's *konoka*.[1] The maker drinks with nobody, but the owner drinks with everyone. The owner sits in the *anna* with his wife alongside him, and couples come to them to drink. The owner gives drink to the men, and his wife gives it to the women. When the dance is over the people say *naka* to the owner.

If we accept the descriptions of both forms as accurate, it seems necessary to assume that something slightly different is being described in each case. In one form there is no difficulty and the affair is clearly understood as an affinal exchange between *konoka*, and this is confirmed by my own limited observation. In the case where men and women are exchanging drink it is difficult to know, in the absence of either observation or native exegesis, whether this can also be interpreted as an affinal interchange, or if some other explanation is necessary.

The former seems possible in Farabee's account where only four people are present, and if the four basic relationships, ego, his sister, his wife, and his brother-in-law, are represented. Some support for this interpretation can be sought in the fact that in everyday life there is only one occasion when a man gives cooked food or drink to a woman and that is during its passage between sisters-in-law when the man acts as a mediator between his wife and sister. We know from Farabee's account that the men sit opposite to the women, and that those of the same sex are diagonally opposed to each other. Thus while the relationships of affinity, kinship, and marriage are represented, a movement in either a clockwise or anti-clockwise direction involves going through a mediator, and there is a formal

---

[1] Təmeta gave an example of a dance festival at which he had been the maker of the drink. The owner to whom he had given the drink was Pïtï (494), who is the husband of Apokïnini (493). Təmeta regards this woman as his own daughter although she is in fact the daughter of his deceased *imoiti*. Since Pïtï is Apokïnini's mother's half-brother and her father was Təmeta's brother (*imoiti*), Təmeta and Pïtï have the double affinal relationship— WB/ZH and DH/WF.

display of the important relationships in a man's life and of their nature. Even if these assumptions are correct there is still no way of knowing what is the relationship of the man and woman sitting opposite each other. In the events which I witnessed, husband and wife sat opposite each other, but it would be unwise to use this as any sort of evidence because there are certain fundamental differences between the two situations—not least that in Farabee's account both pairs drink. There is one small but interesting point—the men who charge into the village carrying a pole come from the north side, while the women have congregated round the bowl at which the man is sitting on the south side.

While this explanation of four basic relationships may be applicable to what Farabee observed, it will not account for the features described both by the missionary and Korokoro where there are six people involved with all the men on one side and all the women on the other. Now it is possible that this is another example of the ritual mentioned above and described as role reversal. It is noteworthy, although it may be coincidental, that the same two informants described the women as dancing on the outside and the men on the inside. While such an explanation would account for men and women giving drink to each other, there is one further possibility which must be mentioned. In the drink party which I observed the maker of the drink and the provider of the meat were the same person, but according to Korokoro this is not necessarily always the case. There may be three pairs involved in the dance festival— the maker of the drink, the provider of the meat, and the owner of both. Təmeta described it slightly differently and said that the three groups consisted of the owner of the drink, the owner of the meat, and those who danced on the drum. An outline of this latter pattern can be discerned in Schmidt's account, but Figueiredo states that the *dou-entu* performs on the drum. Indeed Korokoro's account seems to be more valuable in understanding the roles of the three groups which Figueiredo mentions, although there is still no explanation of the three couples drinking together. Figueiredo states that the Indian who presides over the distribution of the food is the leader of the *dou-entu*, which is exactly what we would expect. Unfortunately there is no mention of the part played by the leader

18

of the *kuriya-entu,* but the inactivity of the third group seems to fit perfectly the role of the maker of the drink.[1] It is certainly interesting that this dormant group only participates in the festival towards its close, at the point when the *kuriya* are to be killed. This suggests a restructuring of the oppositions within the framework of the festival, and there is some evidence to support such an idea.

The explanation would seem to lie in the understanding of the Trio word *sasame.* When I asked an informant why the Trio no longer dance, he answered that previously the Trio had danced when they were *sasame,* but that they do not dance now because it displeases God, and since the Trio are now always *sasame* there is no need to dance. In its simplest connotation this word means 'happy', but its deeper meaning implies a sense of inner contentment and the feeling of belonging not only to the society but to the whole of nature and the universe. Thus when a group of people are *sasame* they are sharing these feelings, and in so doing are expressing a set of common values. It is to achieve this that the Trio dance, but *sasame* is not simply the reason for dancing—it is also the sensation which dancing engenders.

Sasame is expressed in the dance festival in a number of ways; the act of drinking with the owner of the drink was explained as an act which signified that people were *sasame.* Indian informants stressed the importance of the cassava stocks, one held by the men and the other by the women, as a symbol of this feeling.[2] Figueiredo mentions the women dancing with a

---

[1] Among the Waiwai all the members of the village in which the dance is taking place do not join in—at least to begin with (Fock, 1963, p. 68). The principle would appear to be the same, the variation stemming from the different composition of Trio and Waiwai villages which, in turn, reflects the former's preference for village endogamy and the latter's preference for marriage outside the community.

[2] A more utilitarian and economically practical reason was also given. The Trio say that they dance and sing so that the cassava spirits will come and sit on the shoulders of those holding the cassava stem. The stem becomes inbued with the spirit, and when after the dance it is cut up and planted a good crop is ensured. All Trio dance festivals appear to have some economic-religious aspect in as much as they are directed at a spirit which is considered to influence some part of the subsistence economy. Very briefly, small low-flying birds are associated with vegetable products, eagles with game living in trees such as monkeys, and the jaguar with land game such as pigs. The Trio have a song (*ereme*) for each important spirit.

cassava stem, and my missionary informant said that at the dance festival which he witnessed two cassava stems were used, one held by men and the other by women, and that neither was put down for the duration of the dance which lasted throughout the night.[1] One is lead to speculate on whether the *kuriya* do not have the same symbolic meaning. Their peculiar characteristics allow them to survive the course of the festival of which they are the centrepiece until the closing stages when they are ceremonially slaughtered.[2] If the *kuriya* symbolize the *sasame* spirit of the festival, that is to say the temporary replacement of self-interest by group-interest, then their destruction should indicate a loss of *sasame*, a revival of old oppositions and a return to normality.

There are some other features of the dance festival which support this conclusion. In Schmidt's account particularly, but also in Farabee's and Figueiredo's, note is made of the use of tobacco at the beginning of the event. This must be contrasted with the eating of honey at the end of the feast as reported by Figueiredo, and both acts related to Lévi-Strauss's demonstration (1966) of the conjunctive meaning of tobacco and the disjunctive meaning of honey. Then there is in Figueiredo's report the contrast between uniting to eat a communal meal which happens near the beginning of the festival and the groups scattered about the village square to eat the final meal of land turtle and honey. Finally there is the wrestling which follows on the slaying of the land turtles and which, as far as I can

---

[1] Farabee refers to a pole being carried by the dancers, and the way in which it is used would certainly seem to indicate that it is not a cassava stock. However, Farabee gives no indication that this pole has anything to do with house construction and thus similar to the ceremony among the Waiwai reported by Fock (1963, p. 169). Fock appears to have missed the very obvious sexual connotation of what he describes; the house post has to be put in position by men from a different village, is introduced into the house through the doorway, and is set up, clear of the ground, just above the central hearth.

[2] The use of land turtle shells as stools further emphasizes their connexion with hardness and permanency since mythically the Trio stool is carved out of stone, a substance to which the Trio attach the qualities of immortality, permanency, hardness, and strength. However, it must be remembered that the land turtle has a dual nature—hard on the outside, soft on the inside. It is particularly interesting that in butchering the *kuriya* men deal with the hard exterior, women with the soft interior. Perhaps the very duality of its nature makes it an ideal symbol of unity.

judge from the description, is totally unlike the usual form of Trio wrestling and appears to symbolize physical separation. Thus there appears to be in the over-all scheme of the Trio dance festival the form of a rite of passage; there is an initial stage which is concerned with the separation from everyday life and incorporation into the village, and a final one with a return to normal life and separation from the village. During the middle period *sasame* holds sway.[1]

In summary, the dance festival represents social intercourse rather than isolation, friendship rather than suspicion, community rather than individual interest. It is a period during which mythical unity is achieved and during which the empirical diversity and contradictions of everyday life disappear.

---

[1] In some ways the scheme of the Trio dance festivals follows more closely that of sacrifice than a rite of passage, since the emphasis is on the middle period rather than on the entry into and the exit from the sacred world it represents. The inference which can be drawn from this is that for the Trio the dance festival is not a time of Saturnalian turmoil but rather the highest level of cosmic and social order. So firmly was my mind bound by my own categories of thought that it was a long time before I could rid myself of the equation Saturnalia = chaos.

XII

NATURE AND CULTURE

So FAR the basic divisions in Trio society have been aligned under various headings, male/female, known/unknown, inside/ outside, and these distinctions have been shown to have working value in the total social organization of the Trio. In this chapter an attempt is made to relate this series of oppositions to a wider scheme, and to do this one must turn to Trio myths. The Trio are not great tellers of myths, and it is notable that some of the themes which are widespread not only in Guiana but throughout South America are missing. However, there is one Trio myth which all the older men know in greater or lesser detail, and this concerns the origin of women. It is not surprising that this myth is so well known, since it seems to contain the justification of so much that is observable in Trio society. A short version of this myth with a few explanatory notes is reproduced here, and is followed by an interpretation of its meaning.

I

This is how Pərəpərəwa was.[1] He went to throw fish hooks, he went to the edge of the river to catch fish.[2] He did not catch any. Then he did catch one, and he threw it over his head. It hit the ground and flopped around, and he looked but it had gone. It was not there. 'I have just thrown a fish,' said Pərə- pərəwa, 'I caught a fish, a waraku.'[3] He heard a voice from behind him say, 'It is I.' Pərəpərəwa was surprised because it was a woman. The woman, Waraku, said, 'I want to see your village.' So they went, and at that time Pərəpərəwa's village was among the waruma reed.[4]

---

[1] Pərəpərəwa is a Trio culture hero who is now thought to live in the entuhtao.

[2] In another version of the myth, the river is stated to be the Makurutu, a headwater tributary of the Paloemeu River.

[3] An unidentified fish which is the size of a ⅓-lb trout, and has red markings on back, fin and tails, frequently caught and eaten.

[4] Ischnosiphon sp. The most important raw material in basketry.

Waraku was surprised when she saw the village, and said 'Where is your food? Where is your drink? Where is your house?'

'I am without a house,' answered Pərəpərəwa. 'Where then is your bread?' asked the woman. 'My bread is fixed from the *waruma*,' said Pərəpərəwa.[1] 'Come, I have seen enough of your being,' said Waraku, and they returned to the water. She said, 'Wait a minute, my father is coming, and he is bringing food, bananas, yams, corn, sweet potatoes, eddoes, and cassava.'

When her father came he first saw the cassava plant. He came up and up, and they saw the leaves of the cassava plant coming up out of the water. He came, he got closer, and then Pərəpərəwa saw him, and he ran, for he had seen the red eyes of the big alligator,[2] and he was frightened. The woman shouted, 'Come back. Where are you going?' Then the woman caught the canoe when it came in, but Pərəpərəwa stayed far away. Then the woman took the cassava plants, the cuttings of the stocks, and she put them on the ground. She picked up banana sprouts, and put them on the ground. Then she picked up yams, then she picked up eddoes, then she picked up pineapple plants, then she picked up sweet potatoes, pawpaw, corn, cashews; she picked up all these things and took them out. Then the giant alligator went, and he turned his tail. The cassava was carried on his tail, and he went away very quickly. Therefore we say that the cassava is the tail of the snake, the roots of the cassava are the tail of the snake.[3] Then Pərəpərəwa received these things; the woman gave them to him.[4]

'How shall I fix them?' asked Pərəpərəwa. 'Cut a place for them. Cut a field for them,' answered Waraku. 'Right,' he said, and then he planted them. He planted cassava, bananas, yams, pineapple, corn, and all the other things in his field.

That is how it was, and he planted the things which he had,

---

[1] His food was the soft pith inside the reed.

[2] Waraku's father is an *ariweimə*, a giant alligator which is like a large canoe, but from time to time also takes on the appearance of a large snake, *əkəimə*.

[3] *Əkə arokï. arokï* means a long tail, but also means penis.

[4] In another version the woman also provides a machete, a knife and fire. In that version it is quite explicitly stated *weiporəken totï anokanempə*, formerly his meat was baked in the sun.

and they grew. The cassava, the yams, the sweet potatoes, the pineapples, the corn, and the sugar-cane, they all grew until they had finished growing. The Waraku said to Pərəpərəwa, 'Go, dig it. Go, pull it. Go, look at it. The cassava is getting body.' But Pərəpərəwa would not go, and then Waraku was angry with him. The cassava got bigger and bigger, and finally she went to see it. It was big, and the stocks were high, and she dug it. Then she told Pərəpərəwa about it, and gave him instructions. She told him about a cassava squeezer. 'Weave one of these,' she said, 'and then make a sieve.' For Pərəpərəwa was ignorant and did not know about these things. Then Waraku said, 'Make a cassava griddle to bake the cassava on.' Then she made a cassava plate and baked cassava.[1] Then Pərəpərəwa tried some of it and he vomited. He had been eating the inside of the *waruma* reed and therefore was not accustomed to it. He tried everything. She made some drink, and he tried this. But he had to swallow all the new foods quickly, he was not used to them, he almost vomited so he had to swallow without tasting. But he grew accustomed to eating these things. He stopped eating the inside of the *waruma* reed. That is how it was.

II

Even in this short version, the main theme of the myth is quite clear; Pərəpərəwa was living in a state of nature, without cultivated food, fire, and artifacts. All these things were given to him by the fish/woman, Waraku. The fundamental opposition expressed in the myth is between nature and culture, and nowhere is this more obvious than in the distinction between the two sources of heat. The man uses natural heat (the sun), while the woman owns cultural heat (fire). Culinary aspects aside, this distinction is observably present in the actual technological activities of the two sexes; for example, a woman uses

---

[1] Although not explicitly stated it is possible to assume that Pərəpərəwa made the sieve and the cassava squeezer under instruction, but refused to make the cassava griddle and thus Waraku made it herself. The close association between certain tasks and the sex which carries them out is well demonstrated in the following story. A missionary told the Trio the Old Testament story of Joseph in prison with a butler and a baker. When the Trio retold it the story was about two men and a woman shut up in a house—but whoever heard of a Trio man baking bread?

fire in the manufacture of her pots, but a man puts the raw material of his basketwork out in the sun to dry. For a start I wish to consider some oppositions which can be drawn up under the heading of natural heat and cultural heat.

Natural Heat	*Cultural Heat*
Sun	Fire
Dry season	Wet season
Outside	Inside
Activity	Inactivity
Men	Women
Hard	Soft
Permanent	Ephemeral
Spirits	People

The dry season association with the sun is quite explicit; the Trio word for sun is *wei*, and for dry season *weipo* which literally means 'sun on'. The dry season is the time for movement outside the village, hunting and travelling, while in the wet season the Indians tend to remain in the vicinity of their villages. The dry season is also associated with hard earth and the exposure of rocks in the river beds. Hardness is a quality of men, softness of women. However, there are two different types of hardness and softness; one is a purely physical property which is described by the words *akïpïi*, hard, and *amiye*, soft. When I first arrived among the Trio my hands were very soft and the Indians described them as being like those of a woman. The other type of hard and soft, *karime* and *karina*, carries a more metaphysical meaning, and refers to strength and state of health. The word *karime* has already been discussed in its relation to ceremonial dialogue where the connexion between strength and permanency was indicated. The role of rock as a symbol of hardness and permanency has also been previously mentioned, and its opposition in this sense to wood is highlighted in the following myth.

A Trio went for a walk in the forest and before he went he was warned not to answer if a tree spoke to him but only if a rock spoke to him. In the forest he heard a tree fall and thought it was a rock calling to him, so he answered it; ever since then the Trio have been like trees or wood (same word for both, *wewe*) both in terms of softness and ephemerality. People, i.e., the Trio, die like trees, and in this context are opposed to spirits, *wĭripə*, who are closely associated with rock and who are represented by stones in the shaman's rattle.

However, this scheme is neither rigid nor complete and certain symbols are not invariably found in the same position; this, for example, is the case with the sun, whose symbolic value is not limited to its heat property. This can best be demonstrated by introducing another Trio myth.

The Trio have a culture hero called Aturai who, as a child, was captured by the Okomoyana[1] who planned to eat him. He was given to the Okomoyana women to bring up and fatten, but when he was full grown they allowed him to escape and he returned to his own people. However, he had learnt from the Okomoyana women the advantage of having affines, so when he arrived home he told his people to stop marrying their mothers, sisters, and daughters, but to marry other women. Here is a clear case of nature and culture expressed in the opposition of incest to social order, i.e., rules of marriage and affinity. A further series of oppositions can be constructed under these headings.

Nature	*Culture*
incest	marriage rules
moon	sun
chaos	order
periodic	routine
individual	co-operative
death	birth
sky	water
entuhtao	earth
soul	body
above	below
night	day
black	red

Some of the opposed pairs in this list need further explanation, particularly with reference to their position in the earlier

[1] See Chapter II, p. 20.

list. In the first place the connexion of the moon with incest is clearly stated in the Trio version of a myth which has wide distribution through the New World. The moon is a man who committed incest with his sister, who finds him out by smearing black paint on his face. The man, ashamed, then climbs by a ladder of arrows into the sky, and since then has controlled the time at which women menstruate. The aspect of the moon which symbolizes this is its movement, for the Trio regard the moon as travelling from West to East.[1] The contrast here is with the sun and this is made quite explicit in the longest version of the Pɔrɔpɔrɔwa myth which I heard. In the beginning the sun was stationary at its zenith, and it was only with the introduction of culture that it started to move and day began to alternate with night. The regularity of the sun's movement curiously parallels the routine associated with female economic activities, and in direct contrast with the uncertain behaviour of the moon and its association with female menses, a period at which a woman's economic routine is disrupted. However, one must go further than this since the sun has been shown to have two opposing values, one associated with its heat and the other with its movement. First one must introduce certain basic cosmological ideas of the Trio.

There are three layers in the Trio cosmos; the water (*tuna*) which is the bottom layer and under the earth. The earth (*nono*) which is the middle layer, and the upper layer, the sky (*kapu*). The sky and water meet on the horizon, at the *entuhtao*, which is both the source of water and sky, but also the reservoir of soul matter (*amore*). Birth, of course, occurs through women, but symbolically through water as does all creation; the association is quite clear. As stated in the myth not simply the first woman (a fish) but also culture came from out of the water, and the Trio word 'to be born', *enuru*, is also used to describe fish which flounder the surface when they are poisoned. The opposition of sky to water exists in the opposition of death to birth. While the soul of the new-born arrives through water, the soul of the deceased returns eastward to the *entuhtao* by a path through the sky, the direction in which the moon travels.

---

[1] The Trio indicate the passage of a day by the movement of the arm from east to west across the sky. They indicate the passage of the moon by moving the arm in the opposite direction.

The sun is said to spend each night paddling its canoe through the water under the earth to rise again each morning in the east.[1] Thus, by night, the sun is associated with water and below, the source of creativity, but here once again its heat property comes to the fore, and the presence of both destructive and creative qualities can be recognized. The destructive aspect of the sun in its dry season context is quite clear, and on hot, cloudless days the power of the sun is referred to as *kutuma* (painful) and *atuma* (burning). Further, the symbolic value appears to depend on position; the celestial sun is destructive, the sub-terrestrial creative. But still we have not reached a complete answer, which is more easily discernible in the symbolic values of water.

The Trio distinguish two types of water; terrestrial water (*tuna*, water or river) and celestial water (*kono*, rain). It has already been indicated that terrestrial water (or more correctly sub-terrestrial water) has creative qualities. Celestial water has destructive qualities, and rain usually falls in violent storms accompanied by high winds, which are feared because they are thought to contain the souls of the departed (*amorempə*).[2] However, in practice, the intensity of these phenomena is the important thing; the Trio appreciate the value of light rain and the destructive nature of floods. The controlling principles are excess and moderation; the sun becomes destructive when its heat is too intense and here one can make a connexion between intensity and movement. At no time can the sun have been hotter than in the time before culture when it remained stationary at the zenith; a condition most closely approximated to by the dry season, the time when water, the creative essence, is at its lowest ebb. On the other hand, a flood, an excess of the creative essence, is equally threatening.

This same distinction between excess and moderation can be seen to operate in a number of other spheres. Black (*sikime*) is associated with incest, sexual intercourse (in its destructive, aggressive, asocial aspect), rocks, spirits, and the application of

[1] As evidence of this an Indian pointed out that the water in a river is warmer in the morning than the evening, which, for large rivers, is true as far as the relative temperatures of air and water are concerned.

[2] The thing about which the Trio show great anxiety when caught in a storm out in the forest is falling trees. Maripapa (452) was killed in this way.

black paint is multiform and intricate. The verb to apply black paint is *imenuhtɔ*, and the jaguar, the most obvious symbol of the forest world, is frequently referred to as *tĭmenuren*, the painted one. Red (*tamire*) is associated with protection against spirits, women (Waraku, the first woman was painted red), fertility, and its application is uniform and without design except on the face. The word to apply red paint is *imuka* which contains the same root (*mu*) as *imuku*, child, *imuhte*, to be pregnant, and *munu*, blood. The Trio do not regard blood in its normal manifestation as being in any way harmful, and the dangerous condition of the menstruating woman results from an excess of blood and fertility.[1]

One comes back to the same thing starting from another angle. The earth (*nono*) stands in opposition to the *entuhtao* as the place of the body (*pun*) in opposition to the place of the spirit (*amore*). This can be seen at death when the body and soul finally separate, the former being placed in the earth while the latter returns to the *entuhtao*. Furthermore the corpse is placed beneath the floor of the house while the spirit goes to the most distant part of the Trio cosmos. As well as this, the earth is also the place of life, i.e., people, which is between birth and death, water and sky; it is also soft and hard according to season, and thus between wood and rock, the symbols of ephemerality and permanency.

The need now is to explain the connexion between permanency and death. The explanation lies in the distinction between excess and moderation; once something endures too long it threatens the whole order of things, and indeed to turn order back into chaos. Thus, in the beginning, order was created when the sun began to move, but this is even better portrayed in the Trio myth of the long night. The Indians sitting waiting for the return of the sun are turned into stones (Frikel, 1961, b, p. 2). Confusion arises from the failure of things to follow in due order; in one context birth is opposed to death,

---

[1] White (*tĭkoroyen*) seems to lack such marked symbolic value (perhaps my ethnography is at fault) but tends to appear in the betwixt-and-between states. Sick people and girls following their puberty seclusion are empirically white, and as pointed out to me by a Trio white separates black and red in basketwork and beadwork designs. It is interesting that whiteness can result naturally (from seclusion), blackness also naturally (from exposure to the sun), but redness only culturally (by human application).

in another eternal existence is opposed to birth and death, the ephemerality of man. With both fire and water, the destructive element is associated with excess, but they are both creative when they occur in moderation, in their due order, and within their own boundaries. But just as birth and death combine as a symbol of proper existence, so do fire and water. The traditional treatment of the sick (those between life and death) consists of warming the patient by building fires as close as possible to his hammock and then washing him with cold water (or alternatively just washing him with warm water). There is a striking similarity in procedure between this and the Trio method of cracking rock, which is done by heating it with fire and pouring cold water over the hot rock.[1]

One could go on but there seems little point in extending this demonstration; many Trio symbols have no rigid values but obtain their meaning from an interplay of factors which include their position, their inherent characteristic, and the particular incidence of the phenomenon. This fluidity of meaning does not surround all Trio symbols, and there are certain pairs of oppositions in which the values are more stable, their polarity more sharply defined. These polar oppositions seem mainly to appear at the level of action rather than at the level of thought, although, of necessity, there is considerable overlap between the two levels. The important difference is that, at the level of thought, the solution to an opposition is available by adjusting the context and the associated values. This solution does not offer itself at the level of action, since empirical situations, assumed or real, cannot always be resolved by intellectual processes.

In these cases the resolution of the conflict is often achieved by the introduction of a third value, a mediator. This point has cropped up several times in the course of this monograph and this seems to be because these polar oppositions mainly occur at the socio-economic level. Listed below under the rubrics of nature and culture are some of the oppositions noted in earlier chapters.

[1] I have the idea that it is not ultimately important whether the treatment cures or kills, but what is essential is that the invalid be relieved from his state of uncertainty—an anxiety-provoking condition. It seems possible to me that in cases of serious illness this may also be true of my own culture.

Nature	*Culture*
men	women
male activities	female activities
outside	inside
unknown	known
forest	village
anna	house

Now the mediators between these oppositions seem to operate in one of two ways; either they act as a means of communication between the polar terms, or else they tend to strengthen one to the detriment of the other. An obvious example of the former is the shaman, whose mediating role is almost universal, and the Trio shaman is no exception to this. He stands between people and spirits, he is of the earth but can visit the other cosmic levels, he is both curer and killer, depending on whether he is inside or outside. Təmeta (482) succinctly summed up the shaman's position when he said that a shaman is like a menstruating woman, an apt simile which stresses the state of betwixt-and-between in which they both exist; the one suffering from an excess of power and the other from an excess of fertility. In a less well defined way the village leader also stands between inside and outside but, if anything, his duty is to strengthen the inside which he owns and symbolizes. It should be remembered that ceremonial dialogue is one of the few institutionalized mediating devices which the Trio have.

At the subsistence level the distinction between male and female is very obvious when considered in terms of oppositions between nature and culture, destruction and creation, outside and inside, and casual and routine. The converging of these activities occurs in collecting and planting, both of which are connected with the dance festival, itself the major attempt to resolve such diversities and create a united world. For this the *kuriya* seems a perfect symbol since it is game but collected, it embodies the qualities of hard and soft, and as nature it endures for a long time in culture without any processing required. Finally, it is appropriate that, when the distinctions of the empirical world reassert themselves, they should perish at the hands of men and be cooked in the pots of women.

The husband/wife relationship was described as mediating

between the male/female relationship, and, specifically, between the relationships brother/sister and *emerimpə*. While the
Trio appreciate the destructive quality of the sexual drive, in
the husband/wife relationship they seem to recognize the
necessity for its expression. The relationship between *emerimpə*
is casual, and potentially socially disruptive; the relationship
between brother and sister is stable and harmonious. The
relationship between spouses attempts to conjoin these two
aspects, but the spouses also serve as an articulating device in
a more practical context, as a means of communication between affinally related groups. This brings us to the distinction
between inside and outside as expressed by related and unrelated affines. The conflict here is between the need to find a
wife and the unwillingness to leave home; it is a question of
how to keep and eat one's cake. The solution to this difficulty
has been found in marriage with the sister's daughter; an
institution which, perhaps more than any other, allows the
Trio to keep the outside where they think it belongs.

III

Before turning to certain comparative and theoretical points
which arise from this study, a brief summary will be made in
order to synthesize the salient features which have been
described.

The important relevant elements in Trio culture are the
reliance on the resources of the immediate environment, an
economic system and division of labour which maintain a
male/female interdependence, and relative isolation of communities, which is internally maintained by bonds of blood and
marriage and externally by an attitude of hostility and fear
which is supported by beliefs concerning the causation of
sickness and death.

Against the background of these features the other aspects
form a logical pattern. Concepts of property are poorly developed with regard to traditional objects since these are
available from the boundless resources of the environment.
However, this is not true in the case of women, who more than
any other resource are vital not only for the survival of the
individual but for the existence of the society at any level. At a
social level, the conservation of human resources is favoured by

the preference for village endogamy, the enforcement of matrilocality by use of ceremonial dialogue, and discouragement of the outsider by a demand for bride-price and the intense application of avoidance.

A Trio man finds his female partner in the form of a sister, and although this partnership may be quiescent while the partners are married, it never totally fades. An unmarried man's dependence upon his sister means that in the event of her marriage his loss must be made good by another woman. Trio marriage is the exchange of women, and the transfer of this fundamental property brings in its wake an unending series of prestations and counter-prestations.

A man who marries within his own community experiences none of the unpleasantness which befalls the stranger. The attitudes and behaviour extended towards his affines are no more than a confirmation of those which are applicable to them in the role of kin. Thus marriage strengthens the ties which already exist within the community.

It can be seen how simply the conclusions reached from the formal analysis of the relationship terminology fit into this scheme. The removal to proximate genealogical levels of potential affines means that the conventional restraint which exists between two levels parallels that between two male affines, so that the role of kin can become merged with that of affine without involving any disruption of previous status. This is more obvious in the case of female affines and especially the sister who, in one-third of the Trio marriages, can be expected to be the wife's mother.

If looked at from the view of a young unmarried man his total social sphere will consist of kin; it is only in his or his sister's marriage that the actuality of affinity is realized. Thus a man belongs equally to both sides of the family and only in marriage does the potential dichotomy of his social world receive recognition.

The pattern of behaviour within the circle of kin and acquaintances contrasts vividly with that among strangers. As, away from the community, these ties weaken, so the attitude of suspicion and hostility increases. The informality which is possible because the ordering of behaviour is intrinsic in the relationships is replaced by formal institutions; avoidance in the event of new alliances, ceremonial dialogue in the case of new contacts.

The picture of Trio society as consisting of a series of introverted and isolated village communities becomes overwhelming. In general terms, this is the correct one, and although it has been shown that, for a number of reasons, the single village is not a social and economic independent unit, this does not contradict the basic truth of this premiss. The counterbalance to isolation and hostility is the tradition of hospitality, trade, and the more periodic admission of interdependence that is revealed in the dance festival. However, from this one must not be left with the impression that the Trio spend their lives cowering in fear, although this emotion never seems to be far beneath the surface, and it is certainly an attitude which reveals itself at all levels of thought.

Finally, there is the question of how such a society developed. One cannot be certain, but a conjecture which seems to fit is that the watershed region became a retreat area where the remnants of a number of different groups settled, some of whom had possibly suffered already from European contact. Whether or not there was an earlier or indigenous population is not important, but the population density was almost certainly higher than it is now. Mainly as a result of exotic sickness and disease, this population became gradually depleted. The survivors, their attitude to strangers tempered by their unfortunate experiences with them, turned in upon themselves to find security among their kin and co-residents. They had at hand the very institution which would allow the development of this introversion, marriage with the sister's daughter.

19

XIII

COMPARATIVE AND THEORETICAL ASPECTS

IN THIS final chapter I wish to consider certain theoretical points which arise from this study of the Trio, in particular from marriage with the sister's daughter. The literature on this subject is neither intensive nor extensive; it is a trait, which in institutionalized form, is more or less confined to South America and South India.[1] The ethnographers who have reported this type of union have usually been content merely to record its presence; on the other hand some of the social anthropologists who have offered theories to account for sister's daughter marriage have had no first-hand experience of societies who practise it. This does not necessarily invalidate their ideas, and it may even be an advantage, but what I intend to do here is to review these theories in the light of knowledge gained among the Trio.

I

One of the earlier theorists on this subject was Kirchhoff, who saw this type of marriage either as a means to eliminate bride-service, or as a method of providing for a widowed sister (1932, p. 58). Gillin in his analysis of the Barama River Caribs was very much under the influence of Kirchhoff and interpreted avuncular marriage among this group as a means of removing bride-service (1936, p. 96), although he overlooked the fact that with matrilocal residence it is likely that Kirchhoff's second reason is equally applicable. We have already seen with reference to the Trio that marriage with the sister's daughter may eliminate bride-service *per se* but at the same time it reaffirms existing obligations to the sister, now the wife's mother, whether she be a widow or not. Finally the existence of true bride-service among the Trio was questioned, since the

[1] Uncle-niece marriage also exists sporadically in uninstitutionalized form. For example, among Brazilian plantation owners with an aim of keeping the property intact (cf. Freyre, 1963, p. 356).

duties among affines are basically symmetrical, and although a Trio gains certain advantages from marrying his sister's daughter, the removal of all affinal duties is not one of them.

Kirchhoff has been criticized by Lévi-Strauss for the suggestion that avuncular marriage is an archaic form (1949, p. 156), and his attempt to explain unilateral cross-cousin marriage as a consequence of avuncular privilege (1949, p. 539). Certainly, as Lévi-Strauss states, the presence in the relationship terminology of a pattern reflecting marriage with the sister's daughter cannot be taken as evidence of ancient usage, and indeed the very reverse of this has just been suggested for the Trio, that the terminological adaptation to sister's daughter marriage is relatively recent. Lévi-Strauss's more positive suggestion is that the widely spread South American system (not as widely spread as he claims) whereby the grandparents, parents-in-law, and cross-aunts and cross-uncles are equated is a solution for resolving the terminological conflict resulting from oblique marriages and at the same time maintaining intact the four divisions of ego's own genealogical level (1949, p. 155).[1] This conclusion seems to have been reached from his work among the Nambikwara, and although, for a number of reasons outlined below, oblique marriages in that group are not directly comparable with those among the Trio, it is useful to comment on some of the differences.

Firstly, the oblique marriages among the Nambikwara are secondary and privileged unions and the role of these wives is different from that of the first wife (1948, pp. 54–62). Oblique marriages among the Trio are neither secondary nor privileged, but primary and fundamental. This partly contradicts Lévi-Strauss's claim that avuncular marriages are privileged unions because they have been grafted on to some other form (1949, p. 154); while this may have once been true of the Trio it is no longer so.

Secondly, the relationship terminology employed by the Trio does exactly the opposite to what Lévi-Strauss expects; it does not remove terminological confusions resulting from

[1] Lévi-Strauss's view that for some reason (none provided) the Nambikwara terminology is adapted to the feminine perspective has been criticized by Dr. Lave (1966, pp. 193–4), who has shown that this is not 'a curious emphasis on feminine perspective', but 'the most fitting solution to the terminological problem'.

oblique marriages to a different genealogical level from ego, but centres the confusions on ego's level. The result of this is that ego's genealogical level consists of only two categories, and not the four which Lévi-Strauss feels must exist alongside the reciprocal relations which bind potential spouses, brothers-in-law, and sisters-in-law (1949, p. 155). These differences may be logically associated with other differences in social organization, and Lévi-Strauss allows himself a let out clause in saying that, according to circumstances, different groups will accept one solution rather than another.

Lévi-Strauss has stressed the importance of the brother-in-law status in South America (1943, b), but it is in this factor that the main difference between the organization of the Trio and Nambikwara systems seems to lie. A Trio man and his brother-in-law, either his sister's husband or wife's brother, belong to different genealogical levels, between which there is a conventional attitude of restraint. Where this restraint is not intrinsic in the relationship it is replaced by affinal avoidance. This contrasts vividly with the behaviour between Nambikwara affines; a man shows no particular reserve towards his wife's parents and the behaviour between brothers-in-law is marked by familiarity which includes homosexual play (1948, pp. 75–76). Accepting that in each case behavioural differences are repeated in terminological differences, is it possible to state why affinity in one case is marked by avoidance and in the other by intimacy?

This, I believe, has to do with the actual exchange of women. Affinity among the Trio is only realized by the actual event of marriage, but do the Nambikwara brothers-in-law actually exchange women? Although Lévi-Strauss does not say it, he hints that they do not, by saying that the Nambikwara make direct exchanges of sexual services as compared with Tupian brothers-in-law who exchange their sisters (1943, b, p. 407). Certainly the attitude between Tupian brothers-in-law is one of reserve, even hostility, and the very term for such a relationship is synonymous with the word for an enemy (Huxley, 1963, p. 242). This usage closely parallels that associated with the Trio *pito*, a reciprocal term which has the underlying meaning of brother-in-law and denotes equal status. Just as the term *pito* has no place in the Trio kinship group, so presumably the

Tupian 'enemy/brother-in-law' is absent in the case of avuncular marriage. This has more meaning than the suggestion that such a union eliminates bride-service since this is exchange without tears—marriage and trade without war. Seen in this way the Tupian system is not basically different from that described for the Trio.

To finish with the bride-service interpretation of sister's daughter marriage one must refer to its inadequacy in universal application. This is simply done by considering sister's daughter marriage in relation to rules of post-marital residence. In South America temporary matrilocal residence even in societies with a patrilocal rule is not unusual. This is not the case in India, where marriage with the sister's daughter is associated with patrilineal and patrilocal groups,[1] and in such a situation it is obviously difficult for bride-service to be implemented.

The question of post-marital residence brings to the fore another important result of marriage with the sister's daughter. In a society which practises patrilocal residence, a man loses his sister when she marries and moves to her husband's home. His sister's daughter, however, returns as his son's wife, but should he marry her instead, it causes no disruption in the system of post-marital residence. In a society which practises matrilocal residence, a male ego leaves his sister to live in his wife's home. However, if he marries his sister's daughter, the pattern is changed and he remains in his natal community. Thus a practice of matrilocal residence is ideally suited for the development, by marriage with the sister's daughter, of village endogamy and the formation of a residential core consisting of brothers and sisters. The point has also been made that marriage with the sister's daughter confirms, even duplicates, a pre-existing set of ties and obligations between brother and sister.

The interpretation of cross-cousin or sister's daughter marriage as a means of reaffirming kin ties, which was made by Gough (1956), McCormack (1958), and Tambiah (1958), has

---

[1] Aiyappan (1934) saw the explanation of sister's daughter marriage in the extreme form of patrilineal organization, because in South India it is only such people who practise this form of marriage while it is looked upon with horror by the matrilineal groups. This is obviously not an explanation but a related fact. Sister's daughter marriage in a matrilineal society would involve marrying someone related by descent.

been criticized by Dumont (1961), who prefers to regard it as inherited affinity. Recently Yalman has written 'What Dumont calls "affinity" I would translate as rights and obligations between brothers and sisters.' (1967, p. 358), and also, in discussing marriage with the sister's daughter, 'A description of the claims between brothers and sisters explains what appears to be a curious phenomenon much more adequately than Dumont's recourse to the "inheritance" of affinity.' (ibid., p. 359). The Trio stress the importance of the brother/sister relationship and its influence infiltrates into every aspect of Trio life. For a man his sister represents the inside, and the dyadic relationship symbolizes harmony and security; marriage with the sister's daughter not merely reaffirms the relationship but adds the single missing component, the sexual aspect. My own position, therefore, which rests on the Trio material, is closer to that of Yalman than that of Dumont and little advantage can be gained, in understanding Trio society, by separating out inherited affinity from consanguinity.

Dumont has also written that 'it appears logically impossible to couple, in a classificatory system, difference of status and uncle–niece marriage' (1961, p. 90). The Trio system does offer some clue as to how these three features could occur together, although not, it must be admitted, in the normal way of vertical groups of wife-givers and wife-takers with a permanent status distinction between them. These status distinctions are horizontal divisions of the society based primarily on category, i.e., genealogical level, although in any particular case and as far as behaviour is concerned it may be overriden by relative age. This is not immediately obvious in the Trio system because both in thought and action direct exchange is present. Where, however, all marriages occur into the category of sister's daughter, the status distinction between proximate levels is more apparent because each genealogical level is wife-taker *vis-à-vis* the senior level, and wife-giver *vis-à-vis* the junior level. Thus ego is in turn inferior and superior, respects and is respected.

That relative age is likely to play a part in the ordering of a society which practises marriage with the sister's daughter seems to be generally accepted, and the use to which the Trio put this factor has been explained. Mrs. Karvé has probably taken this idea further than anyone else in suggesting that a whole society can be divided into two groups, those older than ego, and those younger than ego. Marriage then takes place with a woman younger than ego who is the daughter of a woman who is older than ego (1953, pp. 223–9).[1] However, if status distinction is to be aligned with genealogical level which may or may not coincide with generation, it is obvious that such a system could only work in small-scale societies. The difficulties which would face a society trying to order itself in this way have been referred to by Needham (1958) in his formal analysis of patrilateral cross-cousin marriage. Lévi-Strauss has pointed to the similarity between patrilateral cross-cousin marriage and avuncular marriage as both being systems in which cycles of reciprocity are closed without forming more than small, local, and discrete structures (1949, p. 557).[2] I consider there to be a further similarity between these two types of alliance; this is the characteristic of discontinuity, and it has led me to propose the formal possibility of a type of prescriptive alliance which I have called Oblique Discontinuous Exchange (1966, b).

The simplest approach to this subject is through a consideration of the equations FZD = M, and MBD = ZD. Leach appears to have been the first person to have recognized the fact that the mother's brother's child and the sister's child will be the same person if an offspring of a sister's daughter marriage (1951, p. 26, n. 7). That, at the same time, the mother and the father's sister's daughter will be the same person, if realized, was not commented upon. Mrs. Karvé in her review of kinship organization in India mentions that when marriage with the sister's daughter occurs over a number of generations the father's sister's daughter becomes merged with the category of mother, and even gives some examples of this occurrence. She notes that when this happens consensus of opinion is against marriage

---

[1] For a criticism of this idea and the evidence on which it is based, see Dumont and Pocock, 1957.

[2] Lévi-Strauss has also used a financial simile in comparing these unions with matrilateral cross-cousin marriage; he describes the latter as a credit system, and the former as cash payment (1949, p. 558). In describing the Trio it would be possible to take this simile even further and say that because of the close tie between brother and sister, the latter's marriage is little more than a tenancy since the brother never relinquishes his right to the goods which he has provided.

with the patrilateral cross-cousin (1953, p. 194). McCormack (1958) does not refer to the existence of either of these equations although they are well displayed in his diagram (p. 40, Fig. 1), and has been criticized on this score by Dumont (1961, p. 94, n. 24) and more especially since McCormack includes Leach's relevant paper (1951) in his bibliography.

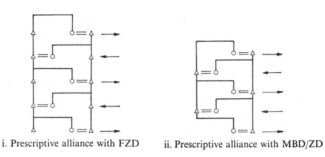

i. Prescriptive alliance with FZD   ii. Prescriptive alliance with MBD/ZD

Figure 14: A diagrammatic comparison of a system of patrilateral cross-cousin marriage with a system of MBD/ZD marriage.

The most recent and detailed examination of marriage with the sister's daughter is by Dr. Lave who notes both FZD = M and MBD = ZD and considers that 'Without ZD marriage, it seems unlikely that one would find these equations in the relationship terminology' (1966, p. 197). Dr. Lave's paper is a formal analysis of marriage with the sister's daughter and from it she draws eight propositions. I have elsewhere commented upon these (1966, c), and the evidence for what I wrote there can be found in the pages of this work. On the majority of points I agree with Dr. Lave, but not in her final definition of the system as one of direct exchange, in which she is supported by Leach (1951, p. 26, n. 7).

My case centres on the discontinuous aspect of marriage with the sister's daughter when it has reached its final development. In such a system not only will the equations FZD = M and MBD = ZD be present, but marriage will be prohibited with the category FZD/M and prescribed with the category MBD/ZD. It is undeniable that a direct exchange element is retained, but typologically it is closer to patrilateral cross-cousin marriage. Their similarity lies in the discontinuous aspect of both systems, that is to say the flow of women is reversed in alternate generations. This can be readily seen in Figure 14 where the direction in which women move is indicated by the arrows. Such a system certainly contains all the attributes which Lévi-Strauss has used to describe patrilateral cross-cousin marriage, and like that type of alliance it seems highly unlikely that a large ongoing system of this type will be found to exist. That it can work on a smaller scale is evinced by Mrs. Karvé's observations in India and my own among the Trio, where small family groups fit the necessary requirements.

II

One of the conclusions reached in this study is that for the Trio the distinction between inside and outside has practical value in the ordering of their cosmos, both social and natural. Certain Trio attitudes and practices enforce the existence of this dichotomy, while others are concerned to resolve its indisputable existence. Marriage with the sister's daughter has been interpreted as one of the latter. This explanation of this type of marriage is particular, but it does seem to contain the seed of a potentially universal explanation of such unions. I do not pretend that the following discussion is in any sense conclusive but I believe that its path leads in the right direction.

If the starting point for the argument is that sister's daughter marriage is a highly refined form of endogamy which operates to maintain the exclusiveness of a community (i.e., the Trio case), then the first stumbling block appears to be the patrilocal society. This difficulty can be readily surmounted by changing 'community' to some form of 'kinship grouping', as will be seen below, but with reference to rule of residence there is one further point which is worth taking up first.

Among the Trio the pressure on the community is external, but in India, and this is admittedly a generalization, internal competition is a feature of patrilineal/patrilocal groups, and assistance is sought outside, particularly from affines. This need not be associated with any form of cross-cousin marriage, but it frequently is. In this context one can refer to Alan Beals's writing about Gopalpur, a village near Gulbarga in central South India. The inhabitants of this village practise marriage with both cross-cousins and the sister's daughter (1962, p. 27), but 'the major securities and satisfactions of life are to be found in the acquisition of a large number of friends and supporters' (1962, p. 22), and it is through marriage that the individual forms ties in other villages, and these relationships are different to those which a man has with his patrikin, among whom he lives and with whom he is in direct competition, both in acquiring wealth and in finding a suitable spouse (p. 32). Unfortunately Beals nowhere makes clear 'the advantages of marrying a sister's daughter' (p. 31), but possibly it is a way of reaffirming the ties with the sister's husband. Here, perhaps, one can distinguish between the ambitious and the non-ambitious, the former creating new alliances with each marriage, and the latter confirming the existing ones. However, this is simply the reason why a particular preference is exercised, and not an explanation of it.

One of the few authors who have dealt with sister's daughter marriage is McCormack, who studied this type of union in Mysore. He noted that a far higher proportion of the non-cultivator castes marry actual or claimed cognatic relatives than do people of the cultivator caste, and goes on to explain it thus:

Chance, therefore, does not account for the higher frequency of matings between non-relatives among the hereditary cultivators. The frequency differences are explained by the fact that the cultivator caste comprises a relatively large, locally-situated group of potential spouses and its members are therefore freer to contract marriages with unrelated families. Hereditary cultivators may marry within their own village, whereas the local populations of the non-cultivator castes are nearly always exogamous due to their small size. The non-cultivators, who are faced with these great difficulties in marital match-making, find their spouses in the families of close relatives, and often even these related families must be found at considerable distances from home (1958, pp. 36–37).

McCormack's reason for these marriages is interesting and can be compared with the situation among the Trio. In one case the class of potential spouses is limited by socio-economic factors, and in the other by a physical isolation which perhaps creates and is certainly reinforced by a conceptual opposition between inside and outside. However, this is not a satisfactory answer since, in order to account for marriage with the sister's daughter rather than cross-cousin marriage, at least in the patrilineal/patrilocal case, a further assumption needs to be made. This is that the shortage of women is so acute that it is necessary in order to obtain a wife to take a woman from the next generation, or as Lévi-Strauss says, make '*une spéculation sur un avenir encore irréel*' (1949, p. 558). This may well have been a problem which faced the Trio, and Yde has attributed to the lack of women both polyandry and an unusual division of labour among the Waiwai (1965, pp. 18–19 and p. 305). Is this—the shortage of human resources which may be actual or assumed—the common element which characterizes all systems of marriage with the sister's daughter? If it is, then the fact is likely to be hidden beneath a mass of cultural accretions, but in itself it is not a cultural solution, because it involves the basic elements of all societies and thus possesses potential universal application. However, it is quite obvious that it is not a universal solution to human shortage otherwise marriage with the sister's daughter would have been far more widely reported. Thus it is necessary to qualify the type of society in which marriage with the sister's daughter is likely to appear. In the first place, this type of union is not likely to be found in a society which contains any one of the following features: asymmetric alliance or no prescriptive rule, matrilineal descent, and a prohibition on marriage between genealogical levels. Features which one would expect to find present are an ideology of direct exchange, patrilineal descent or the absence of any firm rule of unilineal descent, and the informal ordering of the society along lines of kinship (consanguinity and affinity). This, it is understood, is still unsatisfactory for there are undoubtedly many societies with these qualifications which do not practise sister's daughter marriage (the Wikmunkan could be quoted as just such an example).

I can suggest one other factor which may account for the presence or absence of this type of union in a society otherwise 'qualified' to practise it. This is a matter of how any particular society conceptualizes and perhaps symbolizes its own boundaries. One should note that in McCormack's case the lack of spouses among the non-cultivators is not a simple demographic problem, but one of ideas about purity and pollution. In the higher castes purity becomes an ideal in its own right, and since both caste and its attendant purity are transmitted through

women, marriage with the sister's daughter is a ready method of
guaranteeing the requisite purity.[1] But it is clear that if the
maintenance of purity rests with women, then it is women (and
not purity, merely an associated abstract notion) which in fact
are being safeguarded. Among the Trio this is more obvious,
since the institutions concerned with the preservation of human
resources have received no symbolic overlay; they are consciously concerned with people, not with purity.

This is not offered as a conclusive answer, and could hardly
pose as such, since no examination has been made of the reverse
side of the coin—those societies in which marriage with the
sister's daughter has not developed or is expressly prohibited.
My claim, however, is that we must turn to society's own view
of itself and the principles by which it orders and organizes
itself in order to explain the presence or absence of certain
social practices, such as marriage with the sister's daughter. I
will go further than this and hazard the guess that the presence
of this marriage form will be directly related to the society's
belief that not simply its boundaries but its existence is in
jeopardy, whether the threat be from extermination or pollution.

III

Without further summary the reader should now be in a
position to judge for himself just how far the aims avowed in
the Introduction have been achieved. The main purpose of this
work has been to provide a sociological analysis of marriage
with the sister's daughter, and this institution has been examined exhaustively from every angle. The second aim was to
try to show that social institutions say something about the
society in which they occur; thus a particular marriage rule is
not merely an indication that such unions take place (although,
of course, it does say this), but that it is also the empirical
expression of much wider values. If this is not so, then this
essay has been in vain, but if this is right then it is safe to
assume that any single social feature will not be a lone voice

[1] Writing about the preservation of purity among the Tanjore Brahman,
Yalman has described sister's daughter marriage as the nearest equivalent
to marriage with the sister (1967, p. 351). Certainly for the Trio marriage
with the sister's daughter is the next best thing to marriage with the sister.

but will, at least partly, be saying the same thing as the other
institutions of that society. I have tried to demonstrate this with
reference to the practice of marriage with the sister's daughter
among the Trio, and it has been shown quite clearly that this
form of marriage is not an isolated, haphazardly contrived
institution but one which fits perfectly within a whole range of
Trio attitudes to and ideas about the world in which they live.

An objection frequently levelled at this type of interpretation
is that these schemes are not valid because they are merely
structures based on the observer's analysis and the people
themselves are unaware of them. Indeed, Dr. Lloyd, in a recent
work on opposition and similarity in early Greek thought, has
sought comparative material in anthropological writings,[1] but
has found it difficult to determine from these accounts 'the
extent to which present-day primitive peoples themselves
consciously formulate the system that underlies their dualist
beliefs . . .' (1966, p. 63). While this may be true of the examples quoted, the pre-Socratic philosophers who constructed
Tables of Opposites and were consciously aware of the principles of their argument have their equivalent in African
philosophers, who have produced complex and intricate cosmic
theories. That Dr. Lloyd has shown the use of polarity and
analogy as a means of understanding and explanation to
occur consciously among some members of a society provides
the strongest possible evidence of its unconscious existence at
all levels. Indeed most members of any society are unconcerned
with and unaware of the principles (and their associated values
and symbols) by which they order, solve, and explain the
business and problems of life. It is the duty of the social anthropologist to identify and to reveal these underlying principles.

[1] It is encouraging that a truly scholarly discipline such as Dr. Lloyd's
should find such help in social anthropology as this remark indicates. 'The
work done by Hertz and other anthropologists on one type of dualist
notion in primitive thought opens up the way for an interpretation not
only of certain ancient Greek beliefs and practices in general, but also of
some of the speculative theories of the philosophers in particular.' (1966,
p. 41.)

APPENDIX A

TRIO RELATIONSHIP TERMS

Terms of reference for a male ego

1. *tamu, tamusimpə:* FF, MF, FFB, MFB, FMB, MMB, WF, MZH.
2. *nosi, nosimpə:* MM, FM, MMZ, FMZ, MFZ, FFZ, FZ, FFBD, FMZD, MFZD, MMBD, WM, MBW.
3. *kuku:* MM, FM, MMZ, FMZ, MFZ, FFZ, FZ, FFBD, FMZD, MFZD, MMBD, WM, MBW.
4. *ipapa:* F, FB, FFBS, FMZS, MFZS, MMBS, MH, MZH, WMB.
5. *imama:* M, MZ, FFZD, FMBD, MFBD, MMZD, FZD, FW, FBW, WFZ.
6. *tĭ:* MB, FFZS, FMBS, MFBS, MMZS, FZS, FZH, ZH, WF, WFB.
7. *ipipi:* eB, FBSe, MZSe, WZHe, MH.
8. *wəi:* eZ, FBDe, MZDe, MBW.
9. *akəmi:* yB, yZ, FBSy, MZSy, FBDy, MZDy, SW.
10. *kĭrĭ:* yB, FBSy, MZSy (literally 'a man').
11. *wəri:* yZ, FBDy, MZDy (literally 'a woman').
12. *pito:* FZS, MBS, ZS, ZH, DH, WB.
13. *emerimpə:* FZD, MBD, ZD, BW, WZ ('potential wife').
14. *ipĭ:* W.
15. *imuku:* S, BS, ZS, MBS, FBSS, FZDS, MBDS, FZSS, FBDS, MBSS, MZDS, DH, ZH.
16. *emi:* D, BD, ZD, MBD, FBSD, MZSD, FZDD, MBDD, FZSD, MBSD, FBDD, MZDD, SW, BW.
17. *ipa:* SS, SD, DS, DD, BSS, BSD, BDS, BDD, ZSS, ZSD, ZDS, ZDD.
18. *yau:* WF.
19. *yaupĭ:* WM.
20. *konoka:* WB, ZH, FZH, MZH, MH.
21. *ipaeye:* SW, BSW, ZSW, MBW.
22. *ipamĭ:* DH, BDH, ZDH.
23. *emu:* baby boy (literally means 'testicle').
24. *epa:* baby girl (literally means 'vagina').
25. *musere:* young boy (sometimes retained as a name, e.g., (488) and (535)).

26. *papoti*:   young girl (sometimes retained as a name, e.g., (651)).

27. *kǐrǐmuku*:   young man, a youth.

28. *wərimuku*:   young woman (sometimes retained as a name, e.g., (216)).

29. *tamutupə*:   old man.

30. *notipə*:   old woman.

31. *yumme*:   old man or woman (literally means being 'ripe').

Terms of reference for female ego (where they differ from those used by male ego)

1. *tamu, tamusimpə*: HF, and all other relations as for male ego except for WF.

2. *nosi, nosimpə*: HM, and all other relations as for male ego except WM.

3. *kuku*: HM, and all other relations as for male ego except WM.

6. *tĭ*: HF, and all other relations as for male ego except WF.

12. *kori, koko*: FZD, MBD, BW, HZ.

13. *emerimpə*: FZS, MBS, MB ('potential husband').

14. *inyo*: H.

15. *imuku*: S, ZS, FBDS, MZDS, MBSS, FZSS, ZH, MBS.

16. *emi*: D, ZD, FBDD, MZDD, MBSD, FZSD, BW, MBD.

17. *ipa*: BS, BD, FBSS, MZSS, FBSD, MZSD, SS, SD, DS, DD, BSS, BSD, BDS, BDD, ZSS, ZSD, ZDS, ZDD.

18. *yau*: HF.

19. *yaupǐ*: HM.

20. As 12 above: BW, HZ.

21. *ipaeye*: BW, HZ, SW, BSW, ZSW, MBW.

There are fewer direct address terms than terms of reference, but the differences which occur are important.

Direct Address terms used by a male ego (a female ego's usage where different in brackets)

1. *tamu*: FF, MF, FFB, FMB, MMB, WF(HF), MZH.

2. *nosi*: MM, FM, MMZ, FMZ, MFZ, FFZ, FZ, FFBD, FMZD, MFZD, MMBD, WM(HM), MBW.

286 APPENDIX A

3. *kuku:*	MM, FM, MMZ, FMZ, MFZ, FFZ, FZ, FFBD, FMZD, MFZD, MMBD, WM(HM), MBW.
4. *pa, pahko:*	F, FB, FFBS, FMZS, MFZS, MMBS, MH, MZH, WMB.
5. *ma, manhko:*	M, MZ, FFZD, FMBD, MFBD, MMZD, FW, FBW, WFZ, BW, FZD.
6. *yetĭ:*	MB, FFZS, FMBS, MFBS, MMZS, FZH, ZH, WF(HF), FZS.
7. *pi, pihko:*	eB, FBSe, MZSe, WZHe, MH.
8. *wəi, wəihko:*	eZ, FBDe, MZDe, MBW.
9. *kami:*	yB, yZ, FBSy, MZSy, FBDy, MZDy, SW.
10. *yikĭrĭ:*	yB, FBSy, MZSy.
11. *yiwəri:*	yZ, FBDy, MZDy.
12. *pito:*	FZS, MBS, ZS, ZH, DH, WB (*kori, koko:* FZD, MBD, BW, HZ, but rarely used in direct address).
13. *yemerimpə:*	No direct address form.
14. *mi, mihko:*	Reciprocal term between spouses. Older married couples may address each other as *ai* or *aimpə.*
15. *yimuku:*	S, BS, ZS, FBSS, MZSS, FZDS, MBDS, FZSS, FBDS, MBSS, MZDS, MBS, DH, ZH (for female ego not BS, FBSS, MZSS).
16. *yemi:*	D, BD, ZD, MBD, FBSD, MZSD, FZDD, MBDD, FZSD, MBSD, FBDD, MZDD, SW, BW (for female ego not BD, FBSD, MZSD).
17. *yipa:*	SS, SD, DS, DD, BSS, BSD, BDS, BDD, ZSS, ZSD, ZDS, ZDD (BS, BD, FBSS, FBSD, MZSS, MZSD as well for female ego).

18. *yau;* 19. *yaupĭ;* 20. *konoka;* 21. *ipaeye;* and 22. *ipamĭ* have no direct address form.

23. *yemu;* 24. *yepa;* 25. *musere;* and 26. *papoti* are sometimes used in direct address, but 27. *kĭrĭmuku;* 28. *wərimuku;* 29. *tamutupə;* 30. *notipə;* and 31. *yumme* are very rarely so used.

There are four other terms the meanings of which is difficult to delimit; these are:

32. *metati:* This term is rarely used and is difficult to define, but it is used between affines. The Trio word *metati* means 'do you (pl.) hear?', but it is not possible to correlate this with its relationship usage. At Alalaparu it is used as a reciprocal term between a husband's sister and a brother's wife. Siwapun (53) said that she used this term to Tarara (8) and Pakĭri (6), but I never heard her do so.

At Paloemeu it is said to be used between *konoka,* but also said to be Alalaparu talk. Təmeta (482), who had visited Alalaparu, said he calls Orosisi (126) by this term because he calls Orosisi's wife, Sine (82), sister.

33. *yahko:* This term is very widely used by men, but lacks precise categorical definition. It is a reciprocal term, and this fact alone clearly distinguishes it from the other terms for 'brother' to which group it is more closely allied than to male cross-cousin. If a translation of this word is needed, 'comrade' is perhaps the closest English equivalent. It is used between Trio who have not reached or agreed upon a more exact degree of relationship, and also by a Trio to a Waiyana. Its present extensive use may be the result of the large-scale migrations which have recently occurred and have thrown into contact many slightly acquainted Indians.

34. *yarĭ:* I was informed that this term was used in addressing a younger brother but only twice did I ever hear it used, and in both cases it was by a man to a classificatory sister's son.

35. *napa, patu:* An affective term of address used by a man to his own elder sister. *Patu* = pot, but *napa* does not appear to have any meaning unless it is related to *inapa,* the verb 'to provide fruit and vegetables', which is a logical connotation.

Finally, there are six terms which can be described as archaic. I was told them by an elderly informant and upon checking it was found that only the older people knew them. At least one of them, *sikami,* must have been in current use at the beginning of this century, since it appears in a vocabulary collected by de Goeje (1906, p. 73). These terms are:

36. *sikami:* direct address by an elder sister to a younger brother.

37. *sika:* direct address to a child of either sex.

38. *moka:* direct address by a man to a young girl (perhaps of Portuguese origin).

39. *mori:* direct address by a woman to a young girl.

40. *arĭkə:* direct address by a man to his sister's son.

41. *sipĭkĭ:* direct address by parents to their son.

Two of these terms call for brief comment; first, *arĭkə* is noteworthy as being a specific term for the sister's son, and, secondly, there is a current example of Sipĭkĭ used as a proper name, i.e., (311).

20

APPENDIX B

TRIO LANGUAGE

I am deeply indebted to the members of the West Indies Mission for their help in the matter of the Trio language. I have followed and used throughout this work the alphabetic and phonetic system employed by them in reducing the Trio language to writing. This reflects the state of the language analysis as it was in 1963/4; no doubt improvements and modifications have been made since then, and this summary takes no account of such developments. Furthermore, while allowing all the credit for language work to the West Indies Mission, I accept responsibility for all errors on this subject which may appear here and elsewhere in this volume.

Phonetic Alphabet

i. Vowels:
    A, a as in c*a*r
    E, e as in p*e*t
    I, i as in m*e*
    O, o as in d*o*pe
    U, u as in b*oo*t
    Ǝ, ə as in c*u*p
    Ǐ, ǐ a flat u—similar to b*oo*t but with lips kept closed and tongue towards back of the mouth.

There are fourteen diphthongs, and vowel lengthening is achieved by doubling of the vowel.

ii. Consonants:
    P, p.   Not aspirated
    K, k.   Not aspirated
    T, t.   Not aspirated
    H, h.
    Y, y.
    W, w.
    S, s.   Pronounced *sh*
    M, m.
    R, r.   When preceded by A, E, or I it is pronounced as a flap R (near a D sound).
            When preceded by O, U, Ǝ, or Ǐ it is almost an L sound.

N, n.   Turns to M before P, and is nasalized before K or at end
         of a word. N is the only final consonant.
Ñ, ñ.   Written NY, ny.

Pronunciation

Syllables end in vowels except occasionally for N. Vowels are coupled with the preceding consonant. The word *pata* (village) is thus pronounced *pa'ta*, or *imuku* (child), *i'mu'ku*.

APPENDIX C

NOTES ON THE GENEALOGICAL TABLES

There were two main problems in the preparation of the Genealogical Table—one was in the collection of the information and the other in its presentation. Some of the difficulties involved are explained below.

a. Problems in the collection of genealogical data

The Trio do not use names in direct address, and try to avoid doing so in reference. This ban does not extend to children, so reference to a third person is normally by the use of teknonymy. This means that while a person usually knows the name of someone of his own age and younger, many do not know the names of older people, even those of their own parents or spouse. While this difficulty could be overcome in the case of younger Indians by asking the older members of the community, a similar solution was not available to discover the names of the parents of these older people. This accounts for relative scarcity of people at level A on the Genealogical Table and their virtual absence at a higher level.

Secondly most Trio have more than one name, but it was unusual for an informant to know more than one although two informants might each know different ones. In the case of living people it has been possible to untangle all the confusions arising from this. No such claim can be made in the case of dead people, and although some instances were disclosed it is possible that some remain concealed and that certain deceased Indians are represented on the table under two different names.

b. Problems in the presentation of the genealogical data

The main difficulty was in deciding to which genealogical level any individual belongs. As it has been shown (see pp. 90–93), according to the viewpoint taken this level will vary. A number of possible solutions presented themselves; four involved the arbitrary selection of a particular system of descent, and one the viewpoint of an individual member of the society. A test sample of 24 marriages was drawn using these different methods, and the proportion of 'horizontal' to 'oblique' marriages calculated for each one. The results were as follows:

Method	Horizontal	Oblique
Senior level⎱ (descent	12 (50 per cent)	12 (50 per cent)
Junior level⎰ from)	17 (70·8 per cent)	7 (29·2 per cent)
Matriliny	15 (62·5 per cent)	9 (37·5 per cent)
Patriliny	14 (58·3 per cent)	10 (41·7 per cent)
Individual	13 (54·2 per cent)	11 (45·8 per cent)

A further test was carried out with a sample of 38 marriages as seen by three different individuals to see if such a method would result in a strong bias depending on the individual used. The results show that this is unlikely:

Individual	Horizontal	Oblique
Iyakɔpo (52)	21 (55·3 per cent)	17 (44·7 per cent)
Muyopɔ (32)	21 (55·3 per cent)	17 (44·7 per cent)
Atu (80)	20 (52·6 per cent)	18 (47·4 per cent)

The coincidence of these figures was so great that further investigation was made to see to what extent individual cases coincide.

Marriage	Iyakɔpo	Muyopɔ	Atu
52 = 53	O	O	H
52 = 55	H	O	H
109 = 107	H	O	H
107 = 110	H	O	H
107 = 113	H	O	H
11 = 12	O	O	O
7 = 12	O	H	O
3 = 5	O	O	H
1 = 3	O	O	O
9 = 6	H	O	O
22 = 13	O	O	O
233 = 117	O	H	O
61 = 62	O	H	H
62 = 63	O	H	O
81 = 106	H	H	H
81 = 82	H	H	H
70 = 90	H	H	H
39 = 40	O	H	H
92 = 91	O	H	H
232 = 92	H	H	H
89 = 88	H	O	O
73 = 124	H	O	O

73 = 70	O	O	H
71 = 63	H	H	H
23 = 27	H	H	H
23 = 25	H	H	H
23 = 28	O	H	H
35 = 28	H	O	O
35 = 118	H	H	O
79 = 118	O	O	O
32 = 30	H	H	O
59 = 58	O	H	O
78 = 80	O	O	H
83 = 80	H	O	O
83 = 87	H	H	O
93 = 72	O	H	O
24 = 41	H	H	H
90 = ? ?	H	H	O

Between Iyakɔpo and Muyopɔ, and between Iyakɔpo and Atu there is 52·6 per cent coincidence, and between Muyopɔ and Atu 55·3 per cent.

Taking these two sets of figures together they indicate that while the proportion of 'oblique' and 'horizontal' marriages will be approximately the same for any two individuals, in any particular case there is only a half-chance that the marriage will be of the same type.

It was decided therefore that the Genealogical Table should be drawn from the viewpoint of an individual, and, in fact, it has been constructed from that of two individuals—those numbered 1–299 inclusive as seen by Iyakɔpo (52), and those numbered 300–786 inclusive as seen by Korokoro (300). The reasons for this decision are that the individual method did not produce figures which are widely different from the other methods and, in the absence of any conventional rule of descent, it preserves some Trio character while avoiding the possible inherent fallaciousness which the arbitrary selection of some other method might bestow upon it. There are obvious criticisms which can be made of such a method but, even if it does result in a few anomalous situations, it does not give an over-all false impression. The lack of any definite rule of descent is further emphasized by the drawing of the lines of affiliation from the 'union by marriage' lines which join the two parents.

Some modifications have had to be made to the individual's viewpoint because early attempts showed that, while the only accurate method of presentation was along the lines of the diagram in Figure 6, this system was abandoned because it made the chart very complicated and difficult to follow, and, while ideal for close relatives of the informants, had serious drawbacks when one came to consider more distantly related people—a simple example of this being the absence of any clearly defined place for a *pito*, a category which is anyhow not defined by genealogical level. Accordingly certain adjustments have been made in order to eliminate ambiguities. Firstly, wherever there is no evidence to the contrary, marriages have been drawn as 'horizontal'. Secondly, those called *pito* are placed on the same genealogical level as the informants unless there is a sister called *manhko* or *emi* who allows an alternative view. The same solution is applied to the women called *nosi*, who are regarded as belonging to the same level as their husband unless there is evidence to the contrary. The correctness of this procedure is supported by the final result because as is mentioned above (see p. 149) the total number of marriages shown on the Genealogical Table is equally divided between 'horizontal' and 'oblique' forms, proportions which other evidence leads one to expect.

c. Explanatory key to Genealogical Table

Living male. . . . . △
Living female . . . . ○
Dead male . . . . ▲
Dead female . . . . ●
Index number 263
   (placed under one of the above symbols)
Waiyana Indian 318
Union by marriage. . . . . =
Divorce . . . . ⤬
   (only shown in cases in which both spouses are still alive)

(1)

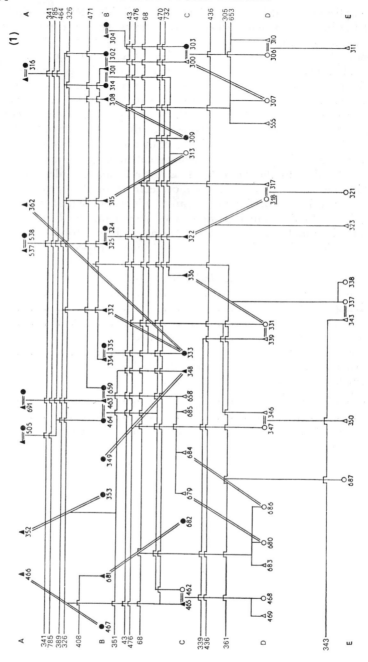

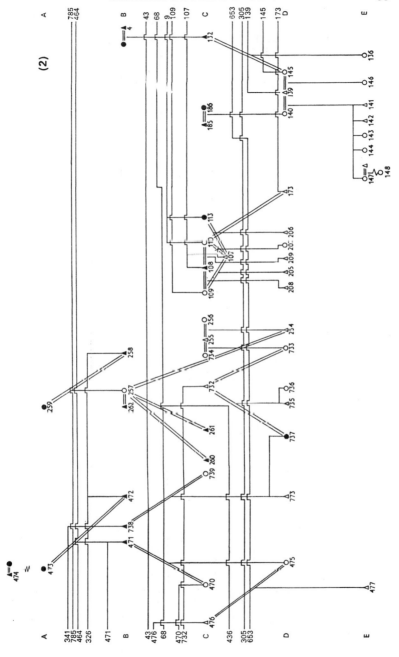

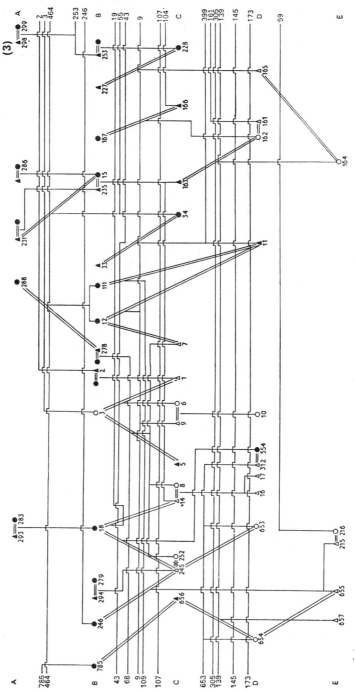

(4)

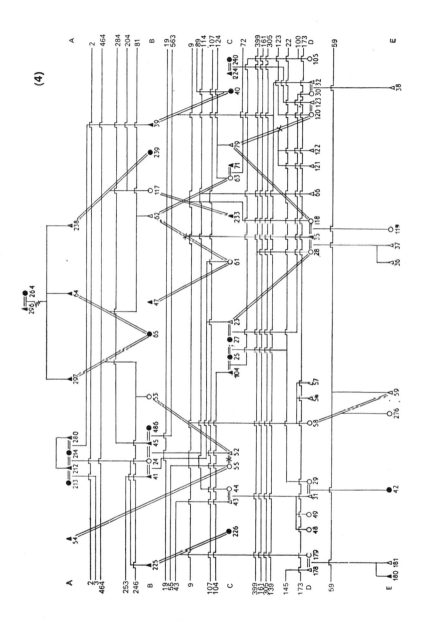

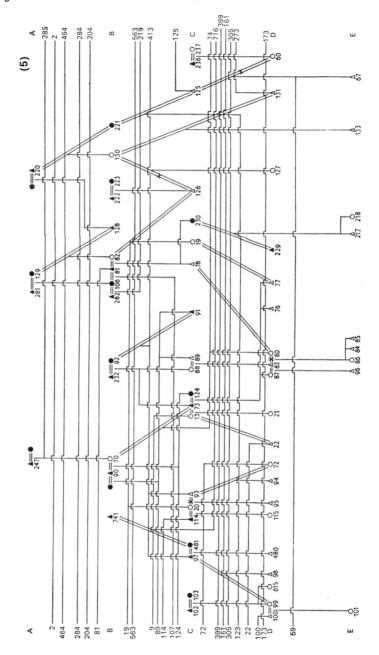

(6)

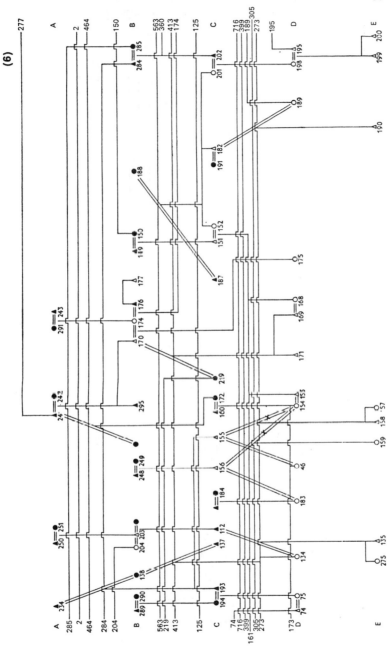

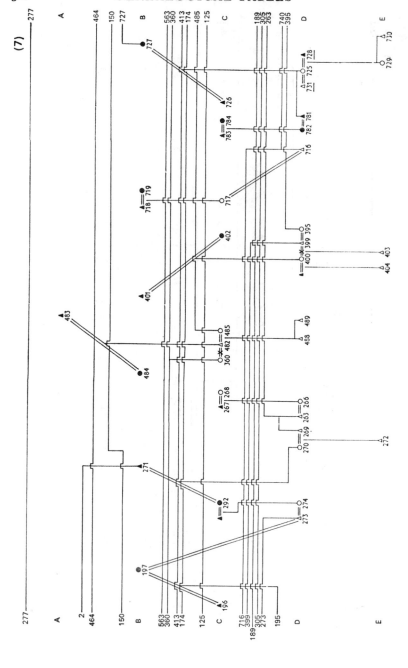

(8)

(9)   277

277

A   389 150 592 591   B   563 457 413 174 485 125 569   C   556   189 263 740 596   D   E

575

558
569 557
576

567

573
572

211   210   525   566

631 632   568   524
595 596

588 589   587   594   593

597

495 497   591 592   590   619

771 700   617 616   618

708

710

599 706   598

498 499   496 630 704

770   769

695

694   692 693 768

709 707

714 715

712 713   711

277

A   389 492 150 700   B   563 457 413 174 485 125 699   C   494 189 263 740   D   E

(10)

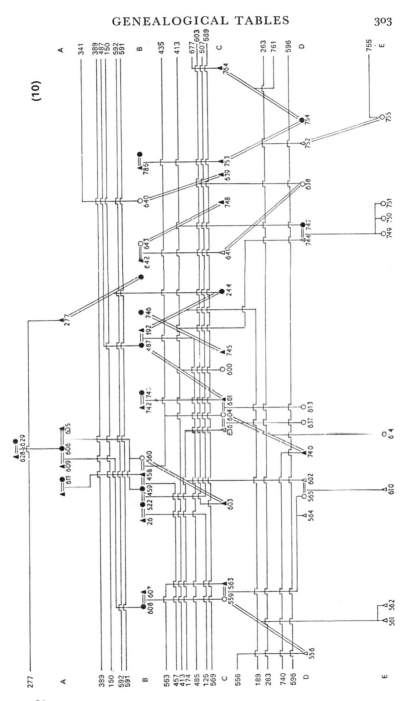

21

(11)

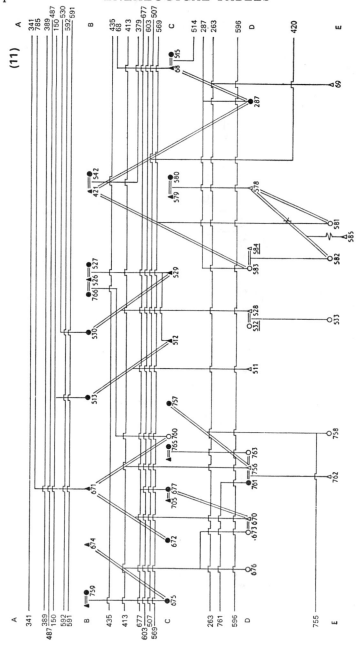

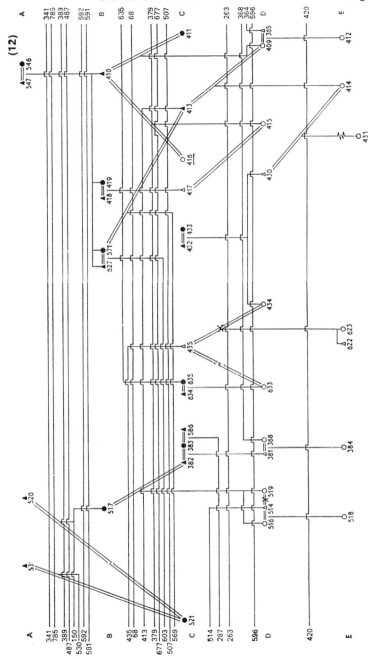

(12)

(13)

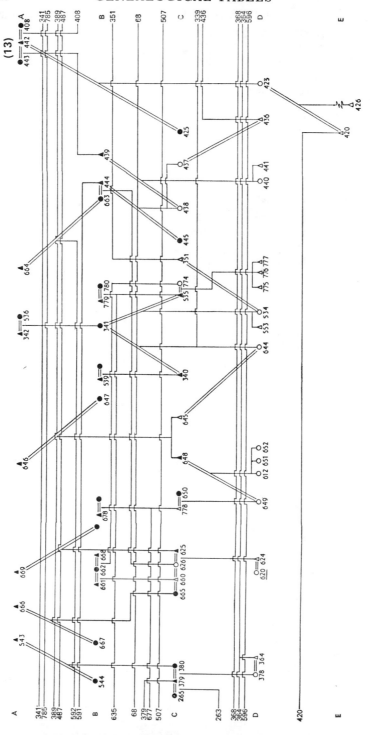

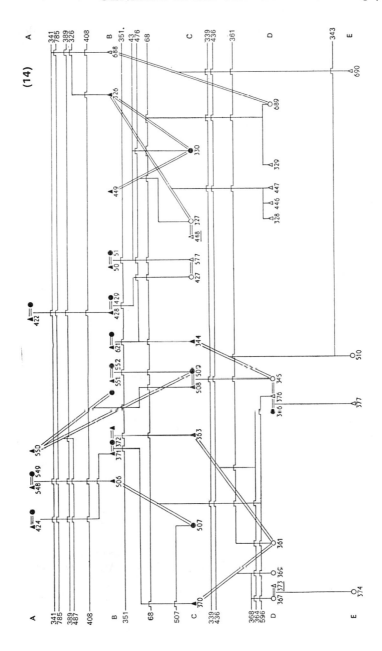

Index to the Genealogical Table

All the data required for the construction of the Genealogical Table are contained in this index. Each entry is formed in the following way.

1. Reference number.
2. Name. Other names when commonly used are included immediately below.   .
   Italicised names indicate a Waiyana.
3. Sex, and living or dead. Male . . . . △
   Female . . . . ○
   Dead Male . . . . ▲
   Dead Female . . . . ●
4. Reference to location on Genealogical Table.
   The number refers to the sheet (1–14), and the letter to the genealogical level (A, B, C, D, E). There are a few cases where people fall outside these five levels; those above Level A are marked +, and those below Level E are marked −.
5. Closest genealogical relationships.
   The letters give the relationship and the number the actual individual. For example number 1, Susuku, has listed against him F2 which means that his father is number 2, Tuhori, who is reciprocally marked S1 which means his son is number 1, Susuku. The letters are those which are conventionally used to indicate a relationship.
   The symbols W or H indicate a second or previous wife or husband. When one or other of the spouses has died and the survivor has remarried, the earlier marriage of the survivor is marked in this way but that of the deceased is not.
6. Relationship to ego, and age.
   This information is contained in the parentheses. The first symbol shows the relationship of the individual to the informants around whom the table is constructed; 1–299 inclusive with reference to Iyakɔpo (52) and 300–786 inclusive with reference to Korokoro (300). The symbols F, M, Z, B, BS, BD, ZS, and ZD represent normal English categories but Trio relationship terms are used for T = *Tamu*, N = *Nosi*, P = *Pito*, and *T* = *ipa*.
   In the majority of cases age has been estimated and an error of 10 per cent either way should be allowed. Attempts at objective determination of age by reference to some datable event did not prove very easy because of the lack of suitable incidents. In the Sipaliwini basin, the visit of Schmidt in 1940–2 is the only outstanding event which has occurred in the lifetime of these Indians.

7. Inverted commas.

A few Indians have certain of the entries against their name enclosed in inverted commas; this indicates that, for the sake of simplicity, this relationship is not shown on the Genealogical Table. A few of the Waiyana have their names enclosed in parentheses which means that they do not appear on the Genealogical Table.

316. Kanaruyc ●. 1/A; H?; S315, 332, 389; D302, 314 (N).
317. Inəsi △. 1/D; F315; M313; W318; D321 (ZS; 30 yr).
     Sisi.
318. *Marina* ○. 1/D; F319; M320; Z617, 620; H317; D321; H322;
     S323 (SW).
319. (*Muru*) ▲. W320; D318, 617, 620.
320. (*Mairena*) ○. H319; D318, 617, 620.
321. Tiyokənke ○. 1/E; F317; M318 (Y; 6 yr).
322. Yayarikə ▲. 1/C; F324; M325; W318; S323 (P).
323. Anasinkə △. 1/E; E322; M318 (Y; 7 yr).
324. Aruntə ▲. 1/B; F537; M538; W325; S322.
325. Tuma ●. 1/B; H324; S322 (N).
326. Sanutu ▲. 14/B; B308, 472, 258; W330; S329; D689; W327;
     S328, 446, 447.
327. Irawĭpən ○. 14/C; F449; M330; H448; H326; S328, 446,
     447 (yZ; 38 yr).
328. Napumi △. 14/D; F326; M327; B446, 447 (ZS; 10 yr).
329. Arantə △. 14/D; F326; M330; Z689 (ZS; 15 yr).
330. Nərui ●. 14/C; F50; M51; B43, 577; H326; S329; D689;
     H449; D327 (eZ).
331. Paikə ○. 1/D; F332; M333; B346; H339; H336; D337, 338
     (ZD; 33 yr).
     Arekoa.
332. Yametĭ ▲. 1/B; M316; B389, 315; Z302, 314; W333; S346;
     D331 (MB).
     Atapepe.
333. Nasari ●. 1/C; F334; M335; Z309; H332; S346; D331;
     H362; D361 (eZ).
334. Tapəmpĭ ▲. 1/B; B301; W335; D333, 309 (F).
335. Irasamoke ●. 1/B; H334; D333, 309 (M).
336. Napeta ▲. 1/C; F301; M314; Z313; W331; D337, 338
     (yB).
337. Wakuri ○. 1/E; F336; M331; Z338; H343 (Y; 15 yr).
     Rasimoi.
338. Mawiya ○. 1/E; F336; M331; Z337 (Y; 3 yr).
339. Yapi △. 1/D; F340; M341; Z644; W331 (BS; 21 yr).
340. Pantapə ▲. 13/C; F539; W341; S339; D664 (eB).
341. Pakĭi ●. 13/B; F342; M536; B688, 738; Z640; H340; S339;
     D644; H535; S553; D534 (M).
342. Amenkaeyae ▲. 13/A; W536; S688, 738; D341, 640 (T).
343. Sanəpə △. 1/E; F344; M345; Z510; W337 (Y; 17 yr).
     Inarupən, Inature.
344. Paiye ▲, 14/C; F621; B476; W345; S343; D510 (eB).
     22

468. Sepera ○. 1/D; F465; M462; B469 (ZD; 8 yr).
469. Tampe △. 1/D; F465; M462; Z468 (ZS; 6 yr).
Sanpe.
470. Sareyuna ○. 2/C; F463; M464; Z462; H471; D475 (yZ; 37 yr).
471. Surekore ▲. 2/B; F472; M473; Z659; W470; D475 (P).
472. Sariku ▲. 2/B; B308, 326, 258; W473; S471; D659 (MB).
473. Pisipǝ ●. 2/A; F474; H472; S471; D659 (N).
474. Amipǐ ▲. 2/+, W?; D473 (T).
475. Ǝkǝwiyae ○. 2/D; F471; M470; H476; S477 (ZD; 18 yr).
Yamakǐ.
476. Amasi △. 2/C; F621; B344; W475; S477 (yB; 34 yr).
477. infant △. 2/E; F476; M475 (Y; 2 months).
478. Parokǐwǐ ▲. 8/C; W479; S720; D393 (eB).
479. Arikepǐ ○. 8/C; H478; S720; D393.
480. Pinarǝ △. 5/D; F97; M481 (ZS; 15 yr).
481. Pansina ●. 5/C; H97; S480; Ĥ741; S740, 716 (eZ).
482. Tǝmeta △. 7/C; F483; M484; W485; S488, 489; W360 (P; 42 yr).
483. Atiyari ▲. 7/A; W484; S482 (T).
484. Manaru ●. 7/B; H483; S482 (N).
485. Kara ○. 7/C; F192; M487; H482; S488, 489 (yZ; 24 yr).
486. Mopepǝ ●. 4/B; H45; S563.
487. Reposi ●. 10/B; F550; M509; H192; D485; Ĥ601; D600 (M).
488. Musere △. 7/D; F482; M485; B489 (ZS; 7 yr).
489. Yan △. 7/D; F482; M485; B488 (ZS; 2–3 yr).
490. Sipǝ △. 8/D; F491; M492; Z493; W502 (BS; 22 yr).
Pǐrǝrmare.
491. Aruwate ▲. 8/C; W492; S490; D493 (eB).
492. Awaintu ●. 8/B; F495; M497; Z594; H491; S490; D493 (M).
493. Apokǐnini ○. 8/D; F491; M492; B490; H494; S500, 523; D501 (BD; 24 yr).
494. Pǐtǐ △. 8/D; F495; M496; W493; S500, 523; D501 (ZS; 30 yr).
495. Matanro ▲. 9/A; W496; S494; W497; D492, 594 (T).
496. Panaka ●. 9/C; F498; M499; H495; S494; Ĥ630; S599 (eZ).
497. Takiruta ●. 9/A; H495; D492, 594 (N).
498. *Kiriwa* ▲. 9/B; W499; D496.
499. Pǐropi ●. 9/B; H498; D496 (M).
500. Imariu △. 8/E; F494; M493; B523; Z501 (Y; 5 yr).
501. Repi ○. 8/E; F494; M493; B500, 523 (Y; 2 yr).
502. *Takiru* ○. 8/D; F503; M504; H490.

782. Makara ●. 7/D; F783; M784; H781.
783. Tapon ▲. 7/C; W784; D782 (eB).
784. Ari ●. 7/C; H783; D782.
785. Wiripə ●. 3/B; B671; H656.
786. Sipoti ▲. 10/B; W?; S753 (F).

BIBLIOGRAPHY

PART 1

Works which contain references to the Trio or to Trio sub-groups.

DE AGUIAR, Braz Dias
1943 *Nas Fronteiras de Venezuela e Guianas Britânica e Neerlandesa*
Rio de Janeiro
AHLBRINCK, W.
1931 *Encyclopaedie der Karaïben* Amsterdam
BAKHUIS, L. A.
1908 'De 5de Wetenschappelijke Expeditie naar Binnenland van Suriname', *Tijdschrift van het Koninklijk Nederlandsch Aardrijkskundig Genootschap*, vol. 25, pp. 94–112. Leiden
BARRÈRE, Pierre
1743 *Nouvelle Relation de la France Équinoxiale* Paris
BELLIN, S.
1763 *Description Géographique de la Guyane* Paris
COUDREAU, Henri Anatole
1886–7 *La France Équinoxiale* (vol. 1, *Études sur les Guyanes et l'Amazonie*; vol. 2, *Voyage à travers les Guyanes et l'Amazonie*)
Paris
1891 'Notes sur 53 tribes de Guyane', *Bulletin de la Société de Géographie*, vol. 12, 7th series, pp. 116–32. Paris
1893 *Chez nos Indiens. Quatre Années dans la Guyane Francais, 1887–91* Paris
COUDREAU, Olga
1900 *Voyage au Trombetas* Paris
1901 *Voyage au Cumina* Paris
CREVAUX, Jules Nicolas
1879 'Voyages d'Exploration dans l'Intérieur des Guyanes', *Le Tour du Monde*, vol. 37, pp. 337–416. Paris
1880 'De Cayenne aux Andes', *Bulletin de la Société de Géographie*, vol. 19, 6th series, pp. 383–416. Paris
1882 'Quelque Mots de la Langue des Indiens Trio', *Bibliothèque Linguistique Américaine*, vol. 8, pp. 39–40. Paris
1883 *Voyage dans l'Amérique du Sud* Paris
CRULS, Gastão
1930 *A Amazônia que eu vi, Obidos-Tumucumaque* Rio de Janeiro
EHRENREICH, Paul
1904 'Die Ethnographie Südamerikas im Beginn des XX

BIBLIOGRAPHY 335

Jahrhunderts unter besonderer Berücksichtigung der
Naturvölker', *Archiv. für Anthrop.*, n.s. vol. 3, pp. 39–75.
Braunschweig
FARABEE, William Curtis
1924 *The Central Caribs.* University of Pennsylvania Museum,
Anthropological Publications, vol. 10 Philadelphia
FIGUEIREDO, Napoleão
1961 'A Festa dos Coletores entre os Aramagoto', *Boletim do
Museu Paraense Emilio Goeldi, Antropologia*, No. 15
Belém
1963 'Os Aramagoto do Paru do Oeste: seus primeiros con-
tactos com a sociedade nacional' *América Indigena*,
vol. 23, No. 4, pp. 309–17 Mexico
FRANSSEN HERDERSCHE, A.
1905 'Verslag der Tapanahoni Expeditie', *Tijdschrift van het
Koninklijk Nederlandsch Aardrijkskundig Genootschap*, vol. 22,
pp. 847–1032 Leiden
FRIKEL, Protasio
1957 'Zur linguistisch-ethnologischen Gliederung der Indianer-
stämme von Nord Pará (Brasilien) und den anliegenden
Gebieten', *Anthropos*, vol. 52, pp. 509–63. Vienna
1958 'Classificação linguistico-etnológica das tribas indígenas
do Pará Setentrional e zonas adjacentes'. *Revista de
Antropologia*, vol. 6, pp. 113–89 São Paulo
1960 'Os Tiriyó'. *Boletim do Museu Paraense Emilio Goeldi,
Antropologia*, No. 9 Belém
1961a 'Fases Culturais e Aculturação Intertribal no Tumu-
cumaque', *Boletim do Museu Paraense Emilio Goeldi, Antropologia*, No. 16 Belém
1961b 'Ometanimpe, Os Transformados', *Boletim do Museu
Paraense Emilio Goeldi, Antropologia*, No. 17 Belém
1964 'Das Problem der Pianakoto-Tiriyó', *Beiträge zur Völkerkunde Südamerikas. Festgabe für Herbert Baldus. Völker-
kundliche Abhandlungen*, vol. 1, pp. 97–104 Hanover
FROIDEVAUX, Henri
1895 *Explorations Françaises à l'Intérieur de la Guyane pendant le
second Quart du XVIIIe siècle* (1720–1742) Paris
1898 'Une Faute d'Impression des Lettres édifiantes', *Journal de
la Société des Américanistes de Paris*, vol. 5, pp. 25–29
Paris
GEIJSKES, D. C.
1960–1 'History of Archaeological Investigations in Surinam',
*Berichten van de Rijksdienst voor het Oudheikundig Bodemonder-
zoek*, vol. 10–11, pp. 70–77 Paramaribo

23

GILLIN, John
1963 'Tribes of the Guianas', *Handbook of South American Indians*, vol. 3, p. 799–860   New York
DE GOEJE, C. H.
1906 'Ethnographie der Surinaamsche Indianen', Supplement to vol. 17, *Internationales Archiv für Ethnographie*   Leiden
1908 'Verslag der Toemoekhoemak-Expeditie', *Tijdschrift van het Koninklijk Nederlandsch Aardrijkskundig Genootschap*, vol. 25, pp. 943–1168   Leiden
1910 'Beiträge zur Völkerkunde von Surinam', *Internationales Archiv für Ethnographie*, vol. 19, pp. 1–34   Leiden
1924 'Guayana and Carib Tribal Names', *Proceedings of the 21st International Congress of Americanists*, pp. 212–16   The Hague
1943a 'Neolithische Indianer in Surinam', *Tijdschrift van het Koninklijk Nederlandsch Aardrijkskundig Genootschap*, vol. 60, 2nd series, pp. 334–74   Leiden
1943b 'Philosophy, Initiation and Myths of the Indians of Guiana and adjacent Countries', *Internationales Archiv für Ethnographie*, vol. 44, pp. 1–136   Leiden
GRILLET, John and BÉCHAMEL, Francis
1698 'A Journal of the Travels into Guiana in the year 1674', *Voyages and Discoveries in South America*, Part 3   London
HOFF, B. J.
1955 'The Languages of the Indians of Surinam and the Comparative Study of the Carib and Arawak Languages', *Bijdragen, Tot de Taal-, Land- en Volkenkunde*, vol. 3, 4th series, pp. 325–55.   The Hague
HURAULT, Jean
1961 'Les Indiens Oayana de la Guyane Française', *Journal de la Société des Américanistes de Paris*, vol. 50, n.s., pp. 135–83   Paris
KAPPLER, August
1887 *Surinam, sein Land, sein Natur, Bevölkerung und seine Kultur-Verhältnisse*   Stuttgart
KAYSER, C. C.
1912 'Verslag der Corantijn Expeditie', *Tijdschrift van het Koninklijk Nederlandsch Aardrijkskundig Genootschap*, vol. 29, 2nd series, pp. 442–514.   Leiden
LA CONDAMINE, Charles Marie DE
1745 *Relation abrégée d'un Voyage fait dans l'Intérieur de l'Amérique méridionale depuis la Côte de la Mer du Sud, jusqu'aux Côtes du Brésil et de la Guyane, en descendant la Rivière de Amazones*   Paris

VAN LYNDEN, A. J. H., *et al.*

1939 'Op zoek naar Suriname's zuidgrens (de grensbepaling tusschen Suriname en Brazilie, 1935–38)', *Tijdschrift van het Koninklijk Nederlandsch Aardrijkskundig Genootschap*, vol. 56, 2nd series, pp. 792–882. Leiden

VAN MAZIJK, J.

1966 *Het Medisch werk van de Surinam Interior Fellowship in het tweede halfjaar van 1965* Paramaribo

1967 *Het medisch werk onder de Trio's, Wajana's en Aloekoe's van de stichting Medische Zending voor Suriname in het tweede halfjaar van 1966* Paramaribo

1968 *Het medisch werk onder de Trio's en Wajana's van de stichting Medische Zending voor Suriname in het tweede halfjaar van 1967* Paramaribo

MENTELLE, Simon

1821 'Relation de Voyage fait en Mars, Avril, Mai et Juin, 1766', *Feuille de la Guyane Française*, vol. 2, pp. 724–6 Cayenne

MIGLIAZZA, Ernesto

1965 'Notas Fonologicas da língua Tiriyó', *Boletim do Museu Paraense Emilio Goeldi, Antropologia*, No. 29 Belém

MILTHIADE, J.

1823 'Voyage de J. Milthiade et F. Loret, d'Oyapock aux Emerillons et à la rivière Inini, en tournant les sources de l'Approuague, en Août et Septembre, 1822', *Feuille de la Guyane Française*, vol. 3, pp. 510–21 Cayenne

NORWOOD, V. G. C.

1960 *A Hand Full of Diamonds* London

VAN PANHUYS, L. C.

1898 'Proeve Eener Verklaring van de Ornamentiek van de Indianen in Guyana', *Internationales Archiv für Ethnographie*, vol. 11, pp. 51–72. Leiden

1904 'About the Ornamentation in use by Savage Tribes in Dutch Guiana, and its Meaning', *Bijdragen tot de Taal-, Land-, en Volkenkunde*, vol. 7, pp. 8–11. The Hague

RIVIÈRE, Leon

1866 'La Guyane Française en 1865', *La Feuille Officielle de la Guyane Française* Cayenne

RIVIÈRE, Peter Gerard

1963 'An Ethnographic Survey of the Indians on the Divide of the Guianese and Amazonian River Systems', unpublished B.Litt. thesis, University of Oxford. Oxford

1966a 'Age: A Determinant of Social Classification', *Southwestern Journal of Anthropology*, vol. 22, No. 1, pp. 43–60. Albuquerque

23*

1966b 'Oblique Discontinuous Exchange: A new formal type of Prescriptive Alliance', *American Anthropologist*, vol. 68, pp. 738–40.   Menasha

1966c 'A Note on Marriage with the Sister's Daughter', *Man, The Journal of the Royal Anthropological Institute*, vol. 1, pp. 550–6.   London

1967 'Some ethnographic problems of Southern Guyana', *Folk*, vol. 8–9, pp. 301–12.   Copenhagen

RONDON, Candido Mariano da Silva

1957 *Indios do Brasil*, vol. 3   Rio de Janeiro

ROTH, W. E.

1924 'An Introductory Study of the Arts, Crafts, and Customs of the Guiana Indians', *38th Annual Report of the Bureau of American Ethnology*, 1916–17, pp. 25–745.   Washington

1929 'Additional Studies of the Arts, Crafts, and Customs of the Guiana Indians', *Bulletin of the Bureau of American Ethnology*, No. 91.   Washington

SAUSSE, André

1951 *Populations Primitives du Maroni*   Paris

SCHMIDT, Lodewijk

1942 'Verslag van drie Reizen naar de Bovenlandsche Indianen', *Departement Landbouwproefstation in Suriname*, Bulletin No. 58   Paramaribo

SCHOMBURGK, Richard

1847–8 *Reisen in Britisch-Guiana in den Jahren 1840–44*, 3 volumes.   Leipzig

SCHOMBURGK, Robert Hermann

1845 'Journal of an Expedition from Pirara to the Upper Corentyne, and from thence to Demerara', *Journal of the Royal Geographical Society*, vol. 15, pp. 1–104   London

SCHUMANN,

1882 'Arawakisch-Deutsches Worterbuch', *Bibliothèque Linguistique Américaine*, vol. 8, pp. 69–165   Paris

STEDMAN, John Gabriel

1796 *Narrative of a five years' expedition against the revolted negroes of Surinam in Guiana, on the wild coast of South America; from the year 1772 to 1777*, 2 volumes   London

DEN TEX-BOISSEVAIN, A.

1923 *Tora bij de Trio's*   Amsterdam

TONY, Claude

1843 'Voyage dans l'intérieur du continent de la Guyane, chez les Indiens Roucoyens', *Nouvelles Annales des Voyages*, vol. 97, pp. 213–35   Paris

VELLARD, J.
  1965 *Histoire du Curare*   Paris
VERRIL, A. H.
  1925 'The Indians of Surinam', *Indian Notes and Monographs,*
        vol. 2, No. 4, pp. 309–13   New York
DE VILLIERS, Baron Marc
  1920 'Journal inédit du Voyage du Sergent La Haye de Cayenne
        aux chutes de Yari, 1728–29', *Journal de la Société des
        Américanistes de Paris,* vol. 12, n.s., pp. 115–26   Paris

                              PART 2

Other works to which reference is made in the text.

AIYAPPAN, A.
  1934 'Cross-Cousin and Uncle-Niece Marriages in South
        India', *Congrès International des Sciences Anthropologiques et
        Ethnologiques,* pp. 281–2   London
BEALS, Alan R.
  1962 *Gopalpur. A South Indian Village*   New York
DINIZ, Edson Soares
  1965 'Breves Notas sobre o Sistema de Parentesco Makuxi',
        Boletim do Museu Paraense Emilio Goeldi, Antropologia, No. 28
                                                          Belém
DUMONT, Louis
  1957 'Hierarchy and Marriage Alliance in South Indian Kin-
        ship', *Occasional Paper of the Royal Anthropological Institute,*
        No. 12.   London
  1961 'Marriage in India—The Present State of the Question',
        Contributions to Indian Sociology, vol. 5, pp. 76–95   Paris
DUMONT, Louis and POCOCK, David
  1957 'Kinship, A Critique of Dr. Karvé's Kinship Organisation
        in India', *Contributions to Indian Sociology,* vol. 1, pp. 43–64
                                                          Paris
EVANS, Clifford and MEGGERS, Betty
  1960 'Archeological investigations in British Guiana', *Bulletin of
        the Bureau of American Ethnology,* No. 177.   Washington
FIRTH, Raymond
  1964 'Essays on Social Organization and Values', *London
        School of Economics Monographs on Social Anthropology,* No. 28
                                                          London
FOCK, Niels
  1963 'Waiwai. Religion and Society of an Amazonian Tribe',
        National Museum of Denmark, Ethnographic Series, vol. 8
                                                          Copenhagen

340   BIBLIOGRAPHY

FREYRE, Gilberto
  1963   *The Masters and the Slaves* (translated by Samuel Putnam)
                                                            London
GILLIN, John
  1936   'The Barama River Caribs of British Guiana', *Papers of the
         Peabody Museum of American Archaeology and Ethnology,
         Harvard*, vol. 14, No. 2   Cambridge, Mass.
GOLDMAN, Irving
  1963   'The Cubeo: Indians of the Northwest Amazon', *Illinois
         Studies in Anthropology*, No. 2   Urbana
GOUGH, E. Kathleen
  1956   'Brahman Kinship in a Tamil Village', *American Anthro-
         pologist*, vol. 58, pp. 826-53.   Menasha
HENFREY, Colin
  1964   *The Gentle People*   London
HUXLEY, Francis
  1963   *Affable Savages*   London
JAMES, Preston E.
  1959   *Latin America*   London
KARVÉ, Irawati
  1953   'Kinship Organisation in India', *Deccan College Monograph
         Series*, No. 11   Poona
KIRCHHOFF, Paul
  1932   'Verwandtschaftsbezeichungen und Verwandtenheirut',
         Zeitschrift für Ethnologie, vol. 64, pp. 41-71   Berlin
LAVE, Jean Carter
  1966   'A Formal Analysis of Preferential Marriage with the
         Sister's Daughter', *Man, The Journal of the Royal Anthro-
         pological Institute*, vol. 1, pp. 185-200.   London
LEACH, Edmund R.
  1951   'The Structural Implications of Matrilateral Cross-
         Cousin Marriage', *Journal of the Royal Anthropological
         Institute*, vol. 81, pp. 23-55.   London
  1961   'Rethinking Anthropology', *London School of Economics
         Monographs on Social Anthropology*, No. 22   London
LÉVI-STRAUSS, Claude
  1943a 'Guerre et Commerce chez les Indiens de l'Amérique de
         Sud', *Renaissance*, vol. 1, pp. 122-39   New York
  1943b 'The Social Use of Kinship Terms among Brazilian
         Indians', *American Anthropologist*, vol. 45, pp. 398-409.
                                                           Menasha
  1948   'La Vie Familiale et Sociale des Indiens Nambikwara',
         Journal de la Société des Américanistes de Paris, vol. 37 n.s.
                                                             Paris

1949   *Les Structures Élémentaires de la Parenté*   Paris
1958   *Anthropologie Structurale*   Paris
1961   *A World on the Wane*   London
1966   *Du Miel aux Cendres*   Paris

LINTON, Ralph
  1933   'The Tanala. A Hill Tribe of Madagascar', *Field Museum of Natural History*, Chicago, Publication 317, Anthropological Series, vol. 22.   Chicago

LLOYD, G. E. R.
  1966   *Polarity and Analogy. Two types of argumentation in early Greek thought*   Cambridge

MÉTRAUX, Alfred
  1963   'The Tupinamba', *Handbook of South American Indians*, vol. 3, pp. 95–133   New York

McCORMACK, William
  1958   'Sister's Daughter Marriage in a Mysore Village', *Man in India*, vol. 38, pp. 34–48.   Bihar

NEEDHAM, Rodney
  1958   'The Formal Analysis of Prescriptive Patrilateral Cross-Cousin Marriage', *Southwestern Journal of Anthropology*, vol. 14, pp. 199–219.   Albuquerque
  1966   'Age, Category, and Descent', *Bijdragen tot de Taal-, Land- en Volkenkunde*, vol. 122, pp. 1–35.   The Hague

RIVERS, W. H. R.
  1926   'The Primitive Conception of Death', *Psychology and Ethnology*, pp. 36–50   London

DE SOUZA, Conego Francisco Bernardino
  1873   *Lembranças e Curiosidades do valle dos Amazonas*   Pará

STEWARD, Julian
  1963   (Editor) *Handbook of South American Indians*, reprinted by Cooper Square Publishers, 7 volumes.   New York

TAMBIAH, S. J.
  1958   'The structure of kinship and its relationship to land possession and residence in Pata Dumbara, Central Ceylon', *Journal of the Royal Anthropological Institute*, vol. 88, pp. 21–44.   London

IM THURN, Everard F.
  1883   *Among the Indians of Guiana*   London

TURNBULL, Colin M.
  1965   *Wayward Servants. The two worlds of the African Pygmies*   New York

WILLIAMS, James
  1932   *Grammar, Notes and Vocabulary of the Language of the Makuchi*
         Indians of Guiana   Vienna
YALMAN, Nur
  1967   *Under the Bo Tree*, University of California Press.
                                        Berkeley and Los Angeles
YDE, Jens
  1965   'Material Culture of the Waiwai', *National Museum of*
         Denmark, Ethnographic Series, vol. 10   Copenhagen

INDEX

musical instruments (*continued*)
rattle (*see also* shaman's rattle), 245
myth, 169, 176, 251, 253n, 259–61, 262–3, 264, 266

Nambikwara Indians, 273, 273n, 274
names, 290
napa, see under relationship terms
Needham, R., xii, 84, 277, 341
Negro (*see also* Bush Negro), 14n
Negro Rio, *see under* rivers
Norwood, V. G. C., 337
nosi, see under relationship terms
numbers, 253

Oedipus, 176
Oelemari river, *see under* rivers
Oikoimə village, *see under* villages
Okomoyana Indians, *see under* Trio sub-groups
Opposites, Tables of, 283
oppositions, vii, 193, 194, 195, 232n, 251, 252, 256, 257, 259, 261–9, 279, 280
Oranje Mts., *see under* mountains
Orinoco river, *see under* rivers
Orion, 43
ornaments, 24, 33–4, 40, 246, 249
ownership, *see under entu* and property
Oyumpi Indians, 29, 34, 38
Oyapock river, *see under* rivers

Paikarakapo village, *see under* villages
paint, body and facial, 34–5, 191, 241, 242, 242n, 246, 266
Paloemeu river, *see under* rivers
Paloemeu village, *see under* villages
pananakíri, 14n, 30
Panapipa village, *see under* villages
van Panhuys, L. C., 12, 337
Pará, 8, 19
Paramaribo, 177
Patamona Indians, 161
patrikin, 65n, 280
Patris, Tony, 23, 24
penis, 260n
Pərəpərəwa (culture hero), 63, 259–61, 261n, 264
pets (*see also* dogs), v, 40–1, 46, 53
philosophers, 283
physical features of the Trio, 23–4, 32–3

Pianakoto Indians, *see under* Trio sub-groups
Pianoi Indians, *see under* Trio sub-groups
Pirəuyana Indians, *see under* Trio sub-groups
Pleiades, 42
Pletani river, *see under* rivers
Pocock, D., 277n, 339
poison, 231
polarity, 267, 283
political allegiance, 216–17, 218, 234
political organization, 229–40, 250
pollution, 232n, 281, 282
polyandry, *see under* marriage
polygyny, *see under* marriage
Portuguese, 23, 27
pots, pottery, 11, 40, 46, 47, 55, 210, 222, 261, 262, Plate 6
pregnancy, 182, 266
prehistory, 9–11, 57
property, 39–42, 54, 269
at death, 222–4
women as, 41–2, 269
Proto-Trio, 9
purity, 281–2
pygmies, *see* Mbuti pygmies

Ragu Indians, *see under* Trio sub-groups
Redfern (American pilot), 13, 14n
relationship terminology, 27, 59, 61–2, 69n, 74, 85, 87, 89, 101, 171, 196, 225, 270, 273, 284–7
two-section, 62, 69n
relationship terms (*see also* affines, terms for, and age groups, terms for)
archaic terms, 287
choice of relationship term, 101–3, 226, 234
genealogical specifications of relationship terms, 61, 62, 66, 67, 70, 71, 81, 82, 149, 171, 284–6
individual terms,
akəmi/kami, 66, 70, 71, 73, 74, 76, 79, 84, 86, 87, 90, 93–101, 142, 143, 144, 184, 186, 202, 284, 286
emerimpə, 62, 66, 71–7, 81–2, 87, 88, 99, 103, 141, 143, 148, 160, 162, 166, 172, 187, 191,

PLATE 1

(a) Visitors arriving by canoe at the Paloemeu Village

(b) Sipə (490) using fire to expand a dugout canoe

PLATE 2

Mikĭpə (20), Kuwĭse (86), and Siwapun (53) dancing at Alalaparu

PLATE 3

(*a*) Clearing the jungle for a garden site

(*b*) Hoeing a garden in preparation for planting cassava

PLATE 4

Tawiruye (61) spreading cassava flour on a griddle

PLATE 5

Eoyari (62) ready to go hunting

PLATE 6

(*a*) Tawiruye (61) coiling a pot

(*b*) Kumiru (204) shaping an unfired pot

PLATE 7

(*a*) A view of the Alalaparu village facing west

(*b*) Another view of the Alalaparu village (the Indians and the house in the foreground are Waiwai)

PLATE 8

(a) Women collecting fish downstream from a poisoning

(b) Young girls drinking beside the Alalaparu River

PLATE 9

Men eating in the village square at Alalaparu

PLATE 10

Women peeling cassava in Susuku's (1) house at Alalaparu

PLATE 11

Women preparing cassava. Sore (109) sitting on the lever of the cassava grater while Mairupə (110) points at the photographer with her lips